African-American Proverbs in Context

SW. ANAND PRAHLAD

University Press of Mississippi
Jackson

Copyright © 1996 by the University Press of Mississippi
All rights reserved
Manufactured in the United States of America
99 98 97 96   4 3 2 1
The paper in this book meets the guidelines for permanence and durability of the
Committee on Production Guidelines for Book Longevity of the Council on Library
Resources.

Library of Congress Cataloging-in-Publication Data
Prahlad, Sw. Anand.
    African-American proverbs in context / Sw. Anand Prahlad.
      p.   cm.
    Includes bibliographical references and index.
    ISBN 0-87805-889-3. — ISBN 0-87805-890-7 (pbk.)
    1. Afro-American proverbs.   2. Afro-American proverbs—History and criti-
cism.   I. Title.
PN6426.P73   1996
398.9'21'08996073—dc20   95-53818
                                                                               CIP

British Library Cataloging-in-Publication data available

To Nick, Laura, and Osho and to the memory of
my great-grandmother, Mrs. Clara Abrams

Contents

Preface

In many ways, it seems that I have been writing this book all of my life. I was born and raised in rural Virginia, surrounded by people who cast the world in vibrant and poetic colors. I grew up on a former plantation, in a community of African-Americans descended from slaves who had toiled there; the Big House still stood at the center of the several hundred acres of land, with the descendants of the slave owners coming and going in automobiles rather than in the horse and carriage of old. I was always hearing stories about those days, sometimes funny, sometimes tragic. And I was fortunate in that one of the community pillars, storytellers, and griots was my great-grandmother, to whom I was very close as I grew up. From her, my mother, and other older people, I learned the beauty of language and metaphor, the grace of the spoken word, aesthetics of poetic and philosophical meaning, and the ways in which all of these can be intricately linked to nature, as well as to private, community, and cultural experiences.

I fell in love with proverbs at an early age. I began collecting sayings from calendars and asking older people what they meant by some of the things that they said. The use of a proverb at a particular moment has always intrigued me and struck me as an aesthetic highlight in conversation. When I was taken on walks through the woods, for example, and shown the beauty and mystery of plants, I might be told a proverb as a part of that experience. Or a story might be told about an enslaved ancestor who performed an incredible feat, with a proverb accompanying the narrative. It was always a particularly rich moment when one of those expressions was spoken in some other context, and the pungent fragrance of cultural and personal history enhanced whatever speech event was happening at the time.

Although I had become a working poet by the time I graduated from high school, it was not until 1975, in a folklore class with Daryl Dance at Virginia Commonwealth University, that I realized what possibilities proverbs had as an academic pursuit. This realization crystalized when a few of the proverbs that I had collected for that class appeared in Dance's *Shuckin' and Jivin'* (1978). So when I enrolled in the folklore program at the University of California, Berkeley, I already knew that I wanted to study proverbs. Many of the papers that I wrote for classes there focused on proverbs in one way or another, and by that time I had begun to write down occasions on which I heard proverbial speech and even to conduct a few interviews. The irony of doing graduate work at Berkeley, however, was that most of the time I was removed from African-American cultural environments; thus, most of my collecting was done on occasions when I traveled home to Virginia for summer or Christmas breaks. I was fortunate to have had the opportunity to study with Alan Dundes, who understood my interests and consistently gave me advice and encouragement. As fate would have it, Wolfgang Mieder was a visiting professor in the folklore program at Berkeley during my years there, and I had the opportunity to work with him and to get further advice and direction.

My good fortune continued in the folklore program at the University of California, Los Angeles. Although I was certain that I wanted to do a dissertation on proverbs, I was relatively ignorant about how to conduct such a study. How should the parameters of such a project be defined, methodologically and theoretically, in order to facilitate the kind of inquiry and insights that I was interested in? Proverb scholar Shirley L. Arora mentored and guided my research in addressing these concerns. If being at Berkeley was an introduction to cultural isolation, though, attending U. C. L. A. was an advanced course. So upon completion of my course work, I decided to move back to Oakland in order to locate informants from whom to collect. The collection process was long and arduous because of my insistence on actual speech events rather than hypothetically constructed contexts gathered in interviews. During the next five years, I explored every context imaginable, including bars, clubs, churches, street corners, basketball courts, PTA meetings, bingo games, card games, public buses, and retirement homes, in hopes of overhearing proverbs being used. Eventually, I found my way to several proverb users who became the primary informants for my research. I suppose that I have not had to confront many of the issues that some collectors do; invariably I ended up working with people who already were or who became friends and who shared much of my cultural background and perspective.

Once I had gathered what seemed to be sufficient data, I struggled with some of the most common paremiological problems in writing my dissertation, eventually focusing on the contextual and sociolinguistic analysis of speech events. Speech act analysis and performance theory seemed the most helpful theoretical perspectives in framing and analyzing instances of proverb speech, and so I based much of my methodology and discussion on these. Ultimately, however, I was unhappy with the analysis in my dissertation, which seemed too conservative and failed to establish a model for examining all of the components of proverbial speech that I had been exposed to in those years of listening to proverbs and to the speakers' comments about them. This book represents a continuing quest to develop such a model, one that will account for the aesthetic, linguistic, cultural, and personal components of proverbial speech events that I have witnessed throughout my life. Although I have relied upon much of the data collected for my dissertation, I have added the results of further fieldwork and research and have completely shifted the theoretical framework through which the information is examined. The chapter on blues, for example, represents new territory, as does my theory of levels of meaning. In many regards, I am doing what numerous African-American proverb masters with whom I have been acquainted have done: probing deeper into the dimensions of proverb meanings, attempting a clear articulation of those meanings, and celebrating the magical times when historical, cultural and personal forces intersect with the present moment.

Acknowledgments

Because I have been involved with this study for so long, there are many people to thank. First I would like to acknowledge those who have been mentors and sources of inspiration, and who have helped me to understand the aesthetics of the worlds of scholarship and academia: Murry DePillars, Daryl C. Dance, Alan Dundes, and Levell Holmes. Others have been more directly involved in the research and writing of this study and deserve special thanks. Shirley Arora, the director of my dissertation at the University of California, Los Angeles, has given me unending encouragement and support, and has read and assisted with this project from its inception. Wolfgang Mieder has been equally giving of his time and expertise at each stage of the project's development. Without the help and support of these people, this book might never have come to fruition. Thanks also go to Jennifer Zarelli and Vickie Thorpe, who helped me with editing, typing, and other technical aspects of the manuscript's preparation, to Chris Watkins, who assisted me with the annotations in the appendix, and to Michael Taft, who read and provided incredibly detailed comments and suggestions during the revision process. I am indebted as well to Alan Dundes for the generous use of the Folklore Archives at the University of California, Berkeley, and to a number of friends who lent unfailing emotional support during the many glitches in the writing process, especially Jenifer Crane, Lorie Feldenberg, Peggy Risch, Stephanie Laverdiere, and Aimee Chitayat.

Of course, this study could not have been done without the help of the people from whom I gathered proverbs. I owe them a special debt for the time they have given and the patience they have shown over the many years when I was scribbling down or taping their utterances and persisting with questions about the meanings of things they had said. They have always been generous and sincere in trying to convey as much about proverbs as they possibly could. These people include: Jean Folly, Clara

Abrams, Laura Tallie, Dorothy Bishop, Malcolm King, Matthew Boyd, Jerome Holloway, and my students from Golden Gate Elementary, Sonoma State University, and the University of Missouri, Columbia. This book is dedicated to them.

African-American Proverbs in Context

ONE

Toward a Contextual Theory

Introduction

This study will examine the functions and meanings of proverbs spoken by African-American speakers in context, beginning with the earliest historical period in which there are substantial records available and ending with present-day examples. One objective is the documenting of some of the most popular proverbial items found in the African-American speech community over time, a simple task that has not been undertaken by previous scholars. But a more primary interest is an exploration of the contextual applications and meanings of these proverbs. A number of works have treated the speakers of proverbs as performers and artists and made an exegesis of their art a focal point of discussion (for example, Yankah 1983; Levy and Zumwalt 1990; Alexander and Hasan-Rokem 1988). Furthermore, several works have examined the relationship between the use of proverbs as a form of artistic expression and the social, cultural, and psychological factors that have an impact upon proverb usage and interpretation and upon functions and meanings of items (Yankah 1989; Levy and Zumwalt 1990). The need for more extensive studies that probe even more deeply into these relationships, however, is great. The present work is similar in focus to some of the other contextual studies of proverbs in that it treats the performance context in which the item occurs—the speech event—as the unit containing meaning rather than isolating and focusing only on the text. I have taken seriously Dundes's metaphor, in which the proverb text is compared to the tip of the iceberg, as a descriptive model for how meaning relates to proverbial usage (1964: 260).

   In developing the methodology and analytical framework for this study, I have incorporated the theories of prominent contextualists (Hymes 1964, 1974; Bauman 1977, 1983, 1986; Ben-Amos 1972, 1977; Ben-Amos and Goldstein 1975). I have also relied upon the works of other folklorists and anthropologists who utilize components of the contextual approach in their studies of various cultures and forms of expression (Briggs 1980, 1985, 1988; Basso 1976, 1979). The analysis throughout my work is based on the assumption that an understanding of a given folkloric speech event relies upon the study of the entire situation in which that event occurs. Of utmost importance is the reconceptualization of what comprises folklore that emerged out of the contextual and performance-oriented approaches. As Ben-Amos argues, "In its cultural context, folklore is not an aggregate of things but a process—a communicative process, to be exact" (1972: 9). It should be stated that there are many areas of inquiry that have not been extensively addressed in the contextual study of proverbs—for example, does the use of proverbs always constitute a performance? In Bauman's terms performance is linked to the responsibility assumed by the speaker: "Performance involves on the part of the performer an assumption of accountability to an audience for the way in which communication is carried out, above and beyond its referential content" (1977: 11). But what are some of the relationships that are found between narrative performances and proverb speech acts, and how are such communicative processes perceived from an emic perspective? What training is involved for users of proverbs, and how does this influence style and meaning? What constitutes innovation in proverb performances? Many of these issues are addressed by Yankah in his study of Akan proverbial speech, as well as by some anthropologists who have discussed proverbs (Yankah 1989; Herskovits 1930; Evans-Pritchard 1963a, 1963b; Messenger 1959; Penfield 1983). Such issues, however, must be fully explored for each new group for which proverb study is conducted.

   Context here is considered in the broadest sense, including the linguistic or discourse speech event, the social and cultural contexts, and personal or psychological contexts pertaining to individuals in a given situation (Yankah 1989: 29–31; Bauman 1983: 362; Ben-Amos 1972: 4; Tedlock 1972: 114–130). While I focus intensively on the dynamics of particular speech events,

I am also interested in the way in which cultural and social forces influence proverb meaning, application, and interpretation. For instance, how do intercultural interactions affect the performance and meaning of proverbial speech events? What are some of the relationships that are possible between proverb meaning and other cultural metaphors and symbols? How do historical and social factors central to the lives of African-Americans influence elements of proverb meaning in speech events?

The methodology and vocabulary of this work are also informed by current theories of speech act theory (Searle 1969; Smith 1978; Holdcroft 1978; Petry 1990). I can echo Yankah's statement that "concepts and approaches employed in this work transcend the traditional boundaries of folkloristics, and span the fields of linguistics, discourse analysis, speech act theory, anthropology, literary criticism, and communication studies" (1989: 10). Yankah's work, in fact, lays the groundwork for many of the components of my own study. The most critical of these are the focus on the creativity of proverbial usage and, along those lines, the opinion that proverbs should be considered creative performances rather than merely quotations, which is the customary approach used by proverb scholars. The notion that proverb speech events involve artistic components implies other associated issues such as aesthetic criteria, evaluative responses to performances, and the relationship between a speaker's social status and his or her performance.

African-American Proverb Research

Studies of African-American proverbial speech have reflected trends in proverb research in general. They have also reflected why these approaches fall short in the effort to gain a comprehensive understanding of proverb function and meaning. Historically, most paremiological (proverb) studies have been text-oriented and can be grouped into six categories: (1) simple collection of texts without analysis, (2) discussions of meaning based on such texts, which regard them as poetry or philosophy, (3) discussions of group character based on proverb texts, (4) historical and comparative analysis of variants, (5) structural or semantic analysis, and (6) the discussion of texts found in literature. A seventh type of study involves the use of proverbs in psychological testing, which usually is not truly a study of proverbs. The first three categories of research implicitly consider proverbs as a type of literary genre comparable to poetry; these include most of the work that has been conducted. From this perspective, proverbs can be interpreted poetically or philosophically, and collections encourage the same sort of reading given to collections of poetry. Needless to say, there is minimal, if any, consideration given to contextual components of these items in the everyday speech events in which they might occur. In some cases, attention has been directed toward cultural and social considerations, but most often proverbs have been studied as indices to national character. Such studies base speculation and conclusions on a priori notions and stereotypes rather than on any scientific or ethnographic investigation of cultures and behaviors. These works tend to be exercises in supporting existent beliefs about particular groups. There are several basic assumptions at work: that proverbs express absolute truths reflecting cultural identity, norms, and values of a particular group; that these truths are readily and universally accessible from the texts; and that there is a direct correlation between proverb truths and the behavioral norms and actual behaviors of members of a group. An illustration of this kind of work is Trench's *Lessons in Proverbs* (1852), a subjective and idiosyncratic discussion that attempts to characterize various nationalities according to the author's interpretations of their proverbs. Hulme (1902) uses the same approach, allowing his examination to degenerate into a forum for the expression of his own racism. For instance, he suggests that the proverbs of the Romans reflect their business-like nature and practicality, whereas those of the Italians reflect selfishness and cynicism (94–111). Another extreme example of this trend is Bergmann's essay arguing the national character of Germans in the interest of Nazi propaganda (1936). These early studies demonstrate the dangers inherent in purely subjective interpretations of proverbs as literary texts and the subsequent attempt to make statements about groups based on meanings derived in such a manner.

Most studies of African-American proverbial speech fall into these first three categories. There are numerous reports and short collections of proverbs without any analysis (Malone 1929; Doar 1932; Stafford 1916; Harmon 1914; Whiting 1952; Spaulding 1972; Dance 1978), with some appearing as short notes in journals and others as brief sections in larger works. While these provide reasonably reliable accounts of proverbs that have existed among African-Americans and can be useful in verification of items found from one period to another, they are of no value in efforts to determine meanings, and, in fact, most such items have passed out of currency. They are thus of more significance as historical data or in studies of textual features of African-American speech than as anything else. While a few researchers have attempted to utilize these collections in the interest of determining the functions and meanings of items in slave culture, such efforts must be viewed with skepticism. Invariably they lead to grouping of proverbs under thematic headings and are based on the same assumptions as those noted in studies of proverbs as reflections of national character—the approach that has been taken in most essays on African-American proverbial speech.

Roberts uses this approach in an essay on slave proverbs (1978), in which he acknowledges the difficulty in determining the contextual application of proverbs within the slave community: "Although the lack of adequate contextual data in existing collections renders impossible a thorough examination of the numerous individual situations to which the proverbs were applied, it is possible to gain a general understanding of slave proverbs through an analysis of their base meanings, those meanings which allow them to be applied to specific situations to begin with" (129). He goes on to discuss textual features of some of the proverbs and to link particular items to social issues and problems that recurred in the lives of slaves. As in many discussions of proverbs, his essay considers them thematically and suggests relationships between proverbial themes and behaviors of members of the slave community. He states, for example:

> The theme of rash action is closely followed by that of undue pride and unrealistic aspirations. Proverbs with this theme include: "Save de pacin' mar' fer Sunday," "Dem w'at knows too much sleeps under de hopper," "Looks won't do ter split rails wid," "Nigger wid a picker han'kcher better be looked atter," "De proudness of a man don't count w'en his head's cold," "Some niggers mighty smart, but dey can't drive de pidgins to roos," and "Temmorow may be de carridge-driver's day ploughing." Although these proverbs would seem to represent the slaves' acceptance of their lot and act to support the position of the slaveholding class, in reality they seek to instill a realistic view of the nature of the slaves' world. (134–135)

Substantial reasons for making this approach problematic will become clearer as my discussion continues, but some obvious points can be made now. First, Roberts's entire argument is founded on the premise that one can know conclusively the "base" meaning of a proverb from a personal reading of the text, a premise that I challenge, especially in a case such as this, where the proverbs are written in dialect and are unfamiliar to the contemporary researcher. A second premise is that, without emic or ethnographic information, one can move easily from a textual interpretation of a proverb to an understanding of how it relates to particular issues in the lives of group members. And third, the author assumes that the proverb text states *a* truth that is closely connected to a particular value and normative behavior pattern. These premises overlook a number of important characteristics of proverbs: (1) they are often paradoxical in nature and one item can convey contrasting values in different situations, (2) there are proverbs within groups that pose contrary points of view or recommend contrasting courses of action, and (3) proverbs are sometimes iconoclastic and are not always used to support the established norms of a particular group.[1]

Similar assumptions underlie the research of Barnes-Harden (1980), who acknowledges that proverbs may have different meanings in different contexts but still insists that "[p]roverbs and proverbial expressions, as well as superstitions, are complementary angles in the universal experience of the Black man. It is the verbal transmission of these folk beliefs that manifest most directly the values and beliefs of a people" (57). For this study, proverbs were solicited from fifty informants, who were asked to write down ten proverbs apiece. The author states that "[a]fterwards discussion of this collection was done for explanatory purposes" (59), but no further details are given about the nature of the discussions, what questions were posed or what responses were obtained. There is no focus on the contextual meanings of any of the items. The assumption is made that the texts convey obvious truths that are connected with general values within the African-American community, and items are categorized under headings reflecting the author's delineation of values, e.g., "Love," "Appreciation," "Respect," etc. Although this article stands as one of the two most comprehensive modern collections from African-American speakers and makes the important point that a number of proverbial items found among African-Americans are much closer to items found in Africa and parts of the Caribbean than to English-derived materials, it is of little help to the researcher interested in elements of meaning or function.

Another important modern collection shares many of these perspectives and assumptions about proverbs. It also embodies the most extreme articulation of the argument that proverbs are one of the most important tools or indices for assessing the character, values, behavioral norms, philosophy, and ethnic identity of a group. Daniel (1979) states of his collection from members of the Sixth Mount Zion Baptist church in Philadelphia:

This proverb collection reflects many Black folks' intellectual convictions and intuitions about 1) things thought eternal, e.g., "To err is human," 2) fundamental value sensibilities, e.g., "It is not how long you have lived but how well you have lived," 3) reliable prescriptions for living, e.g., "Never trouble trouble till trouble troubles you," and 4) the submerged truths found in nature, e.g., "Still waters run deep." (ii)

His convictions about the usefulness of proverbs in the study of identity are further revealed in other comments:

Much has recently been said about the existence and nature of "Black" American identity. "Black belief" has been characterized as everything from a series of hopeless superstitions to a complex metaphysic dating back to the earliest days of African recorded history. Some recent political activists have even tried to create and disseminate synthetic "Black identities" which would be consistent with their political ambitions. In any event, there can be no mistake that the sayings presented here represent a valid index of their users' belief system . . . They are testaments of Black belief. A careful reading and unending reflecting will many times over reward those who seek to understand those kinds of Black people's psyches, how they see and value the world, how they seek to develop their social relationships, and their other world concerns. (iii, vi)

Once again, the proverbs are grouped under thematic categories that "emerged from a content analysis of the sayings" (vii), e.g., "Virtues and Vices," with subheadings such as "Cleanliness," "Honesty and Integrity," "Money and Success," and "Wisdom." Although there are no indications in this article of the methodology used for collecting, it is mentioned in another essay (Daniel, Smitherman-Donaldson, and Jeremiah 1987: 495) that the proverbs here were obtained through written questionnaires, followed in a few cases by interviews. The problems with Daniel's approach are those that apply to this type of study in general and that I have noted above. Proverb texts are viewed here not only as survivals, but also as mirrors of culture, two perspectives that have long since been replaced by more complex models in folkloristic theory. An ironic aspect of this study is that the author's approach seems to serve interests similar to those of others that he criticizes: it validates the scrutiny of black culture by anyone who would chance to draw whatever conclusions they might from the simple observation of folklore texts. The similarity to the works of early European proverb scholars is apparent, as is the opportunity for the use of folklore in the interest of political rhetoric or propaganda.

Work on African-American proverbial speech in the next two areas of textual analysis is almost nil. There are no existent structural studies and only one historical comparative analysis of a proverb from African-American speakers (Green 1984). Following the models established by such prominent scholars as Archer Taylor (1950a, 1950b, 1962) and B. J. Whiting (1931, 1977, 1989), Wolfgang Mieder, the most prominent contemporary proverb scholar in the world, undertakes a study of "Different strokes for different folks," arguing its American, and likely African-American, origin (1989: 322). As is the case with most such essays, the history of the item is the end in itself, and there is no extensive effort to discuss meaning or function; an assumed understanding of the base meaning of the proverb underlies the article. The author indicates, in his conclusion, a tendency to view proverbs as indicators of national character by suggesting that the popularity of the proverb is owed to its reflection of a "major element of the American worldview" (322). In the same work, a chapter entitled "Afro-American Proverbs" (111–128) consists of a brief discussion and overview of studies that have been conducted. This chapter encourages further analysis of African-American proverbial speech, suggesting a number of approaches that would advance our knowledge, including ethnographic, historical/comparative, and thematic. Finally, an appendix of short collections of proverbs from different sources and time periods is provided.

A few articles have considered the use of proverbs in literary contexts, although they do not for the most part concentrate on the meanings of items and do not necessarily focus on literature *by* African-Americans. Brookes (1950) includes in her book on Joel Chandler Harris a short discussion of proverbs found in the Uncle Remus texts. She lists the proverbs with the corresponding page numbers on which they are found, but offers no discussion or analysis of their meanings. Yates (1947) conducts a similar study based on Julia Peterkin's *Green Thursday, Black April, Scarlet Sister Mary*, and *Bright Skin*; Ambrose E. Gonzales's *The Black Border, Laguerre, With Aesop Along the Black Border*, and *The Captain*; E. C. L. Adams's *Congoree Sketches* and *Nigger to Nigger*; and Samuel Stoney and Gertrude M. Shelby's *Black Genesis* and *Po' Buckra*, all literature of South Carolina. She states initially that "[t]he purpose of this paper, however, is primarily that of collecting," but does consider the extent to which the proverbs from the texts are found in the speech of people from the state. Both this and the previous study reflect the assumption that the meanings of the proverbs are obvious from the texts. In the former, no discussion is offered. In the latter, proverbs in dialect are compared to "equivalent" proverbs from the English and biblical traditions.

Two other articles examine proverbs from different kinds of texts. Whiting (1952) surveys the diary of an ex-slave, William Johnson of Natchez, who became "one of the most prosperous and respected free Negroes in Natchez" (145). A list of sentences containing proverbs and proverbial sayings is provided with the page numbers from the diary; however, there is no discussion of these. A final essay discusses the frequency of proverbs in blues lyrics (Taft 1994). Context is explored to some extent in this article, as the author considers proverb frequency in a variety of contexts in order to put their occurrence in blues into some perspective. In this very interesting essay, Taft examines more than two thousand lyrics and provides a list of over eighty proverbs and proverbial expressions, citing each respective source; however, no exploration of meaning is attempted.

It should not be surprising that the few essays analyzing proverbs from a psychological perspective are also focused on values, philosophy, and behavioral norms. Maw, Maw, and Laskaris (1976) conducted a study using proverbs to measure attitudes "toward curiosity-related behavior of Black and White college students." Demonstrating the many problematic aspects of such tests mentioned by Mieder (1978), these researchers first selected proverbs "obtained from several books of German proverbs," and went on to conclude that "black college students chose proverbs indicating greater caution in exploring their environments" (1229). Such tests represent, in many ways, the ultimate result of the assumptions about proverb texts that we have been discussing. Another article of note is Page and Washington's study of proverbs and transmission of values in single-parent, female-headed, African-American households (1987). The authors indicate their perspective by building their thesis on the work of Hulme, who, in the tradition of Aristotle, viewed proverbs as mirrors of cultural and personal worldview. From there they move to a number of unproven assumptions about the relationships between proverbs and psychological states, attitudes, and behaviors; for example, they state, "Once internalized, proverbs, like values, become unconscious as well as conscious standards for action and attitudes toward self and others" (50). The article explores, among other things, "the correlation between proverbs and values along the dimensions of positive self-image" (51). Methodologically, proverbs were taken from Daniel's study (1979) and given to 120 women who were asked to indicate their degree of belief in them on a scale of 0 to 5. Women were also interviewed by students trained for this project. After statistical analysis, the authors discuss some of the proverbs, attempting to account for the correlations between them and etic, thematic categories that they have designed, such as "self-respect," "equality," and "family security." One can see that in many regards this study is fundamentally the same as others that attempt to infer cultural and personal values from proverbial items. Like those others, it is more focused on the normative values of the group than on the dynamics of the folklore within the group. One very positive aspect of this project can be noted, however: the authors document valuable information about the transmission of proverb items from mothers to their children. This study becomes the model for one conducted by McAdoo and Rukuni (1993). In their study of proverbs among Zimbabwean women, they are just as focused on the issue of values and how proverbs can be used to interpret cultural norms, and compare their findings to those of the two earlier researchers.

The psychiatric practice of using proverbs as intelligence tests is illustrated by Penn, Jacob and Brown's essays (1988a, 1988b), in which they report on tests given to African-American subjects. In the first article they compare findings from the Gorham Proverb Test with those from the Shipley Institute of Living Scale. Their assumptions reflect a profound misunderstanding of the nature of proverbial materials and, I would venture, of intelligence as well.

> The Shipley Institute of Living Scale was designed to assess general intellectual functioning in adults and adolescents and to help detect cognitive impairment in individuals with normal original intelligence. . . . The scale appears to be a valid, highly efficient method for obtaining general IQ estimates in either group or individual settings. . . . The Proverbs Test uses interpretation of proverbs to test verbal comprehension. (839)

Needless to say, there is no recognition that the very concept of a correct interpretation of a proverb text is inconsistent with the way in which proverbs actually obtain their meanings—in context. In a second article, these authors do come to the conclusion that cultural background influences one's interpretation of proverbs, and that subjects are more likely to attempt interpretation of familiar proverbs than of unfamiliar ones. Their central assumption, however, remains unchanged; they write, "Familiarity with a proverb increased the probability of its correct interpretation" (847).

Another article considers the issue of proverbs in the lives of children, but is more difficult to group under one of the categories that I have suggested (Hudson 1972). The author administered questionnaires to fourth- and sixth-grade students to ascertain their knowledge of particular items, comparing white students from a suburban, middle-class neighborhood to black students from an urban environment, and students from one grade to the other. Although her study entails the weaknesses of tests that seek to elicit the "correct" responses to proverb texts, she does by the end entertain hypotheses that recognize the creative process in proverbial speech and suggests, intentionally or otherwise, the influence of environmental factors on proverb form. In speaking about the proverb "Do as I say, not as I do," for example, she states: "There is a definite use of non-standard English indicated in the response to the first proverb given in Figure 2. 'As he say,' or 'he say' are both common expressions among urban blacks. It is not surprising that the proverb was completed with this usage, and it is evident that traditional ' . . . as I do' is foreign to the children" (23). Further such indications of environmental influences are suggested by "[s]uch items as 'The longest way there *is by foot*,' 'Good fences make *good protection*,' 'People who live in glass houses *worry about stones*,' 'Good fences make *a lot of money [safe lawns]*,' 'Where there's smoke, *there's pollution*' "(23).

Although components of the ethnography-of-speaking, contextual, or performance approaches have been used in articles and booklength studies of proverbial speech among other groups, only four works on African-American proverbial speech can be said to engage these perspectives. The first of these approaches is discussed by Arewa and Dundes in their seminal article "Proverbs and the Ethnography of Speaking Folklore" (1964), which best articulates the application of Hymes's ethnography-of-speaking model. In this essay, they argue for the study of proverbs in context and offer a number of critical points:

> What are the rules governing who can use proverbs, or particular proverbs, and to whom? Upon what occasions? In what places? With what other persons present or absent? Using what channel (e.g. speech, drumming, etc.)? Do restrictions of prescriptions as to the use of proverbs or a proverb have to do with particular topics? With the specific relationship between speaker and addressee? What exactly are the contributing contextual factors which make the use of proverbs, or of a particular proverb, possible or not possible, appropriate or inappropriate? (36)

They then discuss some Yoruba proverbs, using examples drawn from Arewa's memory in place of actual fieldwork, and utilizing the methodology that they have laid the foundation for. This approach is certainly an advance toward a more complete understanding of proverb application and meaning than the traditional text-oriented studies. What is missing, or at least submerged in the thick of other concerns, is a focus on the art of the proverb speech act, the aesthetic dimension, both personal and cultural, as well as on the private sphere of proverbial meaning and function. While seeming to be covered in parts of the authors' discussion, these considerations are never made explicit, and it is never suggested that they may be the focal points of a proverb study. In general, one might gather from this article that the main focus of this approach is to determine rules that govern the use of proverbs. This focus is echoed by others who have analyzed proverbs from the same perspective (Daniel 1973; Seitel 1969, 1977).

The contextual approach to proverbs is further explicated in Kirshen-blatt-Gimblett's "Toward a Theory of Proverb Meaning" (1973), which perhaps delineates the criteria for contextual study and the complexity of proverb usage better than any other discussion. She indicates that a characteristic of proverbs is that they *seem* to express absolute truths, which is a part of their strategy, but that in actuality they express relative truths and are used to express multiple meanings in different situations. She observes, for instance:

> Sources of multiple meaning in "Rolling stones gather no moss" include (1) what is understood by the image presented in the metaphor (stone roller, stone in brook); (2) what is understood as the general principle expressed by the metaphor (movement promotes efficiency, stability promotes tangible gains); (3) how the general principle is evaluated (tangible gains are worthwhile, tangible gains are not worthwhile); (4) the requirements of the situation in which the proverb is used regardless of what one actually believes in principle (does one want to console or criticize the stable person; does one want to console or criticize the wanderer). (822)

These considerations move the study of proverbs into a sphere of theoretical perspective different from previous ones. Such concerns facilitate the study of proverb complexity synchronically and diachronically and the analysis of personal and social influences in specific proverb speech events. The author stresses the importance of semantic features in the encoding and decoding of proverbs:

Sources of multiple meaning in "A friend in need is a friend indeed (in deed)" include (1) syntactic ambiguity (is your friend in need or are you in need); (2) lexical ambiguity (indeed or in deed); (3) key (Is proverb being stated "straight" or "sarcastically"?) . . . there being other cues which help the listener to understand the statement the proverb is intended to make. For example, stress, juncture, tone of voice, and semantic fit are important. . . . (822)

The author also examines a variety of possible meanings for several proverbs depending on the situations in which they might be used, disproving the notion that there is only one base meaning for a given proverb. She gives sources that might produce multiplicity of base meaning, including "(1) . . . what is understood by the concrete image presented in the proverb metaphor and (2) what is understood as the general principle expressed by this image" (825). In conclusion, she states, "that 'proverb meaning' ultimately emerges from a proverb's use in a specific context and that it is not the meaning of the proverb per se that need be our central concern but the meaning of the proverb performances" (825). Kirshenblatt-Gimblett's final conclusions are consistent with the performance-centered approach to folklore, focusing on all aspects of the aesthetic performance, including the audience, the shaping of the expression by the artist, and all ensuing interactions between the artist and the audience in the communicative process. The importance of this perspective to the study of proverbs is that it advances the discussion beyond the cultural and social level to include the individual and psychological. It also moves away from the focus on general kinds of situations to the specific and particular and beyond the concept of folklore as items toward a concept of folklore as communicative process.

As previously mentioned, four essays on African-American proverbial speech are related to the ethnographic or contextual model: "Towards an Ethnography of Afroamerican Proverbial Usage" (Daniel 1973), "Old Time Negro Proverbs" (Brewer 1933), "Getting the Butter From the Duck" (Folly 1982), and "The Poetry of African-American Proverb Usage: A Speech Act Analysis" (Folly 1991). Daniel's article demonstrates that the focus of an ethnographic approach can be vastly different from the tenets of a performance-oriented perspective. While building his argument on the theories of Burke, Hymes, and Arewa and Dundes, the author maintains his earlier insistence on proverbs as mirrors of culture, prefacing his discussion with quotations from Hulme and Trench. The thrust of the essay is that proverbs can serve as ethnographic tools in uncovering various facets of African-American culture, such as perceptions of wisdom or truth, intercultural interactions, childrearing practices, survival of Africanisms, techniques of persuasion, and extent of cultural assimilation.

The articles by Brewer and Folly are very similar in their approach. Brewer gives a short list of items introduced by brief comments about the prevalence of them among members of the slave and ex-slave communities. To his credit, he questions informants to obtain their explanations for some of the proverbs, a practice that would not become popularly advocated for another forty years. He goes further and tries to relate the proverbs to particular components of the slavery experience and to recurrent problems within the slave community; again, this is a commendable effort and one that is more akin to contemporary, ethnographic and contextual studies than to most studies of his day. He, however, indicates another strong element of his perspective in his concluding remarks: "Crude sayings of a crude people, humble, optimistic, good-humored" (105). Undoubtedly, he feels that the proverbs are a kind of index to the national character of African-Americans from this Texas community.

My own essay (1982) presents the explanations of two informants for a number of proverbs, including their discussion of situations in which the proverbs might be used, their meanings, and who would use them to whom. Though I offer no further analysis of the items beyond the informant explanations, the essay is informed by assumptions of the contextual perspective, principally that proverbs contain multiple meanings in different contexts and that the exploration of these meanings is an important endeavor in itself.

The speech act analysis of proverbs undertaken in my dissertation (Folly 1991) contains some of the same arguments found in the present study. The focus is a contextual analysis of proverbs used by African-American speakers, with a number of situations in which proverbs occur forming the basis for discussion about meanings, stylistic features, and poetic characteristics of proverb speech acts. Several speakers are interviewed in an effort to ascertain more accurate information about the emic perspectives of proverb users and audiences. Some of the conclusions of that study inform the theory developed in the present discussion. One of these is that proverbs in the African-American community often serve functions similar to those associated with other speech genres, e.g., rapping, capping, and the dozens. Another is that proverb meaning operates on a number of different, though interrelated, levels. These points become much more developed in the examination of proverb meaning in this work.

It is evident from this survey that a contextual examination of proverbs used in the African-American speech community is a timely contribution. My overview of previous studies is intended not to discredit them but to place them in the context of contemporary folkloristic perspectives and to expand and deepen the field of inquiry about proverbial speech in general and African-American speakers in particular. I do wish to emphasize the important distinction between the common practice of basing discussions of group norms and behaviors on proverb texts and the analysis of proverbs *in context* to gain insights into areas of social tensions or stresses (Abrahams 1968a: 48). More fundamentally, however, I insist that the interpretation of meaning is a complex endeavor, involving more dimensions than group or individual values, and that analyses of other factors are necessary to a comprehensive proverb interpretation. Such facets include the consideration of proverb speech acts as poetic, artistic performances, the range of communicative dynamics that pertain in particular situations, and personal and social components.

A Theory of Meaning

One of the most significant framings of the central question of proverb meaning, ironically, has emerged from a textual scholar, Norrick (1985), who entitled his study *How Proverbs Mean*. For in examining the dimensions of meaning, from a contextual or textual perspective, we should consider *how* meaning is engendered, which includes a philosophical exploration of the very term itself. In other words, what is meant when one asks, "What does the proverb mean?" In his work, Norrick explores the parameters of what is considered by "meaning," although he is focused primarily on proverb texts. He qualifies this focus:

> One justification for studying proverbs as texts rather than proverbs in texts or interactions is simply that proverbs can and do occur as texts, and not only as larger texts. Besides being anthologized as discrete little texts, proverbs occur as complete texts in group slogans and house inscriptions, as noted above, but also accompanying pictures in cartoons, advertisements etc. . . . . The predominance of proverb meaning *qua* text within contexts like those just enumerated also justifies the study of proverbs as texts. Even when it occurs as an integral part of a larger spoken or written text, the independent meaning of a proverb plays a major role in determining its semantic contribution to the text as a whole. (5)

Norrick essentially conceives of proverbs as linguistic units of meaning that exist independently of contexts, a superorganic approach. The task he then sets for himself is to provide a discussion of their meanings that will serve as a preliminary step to analysis of items in context.

Quite unconsciously, perhaps, Norrick constructs his theory of proverb meaning on an ethnocentric bias found also in the work of other scholars, e.g., Barley (1972). Paraphrasing Barley's argument, he states that a proverb "can be understood and even paraphrased without knowledge of its context or of the objects to which it applies" and goes on to say that Barley "distinguishes between the *external relations* a proverb contracts to its context of use and the *internal, logical relations* between the terms of the proverbs themselves, totally independently of any concrete contextual use" (105). He builds upon this idea, coupled with comments made about proverb meaning found in Wilson (1970), referring to Barley's "internal, logical relations" as *standard proverbial interpretation* (SPI). For literal proverbs the SPI is simply the literal interpretation; for figurative proverbs, it is the paraphrased "base meaning." Thus, the SPI given for "No rose without a thorn" is "there is no pleasant thing without some unpleasant aspect." An SPI gathered from collected texts is problematic, however, for what would seem obvious reasons. First, the interpreter of the proverb brings to it a specific set of sociocultural and experiential filters with which to engage in the process of interpretation. It is assumed by Norrick that such factors will affect the specific application of the proverb but not the SPI, but it has been demonstrated that speakers outside of a tradition may not have any insight whatsoever into the meaning of a proverb simply given the text:

> If, however, we are not familiar with the tradition of application, the metaphoric value (and limits) of a proverb may be impossible to determine. A certain Ashanti proverb, for example, goes *The okra does not show its seeds through its skin.* It is by no means evident that this botanical observation, which does not show *its* seeds through its skin, means, "You can't tell what a man is thinking from the expression on his face." Archer Taylor, in his interesting study of the genre, mentions a number of proverbs that have come down to us altogether without a tradition of application and are thus virtually limitless in meaning. (Smith 71)

I suggest that what holds true here for figurative proverbs also holds true for literal ones, for without familiarity with the tradition, how would one even know that a proverb was literal (Abrahams 1968a: 44–45)? Hasan-Rokem observes that "syntactic analysis of the proverb, alone, is relatively unhelpful in discerning its meaning"(1982: 170), and that "semantic interpretation of proverbs must take into account cultural traditions and the norms of specific ethnic groups" (171). It turns out that the SPI, or base meaning of a proverb, is actually a *culturally (or group) shared* idea of the proverb's general meaning. It is an important point, because this is not the most basic level of proverb meaning, nor is it "standard" in the sense that grammatically correct use of a language, for example, can be called standard. Kirshenblatt-Gimblett's study clearly illustrates that a single proverb may be given different base meanings by different interpreters, and that members of one folk group might belong to other more primary and disparate groups that would influence varying SPI's of the proverbs (Kirshenblatt-Gimblett 1973; Arewa and Dundes 1978). Krikmann notes, "Descriptions of such kind, however, as applied to proverb texts, seem to be rather inexpedient for several reasons: (a) they reflect, above all, the peculiarities of the describer's own world view or consciousness rather than the properties of the object being described" (1984: 54). We cannot reasonably oppose the assertion that culturally shared, general meanings of proverbs exist, but we can reject the notion that the meaning qua text is predominant when proverbs appear in context. We can also suggest that such an assumption would best serve as a point of departure for investigation rather than as a concluding point in justifying textual analysis. In many ways the perspective of text-oriented scholars can be compared to that of linguists who focus on the grammatical standards of language and hypothetically correct constructions that can be generated. This stands in sharp contrast to the performance-oriented approach, which can in turn be compared to the sociolinguistic or "ethnography of communication" perspective that emphasizes the actual forms of language that occur within a given speech community (Hymes 1974).

A number of other studies engage these issues of meaning in different manners. While not a contextual study, Krikmann's discussion of proverbs merits consideration because of the multiple dimensions of meaning that he discusses, and because it represents some of the most serious thought that has been given to the subject (1984, 1985). Krikmann begins by acknowledging three possible approaches to proverb semantics: (1) "the 'purely semantical' (virtual, context-free) mode," (2) "the 'pragmatico-semantical' (actual, context-bound) mode," and (3) "the 'syntactico-semantical' mode" (1984: 46–50). Unfortunately, his view of contextual studies is disparaging; he writes that " 'hunting' for proverbial actualizations, e.g., in such a way as

Mathilde Hain (1951) has done, is an ultimately troublesome, unprofitable and thankless enterprise, however important and desirable its results for paremiological research were" (1984: 48–49). Ironically, many of the theoretical points developed in these articles provide excellent focus for someone engaged in ethnographically based research and support most of the major tenets of the contextual approach. For example, Krikmann notes that, while there may be many potential meanings of a given proverb, "[t]he final and maximally definite meanings of a certain text manifest themselves only in concrete actualizations of this text" (51). His discussions go deeply into the possible denotative and connotative relationships that can exist between syntagmatic and paradigmatic factors of a proverb, developing something of a system for examining proverb meaning. In the second of these articles, he presents a number of "Actualizations," which turn out to be discussions of particular hypothetical situations in which the same proverb might be used and the possible variations of meaning that might apply in each. His "Actualizations" are comparable to discussions of meaning in different recorded contexts, such as are found in Hains.

Honeck, Voegtle, Dorfmueller, and Hoffman (1980) develop a psycholinguistic theory of proverb meaning that offers many insightful components overlooked by more humanities-based discussions. First, they discuss numerous important properties of proverbs, including the following: (1) they can be understood on literal and figurative levels, (2) the relationship between the literal and figurative is constrained, (3) "the figurative level need not be . . . signaled by the syntax or the semantics of the statement itself" (131), (4) "[p]roverbs potentially relate a large number of instances that can themselves be literally and referentially unrelated" (131–132), and (5) "[u]ttered in context, a proverb as a figurative statement is neither necessarily true nor necessarily false" (132). These authors further discuss relationships between proverbial utterances and metaphors that occur in speech events, observing that proverbs are less "context-driven" but more "knowledge-driven" than metaphors. Finally, they develop a theory explaining the interpretation process, identifying four phases: (1) the problem recognition phase, (2) a literal transformation phase, (3) a figurative or theory formation phase, and (4) an instantiation phase (150–151). The attempt at identifying the cognitive process that functions in proverb interpretation is extremely important, for it provides a basis for understanding how proverbs do get their meanings. These phases recognize the proverb utterance as the creation of a particular problem and as an invitation or even an imperative that the listener engage in theoretical analysis in order to resolve the problem. Their discussion gives rise to this interesting definition of a proverb: "a pragmatically deviant, relatively concrete, present-tensed statement used to create a theoretical perspective for grouping referentially and literally distinguishable events" (151). I will return to some of the points made in this article in the discussion of my own theory.

Many studies of proverb meaning in context have been conducted; however, relatively few booklength works have appeared, even fewer that are written in English, and fewer still that focus on groups within American society. Furthermore, many of these investigations employ different concepts of meaning and have differing theoretical or methodological focuses. Thus, there was no single study that I could wholly rely upon in developing my own model. Hain's work (1951) still stands as one of the most significant contextual studies.[2] She examines sixty proverbs with a general description of the situation in which each one is used, including the transcription of the proverb speech act. Her work is invaluable in furthering our knowledge of proverbial speech in context and can become the basis for many different kinds of analytical investigations, such as formal speech act theory or the ethnography of speaking approach to proverbs. Speakers in her study, however, are not considered artists but are described in the simplest ethnographic terms, e.g., "*Die etwa fünfzigjährige Kleinbäuerin B. erzählte*" [the fifty-year-old farm woman](33). As one would assume from this, there is no focus on the cultural or psychological background of proverb speakers, their individual motivations, or the personal elements of their art.

I have already mentioned Yankah's work, *The Proverb in the Context of Akan Rhetoric*, which is the closest in focus to my own. This study not only constitutes a refreshing departure from most works on proverbs but also establishes many insights about the dynamics and creativity of proverbial speech that are based on careful field observation and ethnographic research. The author investigates, among other things, the aesthetic and functional characteristics of proverbs as performance and rhetoric among the Akan, exploring issues of authorship, ownership, application, and interpretation. Because so many of his points will be alluded to throughout my study, it is not necessary to discuss all of them here; however, I might mention a few that are key assumptions underlying my own investigation. One is that proverbs are not quotable behavior but are instead performances. Yankah takes issue with the host of proverb scholars who have emphasized the fixed nature of proverbs and denied elements of innovation or creativity, asserting that "whereas the proverb text may exist as a cultural frame of reference it is subject to 'creative deformation' during performance" (34). A second point is that meaning is not intrinsic to proverbs but emerges out of situational applications and "is best conveyed and assessed in performative contexts" (154). As simple as these two points may seem, they have substantial impact on the way in which my model is developed and my analysis of proverbs is undertaken.

While Mieder's *American Proverbs: A Study of Texts and Contexts* is an excellent discussion of American proverbs in a larger social context, it does not attempt an examination of specific contextual meanings of particular items. The proverbs of a wide variety of American groups are covered, as is the use of items in social contexts such as cartoons, songs, literature, and advertisements. The focus of the discussion in most cases is documentation that proverbs do exist in these various contexts, and there is a brief overview followed by substantial examples or collections of items. Thus, this work is very different in nature from what I propose to undertake and cannot be the basis for the development of a model that will facilitate the kind of intensive focus on meanings in which I am most interested.

Quite a number of articles have appeared that discuss proverbs in context (Jordan 1982; Gossen 1973; Seitel 1969, 1977; Briggs 1985, 1988), and add to our knowledge of contextual meaning. What is important about these studies is that the researchers engage the issue of cultural and social influences on the meanings and performances of proverbs and focus upon the interrelatedness of proverbs and other genres within a cultural group, bringing in functional and aesthetic dimensions. For those essays that are anthropologically based, this represents an interest that is an alternative to the preoccupation with rules governing proverbial speech, although this remains a concern. Other essays are less ethnographic but discuss proverbs linguistically, semantically, or as speech acts (Elchinova 1988; Endstrasser 1991; Lopes 1991; Papp 1988; Yassin 1988; Penavin 1979; Fleischer 1987; Kerdilès 1984; Roventa-Frumusani 1985; Schmidt-Radefeldt 1986). In each case the importance of context in determining meaning is emphasized. While a consideration of proverb speakers as artists with specific, complex motivations for their utterances—in short, an identity and personage—is missing from many of these studies, some sense of the speaker as an important focal point and the issue of competence (if not artistry) is addressed in a few essays (for example, Bornstein 1991; Elchinova 1988; Levy and

Zumwalt 1990; Nuemann 1987; Roberts and Hayes 1987). This is one of the major elements that I attempt to develop.

It has also been pointed out that an investigation of proverb meaning, especially in context, necessarily involves a consideration of function; in fact, these have been the two most researched areas of proverbs. Abrahams sums up most of the functional characteristics of proverbs mentioned in part by previous researchers (1968a, 1972a). Central to these is to "propose an attitude or a mode of action in relation to a recurrent social situation" (1972a: 121). Other functions include the reduction of anxiety, the signalling of group membership, and didactic or evaluative marking. That meaning can be relative to function is the crux of Grice's notion of *implicature* (1975) and of indirect speech acts in general. A proverb speech act may mean literally what it says while simultaneously meaning something more significant idiomatically or indirectly. So the meaning is altered by the intended function of the item in context (Norrick 1985: 27).

I propose a four-part model for the discussion of proverb meaning that embraces all of the dimensions that are often singularly emphasized by various other scholars. The first level of meaning I call the *grammatical*, indicating that it is concerned simply with what the language of the proverb states. One might also refer to this level of meaning as the *literal*, and at this level no distinction is made between a literal and figurative proverb. Traditionally, scholars have often overlooked the necessity for focusing on this most basic level before moving on to levels that involve a knowledge of social norms and a familiarity with particular kinds of social situations as well as with traditional applications of proverbs to those situations. In the process, a number of issues deserving of critical analysis have been glossed over. Furthermore, conclusions with no basis in empirical evidence have become the cornerstone assumptions about proverbs upon which more complex theories are then based. To what extent does one need to understand a proverb at the grammatical level, for example, before he or she can correctly apply it? At what point do children understand and respond to this level? To what extent does the figurative understanding and aesthetic appreciation of a proverb depend upon the grammatical understanding? On the other hand, to what extent is a part of the aesthetics of proverbial speech heightened by incongruities between the literal and figurative message? This level of meaning has been observed most often by semanticists, although it is recognized by scholars in other areas as well. Honeck et al. (1980) are keenly aware of the importance of this primary level of proverbs, as is evident from the description of their properties. Krikmann, in his discussions, also points to this component of proverb meaning and its interrelatedness with other dimensions, writing that "each single word belonging to the tropical image carries into the proverb all the associations and connotations, emotive 'nuances' and 'shades' connected with its literal meaning" (1984: 71).

I refer to the second level of meaning as the *situational*, a term also used by Kirshenblatt-Gimblett (1973). The situational designates the intent of the speaker in the particular context in which the proverb is spoken. For instance, speaker "A" might say to person "B," "If you live in a glass house, don't throw stones," as a way of indirectly criticizing "B." The meaning of the proverb speech act might very well be: "I think that a particular aspect of your life is disgusting and you have a lot of nerve to be talking about someone else." This level, which might also be called the *subtextual*, necessarily embraces the theory that discourse can be viewed as an economic transaction and recognizes that the meaning of the proverb speech *act* for the speaker will likely be somewhat different from the meaning of the proverb speech *event* heard by the listener (Smith 1978: 83–105). It is important to note that we have not yet reached the level suggested by Norrick as the most basic, the SPI, for it is entirely possible that the speaker and listener may not share a common knowledge about a customary application of a given proverb, or, even if they do, that the shared knowledge will not be paramount in the encoding and interpretation of the proverb utterance. Again, this is an area in which unsubstantiated assumptions have formed the basis for later theory. For example, how does a listener who is not familiar with a proverb understand what a given proverb speech act might *mean*? I have found such occurrences more common than researchers generally assume is possible, especially in cases in which proverbs are being used by adults to children. Other researchers have noted this phenomenon in passing, but few studies have centered on it. To do so would require sociolinguistic fieldwork, for paralinguistic features of communication are critical components of encoding and decoding in such situations. Unfortunately, most investigations of proverb interpretation rely on textual examples, some in the form of tests and others in the form of hythothetical speech events, rather than on observation of proverb speech events and subsequent interviews of speaker and listener. The theory of proverb interpretation in Honeck et al. certainly moves in the direction of these issues, but is speculative, with no basis in field observation. Their discussion also fundamentally overlooks this level, and assumes that a listener will, in fact, make linguistic sense out of a proverb utterance. My thesis here is that the linguistic interpretation may be an activity that is separate from a behaviorally related understanding of the proverb utterance. A further suggestion is that not only interpretation, but also proverb application, may often be more akin to poetic expression than to logical reasoning. By this I mean that an intuitive "feeling" may guide speaker and audience more than a logical matching of symbols within the proverb to agents in a given situation. The relationship of musicians to notes as they are playing seems an appropriate metaphor, especially in traditions where no sheet music is used.

The third level of meaning is the *group*, or *social*, level. It is at this level that a shared social knowledge of the general meaning of a proverb comes into play. This level includes not only the generally shared understanding of proverb meaning—Americans might share a base meaning of "A rolling stone gathers no moss" that is distinct from that found among the Scottish (Kirshenblatt-Gimblett)—but also meaning at more specific social levels, e.g., regional, community, ethnic group, and family. This means that speakers in different American ethnic groups might understand the application of proverbs used to each other on one group level but not on others. Traditionally, scholars who have attempted to extrapolate meanings from proverb texts of groups from which they themselves come have been engaged on this particular level. It is on the basis of this level that SPI's can be generated, although even this dimension argues against any such simplistic paraphrasing of proverb texts on a number of grounds. First, as Krikmann observes, to paraphrase a proverb text necessarily distorts its meaning, for an important component of meaning lies in the connotative and denotative associations of particular words (1984). Paraphrasing also implies a reductive perspective of meaning that cannot account for the variety of dimensions present in an actual speech event. My suggestion is that an understanding of meaning even on this level requires a degree of ethnographic information and thoughtful, objective analysis.

The fourth level is one that has received little attention from proverb scholars, primarily because ethnographic and contextual work is essential in obtaining data about it. I call this level the *symbolic*, and this application of the term should be distinguished from Smith's application. Her use of the term hinges on the relationship between the intent in a verbal utterance and the accurate interpretation of it by *the other*. As I am applying it here, the term emphasizes the personal and psychological importance of a proverbial item that extends beyond any of the previously mentioned levels of meaning. For example, "Let sleeping dogs lie" might be used because, in addition to the other levels of meaning present, the speaker is reminded of his or her mother, from whom he or she learned it. The symbolic level of meaning is necessarily concerned with the psychological function of the item for its user and audience, and it should be obvious that one cannot make any credible assertions concerning this level without personal informant information. In an earlier discussion, I suggested the term *symbolic value* to designate the degree of importance of this level for a given speaker in a given context (Folly 1991: 131–133). In one case, for instance, a speaker may have heard the proverb used over and over by a close relative and feel that it is in some way a keepsake. In another case, the speaker may have heard the proverb used on television one time and simply liked the sound of it. In the former case the proverb would have a greater symbolic value for the speaker than in the latter. Issues such as identity (Alexander and Hasan-Rokem 1988) are often involved with this level of meaning.

It is my position that all of these levels of meaning operate simultaneously when a proverb is spoken and, consequently, the job of the analyst is to discover in what ways meanings interact. That various dimensions of meaning operate at once is not a new idea, having been suggested by Halliday (1977), who proposed three levels: the ideational, interpersonal, and textual. The relationship among levels of meaning also becomes an inherent component of the aesthetic consideration of proverb speech acts, for speakers are often aware of such levels, and a part of their artistry in applying proverbs is the interplay of dimensions of meaning.

I would like to refer to some of the studies that have been reviewed in the light of my theory, making more specific some of my objections, and then to give an example of how these levels can apply to a particular proverb speech event. In the studies of African-American proverbial speech that insist on viewing proverbs as mirrors of cultural values, it is actually the social level of meaning that researchers discuss as if it were *the* meaning of the proverbs; there is no consideration of the other levels. Furthermore, it is my contention that even the social level of meaning can be derived only through some ethnographic investigation; otherwise, interpretation becomes a self-reflexive activity. My theory is another way of suggesting that proverb meaning is fluid and dynamic, emerging out of communicative events, and is not, as even Norrick asserts, "fixed." Because of the interrelatedness of these levels, one cannot truly say what "the meaning" of a proverb is, but rather must speak of meanings and levels of meaning that emerge out of speech events. Using an example from my research might make these points more concretely.

The proverb "An idle mind is the devil's workshop" was used in one African-American Texas community to address the issue of young girls engaging in sex and becoming pregnant. The social level of meaning in this community has to do with with the avoidance of premarital sex and pregnancy and the moral taboos that pertain to such activities. But how would a researcher know of this meaning from the text? If, for example, we had extrapolated a base meaning or SPI from the text, we might have come up with something along the lines of "If you're not busy, you'll get into trouble." A researcher inclined to draw conclusions about the values and behaviors of the group from the proverb might then suggest that a stringent work ethic is a prominent concern for the community, and go on to place the proverb under a thematic category such as "Work." In fact, work is only a relative concern of the proverb here, and it is entirely possible that children to whom it was used would never relate it so much to work as to sexual taboos and evaluations of parenting. The proverb could hypothetically occur in specific speech events and carry any number of situational meanings, depending on who said it to whom and what the intent of the communication was. This is one area in which correlation (Seitel 1960) is highly significant. The proverb could be used as a means of criticizing someone who had already gotten pregnant and of "putting down" the parenting of that person. It might also have been spoken to the child or the parent of the child (second person correlation) or to someone else about the mother and/or child (third person correlation). In each of these cases, the meaning of the proverb would be altered. In another situation the proverb could be used to proselytize, emphasizing the religious belief in Satan's determined efforts to win converts. For example, an avid churchgoer might speak the proverb to the parent of a child whom they wished to see join the church. In such an instance, the grammatical level of meaning would be crucial, for the proverb picture is one in which the devil has great influence. The social level of meaning would, however, continue to echo, and contribute to the message that sex is associated with sin and that the church provides a safe haven or respite from temptation and the consequences that would surely follow giving in to that temptation. The symbolic level of meaning could only be obtained through interview of participants of a particular speech event, but, for the sake of analysis, let us imagine that the speaker using the proverb had herself become pregnant before marriage. Let us also imagine that a parent used the proverb to that person in condemning her. Then, the symbolic meaning of the proverb speech event for her might involve feelings of shame, fear, or abandonment. This symbolic meaning would be distinctly different from one the speaker might encode had she as a child heard her mother use the proverb to a close friend about a parent down the street and if laughter had ensued from the proverb speech act rather than, say, a mournful silence. The symbolic meaning in this case might easily have to do with feelings of closeness and bonding and, implicitly, boundaries between an in-group and those on the periphery. I believe that this short illustration makes clear the degree of complexity that can be assumed for each proverb speech event, and shows why I consider many previous studies to have missed the nature of proverb meaning.

African and African-American Proverbs

In considering the relationship between African and African-American proverbial speech, a number of questions immediately arise. Some of these can be answered simply; others are more complex and will be addressed in conjunction with other issues throughout this study. The most easily answered questions are those pertaining to the actual corpus of proverbial items found among the two groups. Based on the printed collections, we can safely say that very few proverbs in currency among African-Americans are of African origin. A primary reason for this is that proverb texts exist as preformed linguistic units, making the retention of items difficult in an extreme situation such as slavery, where language groups were stripped of their native tongues and given new ones to replace them. As Dundes observes:

> One must also keep in mind that many proverbs are metaphorical, and it is extremely difficult to translate the metaphor of one language into another. A literal translation of a metaphor might be completely meaningless in the new language, and there may well not be any sort of even roughly equivalent metaphor available in the metaphorical repertoire of the new language. So while it was a relatively simple task to translate African

trickster tales into English, it was nearly impossible to do the same for most African proverbs. (1973: 246)

In this regard, there are significant differences between the United States and the Caribbean (and other parts of the Diaspora) in the retention of proverbial items as well as of other aspects of African folklore (Raboteau 1978; Bascom 1972, 1977; Dundes 1977; Dorson 1977; Szwed and Abrahams 1977). It is likely that there were items of African origin among the proverbs of the earliest generations of African-Americans, but all indications are that over time the large majority of these have been lost, giving way primarily to proverbs from the English and biblical traditions and including items created by African-Americans on United States soil. Unfortunately, few attempts have been made to document African proverbs among African-American speakers. Taylor encourages such investigations (1973), implying that further research would reveal that a number of items are African. In another discussion he notes the likely African origin of the expression "To hoe one's own row" (1969–70: 7–8). Barnes-Harden also suggests the issue of origins (1980) but does not go on to develop this concern.

The aesthetic and functional relationships between the two traditions is even more difficult to ascertain, largely because of the absence of objective, ethnographic studies of African-American proverbial speech. Such relationships, however, are of great value to a study such as this one. As previously mentioned, various assumptions or assertions have been made about proverbs in the interest of describing characteristics of African-American culture, but no scientific evidence has been offered to support these assertions (Smitherman 1986; Daniel 1979). There are many obvious functions of African proverbs that could not be retained in the colonial and postcolonial setting, many of which were closely connected with institutions that were disrupted and/or destroyed. Proverbs were sometimes used in Africa, for example, in arguing court cases (Messenger 1959; Firth 1926; Finnegan 1970: 408–9), on military flags (Christensen 1958; Finnegan 392), "in formal instruction during initiation ceremonies" (Finnegan 413), in chants during ceremonial dance performances (Finnegan 414), in ritual drumming (Finnegan 392; Yankah 1989), in competitive games (Christensen 239; Finnegan 415–416), and as depictions on royal gold weights (Finnegan 392). All of these are specific cultural forms that were lost during the American colonial period, and thus the need for proverbs to function in these roles was also lost.

Not only were the formal contexts of proverbial speech basically lost in the American context, but proverbs have traditionally played a much more central role in the everyday speech of Africans than in that of African-Americans. All researchers of African proverbs seem to agree on the absolute proliferation of items throughout individual societies, and a proverb about Yoruba proverbs suggests the importance of this genre throughout the continent: "Proverbs are the horses of speech; if communication is lost, we use proverbs to find it" (Priebe 1971: 26). Messenger writes about Anang proverbs: "Proverbs are by far the most numerous and most frequently employed of these forms of verbal art, and are used in all manner of situations as a means of amusement, in educating the young, to sanction institutionalized behavior, as a method of gaining favor in court, in performing religious rituals and association ceremonies, and to give paint and add color to ordinary conversation" (1959: 73). The same basic statements are made by scholars about proverbial speech in almost all parts of Africa. The fact that proverbs are being adapted to other media in contemporary African society—for example, maxims being painted on trucks in Ghana (Oledzki 1979)—further reflects their importance. Although proverbs play a significant role in the African-American speech community, they do not occur as frequently and are not as central as in African societies.

The area of most profound influence of African proverbial speech on that of African-Americans has more to do with subtle functions and aesthetics of speech dynamics in general. That the African-American speech community is fundamentally an oral one certainly owes a debt to African speech aesthetics. More specific sociolinguistic observations on this speech community were made by several researchers during the 1970s, a period of unparalleled scholarly focus on African-American speech behavior. These observations can be grouped into four categories: (1) descriptions and analysis of specific speech forms (Abrahams 1972b; Mitchell-Kernan 1972a, 1972b; Kochman 1970; Brown 1972), (2) analysis of culturally influenced types of strategies (Mitchell-Kernan 1972a, 1972b; Abrahams 1974; Kochman 1970), (3) descriptions and analysis of performance styles and aesthetics (Hurston 1969; Abrahams 1963, 1972b, 1974, 1976; Mitchell-Kernan 1972a, 1972b), and (4) ethnographic considerations of the relationship of forms, styles, and strategies to culturally prescribed contexts of speech events (Abrahams 1976). While none of these researchers deal specifically with proverbial speech, they do provide information pertinent to the relationship of kinds of speech events to each other, as well as contextual, ethnographic, and aesthetic dimensions that can be drawn upon in looking at proverb speech events. The significance of the historical and cultural heritage of African-Americans can no more be overlooked in the case of proverbs than in other forms of cultural expression.

Although proverbial speech is not as central in African-American culture as it was (and is) in African societies, some of the same attitudes towards speech and similar patterns of speech behavior have been maintained. It can thus be postulated that to some extent the use of proverbial speech by African-Americans is influenced by African as well as by European aesthetics. Although no scholar has focused on the issue, there are likely significant differences in functions of proverbs within European and European-derived cultures and African and African-derived societies, such as the degree of variation in form of spoken proverbs (Crepeau 1978).

Further, a special fondness for indirection and metaphorical speech by African-Americans has been noted (Hurston 1934; Gates 1988; Smitherman [1977] 1986; Abrahams 1976) and its probable debt to African culture recognized. Some scholars have also discussed at length the close relationship of proverbial speech to the very strong emphasis on metaphorical speech that exists within various African societies. Finnegan notes, "In many African cultures a feeling for language, for imagery, and for the expression of abstract ideas through compressed and allusive phraseology comes out particularly clearly in proverbs" (1970: 390). She goes on to point out, as other researchers have, that the structural unit that we refer to as a proverb is frequently considered a part of a larger emic category of speech by particular societies, and that indirection is a primary criterion of these larger categories. Similarities in the function and locution of some of these African forms and African-American forms of speech can be noted.

About Azande proverbs, for example, Evans-Pritchard notes that the term *sanza* is used to refer to "a wider category of double-talk, speech (and action) intended, usually with malice, to convey a meaning other than their overt sense, and I suggested that this kind of speech might be connected with witchcraft beliefs and political institutions. To give a simple example: a man is drunk and his wives make seemingly innocent remarks to make fun of him without his knowing it. They peck at him, Azande say, after the fashion of a perforated bag (*kokoro mongu*) . . . So a man is made fun of by remarks with a double meaning without his being aware of it" (1963a: 4).

Finnegan tells us more about *sanza*:

> Besides its sense of proverb, *sanza* also refers to ambiguous or hidden language in a wider sense. Usually this form of speech is used in a malicious way, often with the intention of speaking *at* someone while seemingly making an innocent remark. By using this form of speech, as with the narrower class of proverbs, a man can get at another while at the same time keeping himself under cover; the sufferer will not be able to make overt trouble, and in any case the insult, being hidden, can be withdrawn without loss of dignity. This oblique and veiled form of speech is one which, as Evans-Pritchard shows in some detail, fits the suspicious and competitive outlook of the Azande. (1970: 424)

Given these descriptions of *sanza*, obvious comparisons can be made between it and African-American speech forms such as *signifying* and *marking* that utilize indirection as a strategy for making critical commentary. Mitchell-Kernan describes signifying as "a way of encoding messages or meanings which involves, in most cases, an element of indirection" (1972b: 315). Further characteristics of this speech form often include an intention to embarrass or diminish someone's status in the eyes of others. Kochman notes the intention "to compel belief and arouse feelings of anger and hostility" (1970: 157). It will be shown in my discussion in several chapters that a similar use of proverbial speech is found among African-American speakers.

These comparisons not only suggest aesthetic and functional similarities in some usages of proverbial speech by Africans and African-Americans but also raise questions about the emic category in which proverbs are placed as well as about the structure and variability of items. Does the African-American category of "sayings" correspond with the scholarly notion of proverbs, or is it broader and inclusive of other kinds of items? Do these sayings follow generally the structure and form of the scholarly category, either as transcribed texts or as spoken utterances? Is the degree of variability found in many African societies also found in African-American proverb usage? In other words, how fixed is the proverb in speech utterances? While these questions are of some concern and will be addressed to some extent, they are not primary issues in this study. It is clear that a large percentage of African-American sayings do correspond to the etic category "proverbs," and that items are relatively fixed over time. That there are items that do not correspond is certain, and a few of these are mentioned; however, a full investigation would require research methods different from those that I have applied to this study. It seems more urgent simply to establish some coherent and scholarly foundation that demonstrates the core of the African-American proverb tradition and elements of usage and meaning first, before engaging in research that explores the more unique and culture-specific items and usages. For this reason, the present work leans heavily toward the standard method of annotation, focusing on those items that can be annotated from existent collections or of which I could find at least two instances in current usage. The burden of proof of proverbiality and currency in oral tradition for items that do not meet these criteria, and that may deviate from the forms or functions of those discussed in this study or elsewhere, must rest with the researcher who undertakes the task of examining such items.

Proverb Definition

Although there is so far no ideal definition of the proverb, certain characteristics are generally ascribed by scholars to this genre. Proverbs are said to be short statements that seem to express ageless wisdom or truths and that contain elements of English poetry—for example, rhyme, assonance, alliteration, parallelism, imagery, and metaphor. Structurally, proverbs have been described as "a description made up of two or more elements, and these elements often conform to the two parts of the balanced structure. These two or more elements are usually tied together either by a verb of equivalence or a verb of causation" (Abrahams 1972a: 120). An example is "A rolling stone" (first element) "gathers" (verb) "no moss" (second element). Dundes also offers a structural definition of the proverb as "a traditional propositional statement consisting of at least one descriptive element, a descriptive element consisting of a topic and a comment" (1975: 115). In this definition, "topic" refers to the object spoken about, and "comment" to what is said about it. For instance, in "Two clean sheets don't smut," "sheets" would be the topic and that they "don't smut" is the comment about that topic. Proverbs have also been defined functionally as "descriptions that propose an attitude or a mode of action in relation to a recurrent social situation" (Abrahams 1972a: 121). True proverbs must be further distinguished from other types of proverbial speech, e.g., proverbial phrases, Wellerisms, maxims, quotations, and proverbial comparisons. The terms "quotations" and "maxims" are applied to proverbial sentences derived from literary sources, with the implication being that these often refer to those sources more than to the conventional wisdom of the society. Wellerisms are a witty type of proverbial statement that usually include not only a declaration but a secondary statement ascribing the utterance to a particular character; an example is " 'There's no accounting for taste,' said the old woman as she kissed the cow." Though named for the character Sam Weller in Charles Dickens's *Pickwick Papers*, Wellerisms are found in many traditional societies, and predate the literary nomenclature by many centuries. Proverbial comparisons are, as the term implies, similes, e.g., "as white as snow," "like a hog loves corn." Proverbial phrases have been defined by Taylor (1950a: 906) as variable in tense and person, in contrast to true proverbs. The proverb is a self-contained, complete idea that can be used as is; the proverbial phrase *has* to be modified in some way in order to achieve a complete statement. For example, "Haste makes waste" is a proverb and can be used as is, whereas "to be up the creek without a paddle," "to blow your own horn," "to bury the hatchet," or "to be a snake in the grass" are phrases that have to be modified in order to make a complete statement. Abrahams is more extreme in his delineation: "The study of proverbs has been severely complicated by the grouping of conventional conversational devices that share almost nothing but their brevity and their traditional currency. Almost certainly this complication is due to the fact that proverb dictionaries were written not for the purpose of defining this genre but for storing any device useful in developing oratory techniques" (1972a: 123). He continues, focusing more on the functional aspects of the two kinds of speech:

> While proverbs are often used to flavor conversation or oration, they are self-contained units; they have a moral weight of their own and an argument that is virtually self-sufficient. On the other hand, the formulaic intensifiers exist for no other reason than to decorate speech. These are devices of hyperbole; they take an ongoing argument and lend it wit and color . . . Beside these formulaic intensifiers there is a multitude of other adjectival phrases that are sometimes referred to as proverbial. But as noted for the other intensifying devices, their rhetorical function is quite unlike that of true proverbs. (1972a: 123–124)

Whether or not one agrees entirely with these parameters, one must acknowledge that there are differences in form and function. In this study, I am concerned primarily with "true proverbs," and, in most cases, with metaphorical items, since these kinds of proverbs allow and even facilitate the most complex social, linguistic, and semantic relationships and therefore have more potential to increase our understanding of the ways in which meanings operate in proverbial speech events. In a few cases, proverbial phrases are considered for what they can add to the present analysis.

PART ONE

1930s–1960s

TWO

Proverbial Speech among the Ex-enslaved: Speech Events with European-Americans

Sources of Proverb Speech Acts

Locating examples of proverbs used in context during the period of slavery is a nearly impossible task. Several sources give indications of proverbial meanings and functions but also pose substantial problems. First, there are the instances of proverbial speech in literary works by European-American authors, such as *Uncle Tom's Cabin*. Such cases naturally raise issues of authenticity and accuracy: to what extent do the speech events in the novel reflect recurrent uses of the proverbs that were common in the culture? While the perusal of collections from this period might substantiate that some of these items were current in tradition, it cannot supply us with information on their meanings. A second source is the genre of slave autobiographies. But again, these are literary documents, and some of the same issues are relevant here. Many such narratives were actually written and edited by abolitionists who were told stories by illiterate slaves (Osofsky 1969: 12). Some of the more outstanding ones—for example, the narratives of Solomon Northup, Henry Bibb, and William Wells Brown—contain only a few passages of dialogue between characters and almost no proverbs. Like Frederick Douglass's, which does contain proverbs, they employ a formal literary style. The proverbs used by Douglass are addressed to the audience rather than by one character to another, and the question that arises is whether these were current in the African-American community or if they are instead items used by the educated and literate. Furthermore, if they were commonly used by African-Americans, does Douglass's use of them reflect innovation or tradition? There is no accurate way to answer such questions.

A third category includes documents such as letters, diaries, and newspaper columns that may incidentally contain examples of proverbs. These also tend to be literary in nature and more often than not exemplify the use of proverbs to an audience that is not physically present. In some of these, as in the autobiographies, there is often a conscious effort made to avoid dialect, and this would certainly influence the use of proverbial items. A study of one such diary (Whiting 1952b: 149–152) reveals the use of numerous proverbial phrases but only four proverbs: "Honesty is the best policy," "Birds of a feather flock together," "Butter will run," and "What is to be, will be." Another proverb is found in a group of tales told by a former slave, Jake Mitchell, and written and published in a newspaper column by a white editor, Robert Burton: "De one what rock cradle most, in ginnerly rule de roos' "(Sport and Hitchcock 1991: 200).

Proverbs can also be found sometimes in the transcriptions of sermons by former slaves. Many of these are quotations drawn from the Bible and are used didactically, as one would expect. A few, though, illustrate proverb speech acts in which the minister responds to events that occur unexpectedly during the church service and show innovation in form and performance. One minister says in response to a dog entering the church, "**Cast not your pearls before a hawg** [before swine], nor feed holy things to er dawg" (Brewer 1947: 135). Another is used during the collection to encourage the congregation to give more money: "**God loves the buffalo**" [the cheerful giver] (Bradford 1935: 7). A third indicates that the flair for the creation of proverb-like metaphors that is commonly found in African-American sermons today also characterized sermons in earlier times: "Did you ever hold the hand of a galvanic battery? **The more the juice the tighter you hold**" (Courlander 1976b: 361). Once more though, the literary element is involved in these texts, as they were captured by European and, in a few cases, African-American writers.

Transcriptions of interviews with ex-enslaved people or their direct descendants are a fifth source of proverbial speech. These are also far from ideal examples of proverbs in context, but offer the clearest illustrations of actual recorded interactions in which proverbs are used. Rawick, who compiled the largest corpus of these narratives (1972)[1], notes the characteristic social dynamics of the interviews:

> Most of the interviewers were white, most of whom were white women, and the respondents were old blacks, almost invariably very poor and totally destitute, and often dependent upon public charity and assistance from white-dominated charities and public officials. The white interviewers were frequently related to the local elite, a relationship that was known by the old black men and women being interviewed. (Rawick 1972: Supplemental Series 1, volume 3, Ga., part 1, xxxii)

He also notes particular problems with using these documents, warning against their consideration as "a reliable source for those seeking to study black speech patterns and black English" (Rawick 1972: S. S. 1, v. 3, Ga. pt. 1, xxix). The language patterns and dialect were recorded with varying degrees of concern for accuracy by collectors with no formal training, as a rule "taken down in pencil or pen, most often after the interview, from memory or from scattered field notes supplemented by memory" (Rawick 1972: S. S. 1, v. 3, Ga., pt. 1, xxx). It may be that features such as introductory formulas of proverbs, for example, were added, changed, or omitted by collectors not focused on such details. It seems safe to assume that the actual proverbs reported were those that were used and that the general responses and anecdotes recorded were actually related; at least, this is the consensus of Rawick and other scholars who have worked with these narratives. One might reasonably surmise, however, that items which were more culture-specific to the speakers would have had less chance of being remembered or accurately recorded than items with which the collectors were already familiar. Thus the dominance of proverbs that were shared by Euro-Americans cannot be taken as an indication of the range of proverbial speech that existed among the informants.

A second problem is that we do not have the kind of contextual information that would give us a clearer sense of two individuals interacting with each other. This makes it difficult to determine where social forces begin and personal motivations leave off. Of course, this also raises a more fundamental issue; whether or not those involved in these interactions were capable of perceiving and relating to each other as individuals. Might the dynamics between interviewer and informant not be similar to those described by Basso in his work with the Western Apache (1979)? In other words, it might be that members of each group regarded each other more as symbolic constructs than as individuals. To suggest this is to bring proverbial speech into focus as a device for assisting in negotiations between not only personal but also cultural Self and Other. The analysis in this chapter, then, leans toward the sociocultural spheres. Though I have made an effort to use whatever information is available to imbue the speakers with personal identities, they remain in many ways representative voices of their perspective cultural groups.

A number of positive things can be be said about these narratives as sources of analysis. First, they contain more examples of proverbs than any other source. They also allow us to identify some of the common proverbs in use among African-Americans, both in the period in which the interviews were recorded (the late 1930s) and probably during the period of slavery. Further, these accounts serve as important illustrations of interactive speech events between African- and European-Americans. These events are informed by very specific social and political forces and contain multiple facets of context. From them we can glean information about the cultural and social dimensions of proverb meaning and function as well as about certain situational meanings and applications of items. For these reasons, I have chosen to focus primarily on this latter source.

Social/Cultural Dynamics of the Proverb Speech Events

In many ways the isolated proverb speech events in the ex-slave narratives are microcosmic examples of broader social realities inherent in the South and in America in general, and are therefore weighted with political and social implications and charged with the tensions of race relations in this country. There is in the very nature of the interactions comprising these interviews the recognition that the African-American speakers occupy a socially inferior status. They have not initiated the interactions but are complying for a number of reasons: they fear repercussions should they refuse, and they are under the impression that the interviewers can assist them in gaining access to basic services and goods. The conversations, then, pose much the same dilemma that the confines of slavery did, and the dynamics influencing Africana speech behavior in that context persist here. Interviews involving these components would have to be especially tense, delicate and complex, and would necessitate the most strategic uses of language possible for the ex-enslaved speakers.

It is clear that the social nature of these interactions frames the perfor-mance contexts of the speech events and has a great impact on the speech dynamics, choice of items, and levels of meaning that are brought to bear in the encoding of the proverb speech acts. One of the major aspects of these speech events can be called the "ritual of disguise," which refers to the consistent employment of hidden meanings and coded speech by African-Americans to and around European-Americans that has been so widely documented and discussed that no argument need be made for it. Rhetorical forms of communication with European-Americans have become stereo-typical and institutionalized in the Africana community and are often known as "masks," a trope reflected from the earliest times to the present in oral tradition, literature and social essays of writers as diverse as Dunbar ("We wear the mask that grins and lies" [Davis and Redding 1971: 212]) and Fanon (*Black Skins, White Masks* 1967). The cultural recognition of such traditional speech and behavioral forms and the ritualized enactment of them is reflected in such expressions as "puttin' on ole massa," or "shuckin' and jivin'." The art of the rhetoric, or the sociolinguistic performance, lies in the speaker's ability to placate the Euro-American addressee by acting out behaviors in accordance with that addressee's expectations, often by re-ferring to Euro-canonical texts while subtly registering personal statements or offering subversive, social commentary.

That folklore genres are often central to these "masks" has also been established by writers, artists, and scholars. Spirituals, for example, were often sung to deliver coded messages (Lovell 1972; Epstein 1977) and, in much the same fashion, tales, legends, and jokes also expressed hidden social commentary (Levine 1977; Roberts 1989; Hughes and Bontemps 1958; Fry 1975). Scholars have noted frequent occurrences of work songs and hollers, often performed in the presence of whites, that registered severe criticism of European-Americans and institutionalized oppression (Levine 1977). Any researcher concerned with the texts of the WPA interviews should logically consider that this institutionalized component of Africana speech behavior influenced these interviews. Rawick does note the frequent intermingling of "natural" and "fictive" discourse (Smith 1978: 73) that characterizes the ex-slave narratives and that reflects the tendency of informants to blend traditional motifs, i.e., from tales, legends, memorates, etc., with the recounting of personal or community history.[2] Of course, this occurs quite naturally because the interviewers are primarily asking the informants to recall memories of the past, and, as Rawick and others have suggested

(Raboteau 1978), much of the history lies in the realm of oral tradition. To go a step further than Rawick's observation, I suggest that these folklore motifs and genres are often components of the "mask," and function as a part of the ritual of disguise. The ritual of disguise is critical when considering speech events in which proverbs are found, for proverbs are often one of the most important genres in "masking," as evidenced by their frequent occurrence in segments of discourse characterized by elaborate and metaphorical speech.

I suggest that a second ritual is also salient in the speech events of informants in these narratives: the "ritual of defense/attack." Though less acknowledged by researchers as a general trope than the ritual of disguise, the strategies by which this one is executed have received significant attention: these are the strategies of argumentation, persuasion, and insult that have been discussed in the context of such distinctive speech forms as the dozens, "capping," "rapping," "signifying," "sounding," and "marking" (Abrahams 1970, 1974, 1976; Mitchell-Kernan 1972a, 1972b; Kochman 1970; Whitten and Szwed 1970; Brown 1972). Abrahams (1972a) and other scholars have generally agreed that proverbs often function as a means of offering solutions to recurrent problems, but a study of proverbs in context suggests that they frequently play a far more significant role. In the contexts of these speech events between Euro interviewers and Africana informants, proverbs often form a part of the defense and attack strategy. Informants routinely have to defend themselves against criticism, condescension, and denigration of their persons and culture, as well as against logically constructed arguments about one topic or another. Proverbs commonly play a role in this defense; however, in most cases informants are quick to move from the defensive to the offensive position in these interactions, and proverbs are often a pivotal device in this strategy. It has been suggested that folklore items many times reflected the fantasies of enslaved people, allowing them to affirm their vision of social justice (Levine 1977). As a part of the ritual of defense/attack, proverbs sometimes function to project visions of the social order desired by Africana speakers, and can thus be viewed as contributing to what Roberts has called "culture building" (1989) in these speech events. In other examples, proverbs are clearly used as a part of strategies of insult.

Because of their directive and expressive functions, as well as their usefulness in argumentation, proverbs are generally well-suited for use in the contexts of these interviews, but a number of more specific characteristics make them ideal for the rhetorical strategies of many of the speakers. First, proverbs by their nature refer to the established canon in communicating a message and provide anonymity for the speaker. This is an especially important feature in cases where speakers wish to voice criticism or to make social or personal commentary (Roberts 1978: 130), and is reflected in the frequent use of introductory and closing formulas that refer to the Bible, or "The Good Book." Second, indirection is one of the major components of proverbs and one of the most necessary facets of these speakers' communications. Third, proverbs, just as jokes do, often present a hypothetical world that is representative of elements in the actual world and in the interactional situation in which the utterance occurs. In contrast to jokes, however, there is less danger that the proverb will be interpreted as insolent, insulting, or as making light of situations that communicants may feel should be taken seriously. Fourth, proverbs are the most effective folklore genre in constructing and supporting logical argument and persuasion, carrying the weight of authority and social propriety and structurally resembling the statements of syllogisms. Fifth, proverbs can succinctly encapsulate the main point of a segment of elaborate and decorative discourse, focusing the listener's attention on that point and driving it home. And sixth, as Yankah notes regarding Akan proverbs (1989), those in the narratives also function to manipulate the mood and attitude of listeners and create the impression of unity or agreement between Africana speakers and Euro interviewers. References to biblical canon frequently contribute to this component of the speech events as well.

The political and social components of these interactions are vital in discussing the contextual meanings and applications of proverbs, for they are ever present and interact with the immediate and personal elements of a particular encounter. We are able to obtain information about the *social* levels of proverb meaning from many of the examples. We can gain insight into the social meanings of items not only within the Africana community during the 1930s, but often within the European-American community as well, for informants on occasion refer to the common, Euro meaning of items as a part of their own applications and innovations as they use those same proverbs. Hence, the interplay of different social meanings that have emerged out of the social context is an area of focus, just as is the interplay between social and situational (perhaps the most prominent level found in the examples) meanings. Unfortunately, there is little data that would facilitate a discussion of the symbolic level of proverb meaning in these narratives, but a knowledge of the other levels can assist in determining symbolic meanings when we encounter the same items later on in our study.

It should be pointed out again that the narratives are not ideal sources for the examination of proverb meaning in context; they are simply one of the best available sources. Although I consider the informants and interviewers as persons engaged in speech events, the texts, in fact, are transcriptions that have been literalized to varying degrees. We have no way of supplying the kind of contextual information that make these examples more three-dimensional, and I have relied heavily on cultural and historical data in this effort. Hence, the cultural and social levels of meaning are more emphasized than the personal, and speech events at times may come across as somewhat prototypical.

Proverbial Speech and "Masking"

It becomes obvious in reading the texts of the ex-slave narratives that speakers are acutely aware of the necessity for rituals of disguise and defense/attack. On repeated occasions, they relate stories that indicate the importance of disguising their communications both in the context of slavery and in the contexts of these interviews. We receive glimpses of ways in which certain social metaphors functioned, and several examples demonstrate the use of proverbs either in disguising communication or in attesting to the practice of coded speech.

In the following example, Mr. Thomas McIntire speaks about the use of such a social metaphor, indicating that the expression "yer auntie is sho' a comin'" was commonly used and understood among African-Americans to mean that freedom was imminent, though its meaning remained hidden from whites.

> Example #1
> But I members hearin' my folks talkin', en 'twuz'nt jes' eats dey wanted. Dey wanted ter be free, en larn dey chillun, like Marse Jim's chillun, so dey cud grow up en have som'thin fer dem selves. I'd offen hear em sayin' 'nebbr min' chillun, fer **yer auntie is sho' a comin'.**' Dat wuz jes' a blind fer sayin', 'Freedom's comin'.' Us chillun soon learnt what it meant, but de white folks nebber did learn. (Rawick 1972: S. S. 1, v. 5, Ind. and Ohio, 409)

Another example is a bit more complex.

Example #2

Jus' fore de war, a white preacher he come to us slaves and says: 'Do you wan' to keep you homes whar you git all to eat, and raise your chillen, or do you wan' to be free to roam roun' without a home, like de wil' animals? If you wan' to keep you homes you better pray for de South to win. All day wan's to pray for de South to win, raise the hand.' We all raised our hands 'cause we was skeered not to, but we sho' didn't wan' de South to win.

Dat night all de slaves had a meetin' down in de hollow. Old Uncle Mack, he gits up and says: 'One time over in Virginny dere was two ole niggers, Uncle Bob and Uncle Tom. Dey was mad at one 'nuther and one day dey decided to have a dinner and **bury de hatchet**. So dey sat down, and when Uncle Bob wasn't lookin' Uncle Tom put some poison in Uncle Bob's food, but he saw it and when Uncle Tom wasn't lookin', Uncle Bob he turned de tray roun' on Uncle Tom, and he gits de poison food.' Uncle Mack, he says: 'Dat's what we slaves is gwine do, jus' **turn de tray roun'** and pray for de North to win!' (Rawick 1972: Series 1, v. 4, Tex., pts. 1 and 2, 11)

Several communicative and rhetorical components are apparent in this speech event. The speakers in both examples are relating anecdotes that illustrate the ability of the slaves to outwit the enslavers; most importantly, they are relating the stories to a European-American. In both examples we can interpret commentary at the sociopolitical and perhaps at the personal levels. At the social level, the message is that European-Americans have been historically outwitted by Africans, and that one arena in particular in which this has occurred is that of oral communication. It is not difficult to imagine that at the personal level, the speakers may be directing this commentary to the particular interviewers whom they are addressing. A possible message is that they (the ex-slaves) are more verbally and intellectually acute than the interviewers, and, further, that it is partially the interviewers' own underestimations of the speakers' ability that makes deception possible.

In examples one and two, proverbial expressions are at the core of the communications—"turn the tray round," "bury the hatchet," and "auntie's comin'." With "turn the tray round," we can observe the interplay among several levels of meaning. First is the grammatical level that obtains in the context of the story—one character is literally moving the food around on the table. Second is the situational level of meaning, in which the expression is specifically applied to a character in the story, tricking the

other into ingesting his own poison. Third is the social level that applies
to the story, and at which the expression comes to stand for outwitting an
opponent. Fourth is the situational level applying to the interaction between
the interviewer and informant, at which the speaker may be somehow
misleading the interviewer. And fifth is the social level that applies to the
interview situation, in which the general meaning of outwitting an opponent
emerges. One can note the creativity of the speaker in orchestrating the
different levels of meaning here, presenting a narrative that supposedly
explains the origin of the proverbial expression but that, in fact, operates as
a dramatic parable to the interviewer. Interplay among levels of meaning for
"yer auntie is sho' a comin' " is also evident. First is the grammatical level
that means simply that one's relative is coming to visit. At the social level,
as provided by the informant, however, the expression means that slavery
will soon be over and that freedom is coming. The situational level that
is mentioned here involves the use of the expression by adults to children,
perhaps to inspire and encourage them and to address some of the emotional
damage that inevitably occurred as a result of slavery.

In several other examples, proverbs are also used in speech events in
which speakers indicate the importance of tact and indirect communication
during the interview process. The following such example contains not only
a proverb but a possible allusion to a popular folk tale, "The Talking Skull
that Refused to Talk."[3]

Example #3
Does I 'member anything 'bout how de slaves was treated in slavery time?
Well, I 'members a little myself and a heap of what others told me. Wid
dis I done tole you, I believe I want to stop right dere. **A low fence is
easier to git over than a high one. Say little and you ain't gwine to
have a heap to 'splain hereafter. Dere is plenty of persons dat has
lost deir heads by not lettin' deir tongues rest**. (Rawick 1972: S. 1, v.
3, S. C., 27)

It is obvious from the speaker's response that the interviewer has asked
him for some of his recollections of the slavery period, a question that
was routinely asked by the WPA interviewers. Sadly, it is apparent from
the notes of those workers that they were far from cognizant of the farcical
nature of posing such questions, given the social circumstances surrounding
the interviews. In many regards, the speakers are often quite frank, or,
at least, obvious in their sentiments, perhaps because the interviewers'

preconceptions about them were so firm that negative or pointed commentary was misconstrued or simply went unheard. Evidence of this will become more visible as more examples are considered, and particularly in cases where the interviewers' comments are available for scrutiny. To an unbiased observer who is aware of the social dynamics of the conversation from which example #3 is taken, the meaning of the speaker's communication is blatant: he does not wish to talk about the treatment of slaves because he fears that the interviewer—who is implicated by social codes, heredity, social conditioning, and perhaps personal choice—might be offended and, as a result, cause the speaker harm. In other words, it is far from prudent for the speaker to reveal his sentiments about whites, some of whom may have been the interviewer's relatives.

The proverbs here are not ones that show up in any of the collections of "slave proverbs" or in later collections of proverbs from African-Americans; however, they are structurally and functionally proverbial in this speech event. In the first of these, the "fence" becomes a metaphor for speech acts, for words uttered, and the proverb portrays them as enclosures that one builds around oneself, that one constructs between the self and other persons or objects. The metaphor further states that it is wise to build as low a fence as possible (to reveal little) in the event that one needs to reach the object on the other side, in this case anonymity. In essence the proverb is a testimony to the wisdom of keeping one's true feelings hidden in this particular speech event and, conversely, of the foolishness and danger of revealing those feelings.

The interplay between the grammatical and situational levels of meaning are an important component of the creativity and rhetorical strategy of this speaker. The proverb picture obtained from the grammatical level of meaning is somewhat humorous and engaging in and of itself. The use of such an image must, to some extent, distract the listener's attention away from the actual speaker, and perhaps help to diffuse whatever tension might have resulted from a more straightforward refusal to submit further information. The remarks that follow the proverb (especially if the folktale is being alluded to) further shift attention away from the speaker or, one might say, away from the natural and toward the fictive. The situational meaning—the prudence of revealing as little as possible about the treatment of slaves—is thus underscored, though registered. At this level the speaker is also making a comment about the cruelty of Europeans: those who lost their heads did so at the hands of Euro-Americans.

A fourth example is more open to interpretation. The interviewer, unlike most, provides the entire text of the interview, including the numbered questions that she posed to the speaker and then the speaker's replies. The questionnaire is thorough and covers every conceivable facet of life during the slavery period; however, the nature of the responses from the speaker (Mrs. Mary Jane Simmons) is unusual—she answers the questions in as few words as possible, providing a bare minimum of information and no opinions or commentary. From reading the text, one receives the portrait of a woman who never questioned authority and was never aware that any other enslaved person did either, who does not believe in any superstitions, and who is not aware of any of the common beliefs or practices of African-Americans during the time in which she lived—all of which is difficult to imagine. It is in this context that the proverb is used as a response to the interviewer's final question.

Example #4
To what factor or factors do you ascribe your ripe old age?

I have kept the commandments from my youth, and have always lived a very quiet life. My motto has always been **"Never to bite off more than I could chew."** (Rawick 1972: S. S. 1, v. 4, Ga., pt. 2, 570)

I suggest that the proverb conveys not only the speaker's general philosophy of avoidance of conflict but also a particular avoidance in this speech interaction. "Biting off more than she could chew" could be, at the situational level, equivalent to talking too openly or revealing any of her personal feelings on the topics that the interviewer has asked her about. We might speculate that perhaps a social level of meaning in that setting had to do with using discretion in behaviors that concerned white society.

The proverb in the next example also functions as an avoidance mechanism, allowing the speaker, Mr. Henri Necaise, to "turn de tray around" on the interviewer by sidestepping the original question and commenting on a related, but different, topic.

Example #5
It ain't none of my business now, whether de niggers is better off dan slaves. I don know 'cept bout me, I wasn' better off. Yes, I did earn money atter I was free, but atter all, **you knows money is de root of all evil, ain't dat what de good Book say?** When I was a slave I only had to obey my marster an he furnish me everything. (Rawick 1972: S. S. 1, v. 9, Miss., pt. 4, 1633)

The speaker obviously feels that the comparison between slavery and the antebellum South is a dangerous topic to discuss with the interviewer. Furthermore, he seems annoyed that the interviewer has raised the issue, perceiving the question as a kind of trap, a catch-22 in which any way that he answers can prove disastrous. There are several ways of interpreting his response, any of which registers criticism of the treatment of African-Americans. We might consider that he opts for an answer that perhaps many of these speakers believed the interviewers preferred, chiefly because it fit with the popular Euro-American idea that enslaved people favored and were content with enslavement. From this reading of the passage, the speaker is disguising any preference that he might have had for the freedom to earn a wage, citing the proverb to support the premise that money is undesirable, that it in some way spoils human innocence. So, by way of his rhetorical strategy, he effectively avoids making any comment that might disturb the interviewer and manages instead to pacify him or her by presenting the mask that he or she was accustomed to seeing when interacting with African-Americans. This mask is constructed from the social level of proverb meaning that was found in the dominant culture, and by foregrounding this meaning, the speaker suggests his docile agreement with it. We must also entertain the possibility that the situational meaning is sarcastic and that the speaker is making fun of the interviewer and his canon. From this perspective, the proverb might be laden with hostility about the failure of the dominant society to provide any viable means for freed slaves to advance socially and economically.

Variety in Proverb Application

Although most of the proverbs occur no more than once in the texts of these narratives, "You reap what you sow" occurs no less than six times, used by six different speakers. Judging from its frequency, we can surmise that it was one of the most popular proverbs among African-Americans at the time that these interviews were conducted and, perhaps, during the slavery period as well. Its recurrence in the narratives provides an opportunity to examine a wider range of applications than is possible with other proverbs. As I will demonstrate, this variety of applications includes the utilization of social, situational, and symbolic levels of meaning, and not only provides us with information concerning the use of social and personal metaphor, but is also an indication of the kinds of recurrent situations in which this particular proverb was applied.

In the previous examples, we saw proverbs and expressions used in speech interactions in which speakers actually address the issue of masked or disguised communication; however, with this proverb, speakers engage in such disguised communication while addressing other personal and social topics. In the first three of these the topics and commentary are decidedly social. The speaker in example #6 applies the proverb negatively to Euro-Americans who have sought to keep African-Americans enslaved. The superiority of divine and natural law over that of human striving is suggested, and the speaker openly indicates a political conviction and a personal anticipation of the "day of reckoning" that is in contrast to the more cautious arguments of speakers in previous examples.

> Example #6
> President Roosevelt is 'nother good man. He has looked down on de poor and 'tressed in dis land wid mercy; has give work and food to de poor people when nobody else would. When he turn dis way and turn dat way, them men up ther where he is, try to stop him from helpin' us, but de Blessed Master is gwine to hold his hands up. They ain't gwine to be able to stop him, 'cause he has done so much good in de world. Dat man is gwine to be 'membered by de people always, but them dat has fought him and worked against him is sho' gwine to be forgot. Nobody wants to 'member them for de evil they has done. **You knows dat if you sows evil you is sho' gwine to gather evil in time**. They ain't gwine sow much longer; their harvest time is right out dere in sight, but de President is gwine to live on wid us. (Rawick 1972: S. 1, v. 3, S. C., 51)

There is little that could be misconstrued in the application of the proverb here. The speaker correlates (Seitel 1960) the "sowing of evil" with the actions of racist politicians and others who would stand in the way of governmental programs designed to assist and support poor and disadvantaged citizens. Rhetorically, the proverb comes near the end of a narrative speech event similar to a short sermon, containing poetic turns of phrases and impassioned discourse. It summarizes or serves as the moral of the speech event, and is further explained by the comments that follow it and extend the metaphor of the proverb.[4] The grammatical level becomes important in this creative version and application, for a tremendous poetic leap is made from the literal idea of sowing to the image of "sowing evil," and this picture is elaborated upon in the ensuing remarks about "harvesting time."

The picture of "sowing evil" is an odd one, if we follow the grammatical sense of the proverb, and provides a dimension of humor. Two levels of social meaning are likely to pertain here: that of the dominant culture and that of African-Americans. It is safe to assume that one level of social meaning current in the dominant culture related to religious doctrine, and the application of the proverb by Euro- to African-Americans as a tool for instilling docility is evident from other examples. Also clear from other examples is one social level of meaning current among African-Americans—the justification for their right to a share of the American wealth, services, and goods. Here, the first of these social levels helps to disguise and protect the speaker. The second amplifies the situational meaning, that those who have worked against Roosevelt will soon wither away. Included in this second level of social meaning, and part of the amplification of the situational meaning, is a degree of anger, bitterness and the desire for revenge against those who have worked to perpetuate the oppression of African people.

The next example reveals even more about the way in which proverbs were used by African- to European-Americans. As in example #2, the speaker is telling the interviewer a story, perhaps a legend that had been in circulation among members of the African-American community since the period of slavery. A pertinent question about such instances is, why is the speaker choosing to relate the legend to the interviewer? While the data provided by the interviewer is insufficient to determine the reason, we can surmise certain possible motivations. The legend is one that demonstrates the recurrent theme of the enslaved outwitting the slaveowner. It further indicates the specific strategy employed by the enslaved man, and this becomes a central aspect of the message. Two components of the strategy are prominent: (1) the use of biblical authority to successfully argue a case and, more specifically, the use of that authority to defeat an assault that is based on that canon; and (2) the importance of literacy in pursuing an argument.

Example #7

Billy come to de house marster says Billy you preachah? Billy say yas sah. He says, Billy you'se cut dem collads, Billy says yas sah. I'se got some greens. He says now Billy you preachah, git me de Bible and sayd read dis, he shore hates to, but Marster makes him do it, den he shore tares loose on Billy bout stealin, finally Billy says now Marster I can show you in de Bible where I did not steal, he tells Billy to find it and Billy finds it and reads, "**You shall reap when you laborth**." Marster sayd to Billy get to hell outn here. (Rawick 1972: S. S. 2, v. 3, Tex., 606–607)

It is only logical to conclude that the speaker was at some level communicating to the interviewer several different things: his pride in his cultural heritage, a culture that had managed to survive by outwitting the enslavers; a belief held by many African-Americans since the inception of slavery that they were smarter than European-Americans; an awareness that European-Americans had attempted to use Christianity as a mechanism to instill submission and justify oppression; and the belief that African-Americans were entitled to the material benefits of the American system because they had been the primary work force for production of those goods—whether or not the American legal or social system recognized that right. All of these sentiments are encapsulated in the use of the proverb.

The social meanings discussed for the previous example apply here both in the fictive and in the natural contexts, and the story can be viewed as a discourse on the subversion of canonical texts to engender meaning appropriate for the enslaved, or the emergence of liberation theology. In the context of the story, Billy reinterprets the Euro, social level of meaning and applies it socially and situationally. Socially, slaves were entitled to the benefits of the system; situationally, he was entitled to the greens that he had grown. At the level of natural discourse, both meanings are also salient. Socially, the speaker is arguing the entitlement of African-Americans in the antebellum period to benefits of the system and, situationally, his own right to government assistance.

To return for a moment to an earlier point, it is quite interesting to observe this tale being told to a Euro-American. In the context of African-American culture, it was very likely a humorous tale, one which served several functions: it provided an outlet for the expression of anger and a mechanism for the criticism of slaveowners and the plantation system in general, and it celebrated the slaves' sense of pride in their abilities to successfully outwit the oppressors and to obtain the necessary goods to maintain their own culture (see Levine 1977, Roberts 1989). So it would seem a rather bold and even defiant move on the part of the speaker to relate the legend to the interviewer. Perhaps this is permitted by the thin veneer of the story and of fictive discourse in general. Certainly, we would not expect the interviewer to find the story humorous, at least not in the same way that the speaker would. At the core of all of this, however, is the reinterpretation that the speaker gives to the proverb, the implications of which amount to no less than the reinterpretation of the canon holding the institutions of American society in place. Of note is the consistent social level of meaning in examples #6 and #7, while the applications are so different. In one, the proverb has a negative correlation—the sowers are oppressors and the harvest is devastation. In the other, the correlation is positive, first person—the sowers are the oppressed and the harvest is their share of the American wealth.

The dynamics of example #7 are even more evident in example #8, in which the interaction preceding the use of the proverb is accessible. It seems that the interviewer has attempted to put the speaker, Mr. Mack Taylor, "in his place" by referring to the religious virtues of piety, long-suffering and patience, a common tactic of Euro-Americans intended to repress the anger and rebellious spirit of enslaved people and of later generations of African-Americans.

Example #8

Howdy do sir! **As Brer Fox 'lowed to Brer Rabbit when he ketched him wid a tar baby at de spring, "I 'is got you now!"** I's been waintin' to ask you 'bout dis old age pension. I's been to Winnboro to see 'bout it. Some nice white ladies took my name and ask some questions, but dat seem to be de last of it. Reckon I gwine to get anything?

Well, I's been here mighty nigh a hundred years, and just 'cause I pinched and saved and didn't throw my money away on liquor, or put it into de palms of every jezebel hussy dat slant her eye at me, ain't no valuable reason why them dat did dat way and 'joyed deirselves can get de pension and me can't get de pension. 'Tain't fair! No, sir. If I had a knowed way back yonder, fifty years ago, what I knows now, I might of gallavanted 'round a little more wid de shemales than I did. What you think 'bout it?

You say I's forgittin dat religion must be thought about? Well, **I can read de Bible a little bit. Don't it say: what you sow you sure to reap?** Yes sir. Us fell de forests for corn, wheat, oats, and cotton; drained de swamps for rice; built de dirt roads and de railroads; and us old ones is got a fair right to our part of de pension. (Rawick 1972: S. 1, v. 3, S. C., 157)

A number of significant features of this speaker's discourse are readily apparent. The first is the initial application of metaphor to invert the social order and status of the speaker and the interviewer. By casting himself in the metaphorical role of Brer Fox and the interviewer in the role of Brer Rabbit, the speaker reverses the social roles that exist in the real world, becoming the one with the upper hand and moving the interviewer into the subordinate position. Because of the lighthearted tone of the speech event, any serious implications of this maneuver are played down. A compelling aspect of this initial strategy is the masking of the identity of the speaker, as he shrouds himself in the dramatic role of a traditional, fictive character. Also important is the nature of the role assigned to the interviewer, for Brer Rabbit is the ultimate trickster and can only be captured for short periods of time before he devises some method of escape.

It is clear that the speaker assumes that the interviewer is capable of assisting him in obtaining his pension, and the remainder of his discourse consists of his feelings about the government's policy of benign neglect. In response to his entreaty, the interviewer resorts to the familiar rhetorical strategy of referring to the Bible to encourage a submissive attitude. The speaker becomes even more adamant at this point, perhaps reacting in part to the implicit condescension contained in the interviewer's response. He cites the proverb, as does the speaker in example #7, reinterpreting it to apply in precisely the same way. As in other examples, further elaborative and explanatory comments follow the proverb. The social and situational meanings here are identical to those in example #7, as is the rhetorical and argumentative strategy in which the proverb is located.

In several other examples of discourse containing this proverb, the application and message are not quite so easy to determine. Example #9, in fact, illustrates several facets of these other texts that contribute to this ambiguity of meaning. One facet is that the interviewers usually had an investment in painting portraits of the speakers that fit the docile images that Euro-Americans had constructed and fought so hard to maintain. In the interest of maintaining these images, much of the speakers' communications are misinterpreted, ignored, falsified, or otherwise presented in a manner so as to make them consistent with the interviewers' objectives (Rawick 1972: S. S. 1, v. 2, Ga.,ix—xlviii). This changes the nature of the texts quite dramatically in some cases, from ethnographic to journalistic or even literary, and, in many instances, the comments of the speakers are edited and abridged to illustrate points being made by the writers, e.g., example #9.

Example #9
Reflecting the sentiment of the majority of the slaves I have interviewed, she is opposed to capital punishment. She also believes implicitly that a divine punishment is reserved for those who transgress moral law. As **"people sow, so shall they reap,"** and "it is not given to man to judge his

fellow man," are the two maxims she holds in highest reverence. (Rawick 1972: S. S. 1, v. 3, Ga., pt. 1, 49)

The commentary of this particular interviewer is even more suspect when we consider that she has two different accounts of the interview appearing in different volumes.5 In one account there is more actual dialogue attributed to the speaker, and in the second account she adds further personal comments to the text of example #9: "Slavery was both wrong and right: wrong in that it deprived black humanity of the fruits of it's [*sic*] own labor: right, in that it undertook to improve the negro morally—practically expresses her views on that subject" (Rawick 1972: S. S. 1, v. 4, Ga., pt. 2, 488). Nowhere in the text do I find evidence that these are the sentiments of the speaker; to the contrary, given the social level of meaning reflected in other examples, it is likely that the use of the proverb implicated the injustice of the dominant culture and argued for social equity, no matter what the question to the speaker may have been, and that this is a classic case of the interviewer entirely missing the meanings that the item may have held for the speaker. Unfortunately, because it has been taken out of the context in which it was spoken, there is not enough contextual narration to argue conclusively the meaning that was intended.

Two other instances demonstrate that the proverb could be used to support opposite opinions about the same phenomenon—in this case, the existence of hell. These examples also demonstrate, as did #6 and #7, how two speakers can express the same base assumptions or social level of meaning while using the proverb to argue different sides of a more specific issue—the application of situational levels of meaning. In example #10, the speaker is arguing a belief in the nonexistence of hell; according to his argument, suffering and punishment occur before death. Fundamentally, the speaker's argument represents an attempt to make sense philosophically out of the slavery experience, reconciling it with biblical tenets. The essence of his philosophy includes several components: God could not possibly require a person to endure slavery *and then* also to go to hell; if there is an afterlife, it must be a place where the spirits of all persons enjoy equal status; and religion boils down to the sincere observance of compassion and civility in one's earthly life. Philosophically, all of these components fly in the face of the socially endorsed religious beliefs of the time and are implicitly damning of slaveowners and later generations of European-Americans. Moreover, they are also revolutionary in advocating the absolute equality of human beings. A distinct feature of this proverb speech act is the additional symbolic level of meaning that is apparently involved. In connection with the social and situational meanings, the proverb seems to carry some deeply personal and idiosyncratic meanings for this speaker.

Example #10
What I thinks about religion?
Well, now listen, God Almighty give every boy [everybody] de same spirit—the Spirit of God. God ain't made no hell for us. I been reading de Bible about 50 years and I ain't found it. God made us for his own glory. "For your disobedience you shall be striped with many stripes." Dis in de flesh. "Religion is de way I treat my fellow man." "**I gwine reap what I sew** [*sic*]." "De flesh is goin be punished befo he die, but the spirit belongs to God, and he goin take care of it." Misses I never done nuffin in my life what I know was wrong. My Missus taught me to live right and tell de truf. I's old nigger, and I believes according to de Bible dat everybody goin to same place. (Rawick 1972: S. S. 1, v. 8, Miss., 828)

Mrs. Ophelia Jemison, the speaker in example #11, does believe in hell, and her discourse is a personal testimony that takes the form of traditional conversion narratives.[6] As in some other examples, the proverb occurs as the summary or moral concluding a narrative speech event containing poetic and elaborate speech.

Example #11
Hell one turrible place. What de wicked do on dis ert, it jes lak dat in hell . . . Cussing, shooting, fighting one anodder, but dey being sperrits caint do any hurt. De fire down her is a big pit ob brimstone, a roaring an' a roaring. When I was seeking de Lord befo' I conberted (converted) 'e place me in hell to conbince (convince) me. I stay down dere mos' a hour, den I knowed dere a hell.
    I see de souls biling in de pit ob brimstone. Oh! God hab mercy on me soul. I'se a had (hard) believer, nebber did I 'tink dere could be a hell, but I knowed now ef you doan pray hell go be you home. It no flower bed ob ease down dere. **What you sow in wicked doings you sure reap down dere**. (Rawick 1972: S. S. 1, v. 11, S. C. and N. C., 223)

Certainly, the speaker is applying the proverb to support her contention that hell exists, but implicitly to suggest that behavior will be the determining factor in who is sentenced there. This concern with behavior, and at the same time with the purity of the spirit, is, in fact, the place where these last two examples intersect. Just as the speaker in example #10 suggests that an omniscient power will judge the spirit, irrespective of race or social class, so does Ms. Jemison. Despite the differences in focus, the underlying theme is equality of human beings in the sight of "God." In neither example can we be sure of the degree to which the proverbs express social sentiments: no one group is implicated by the speakers' remarks. But we can conjecture that the topic of afterlife was another recurrent issue to which this particular proverb was applied. It is possible, however, that the situational inference of this latter example is that Euro-Americans are going to hell because they have been among the wicked "on dis ert."

The final example of this proverb represents a departure from any of the applications in previous examples. The speaker, Mrs. Hager Brown, is relating a story about the funeral of a community member. Apparently, the son of the deceased woman is found drunk on the porch during the funeral procession, and later overturns his mother's casket during the church service.

> Example #12
> Hager: "I can shout! All the 'Piccolo' I want. Well Francis say, 'I yeddy! I yeddy bout duh boy!' Georgia dead and come long wid body, boy out there porch dead drunk! I say, 'Here we gone to bury boy Mama and boy gone!' Nice caslet. Church ketch fire." (All shouting—warming up with spirit). "Gin to shout. Boy gone up. Turn he caslet over. **Man shill, 'Reap what he sow.'** Bible say, 'Honor you Father and Mother.' You reap or chillun reap. What-some-ever you ain't reap—chillun reap." Some look in porch. Taking Georgia to graveyard.
> 'Who dat dere?'
> 'Dat boy.'
> 'Lie dere dead drunk.
> Zackie: "Likker'll make you not know you mama." (Rawick 1972: S. S. 1, v. 11, N. C. And S. C., 77)

The proverb functions as a criticism of the deceased party, implying that the boy's drunken behaviors are somehow the "harvest" of the parent's deeds. We have no way of ascertaining the relationship between the speaker and the deceased, but it is clear from other comments made during the interview that she holds this particular family in low regard. In essence, the use of the proverb indicates that the boy's character and actions come as no surprise given the character of his mother, or even of someone in an earlier generation of the family. We can infer from this application a third recurrent problem or kind of interactional situation in which this proverb may have been commonly used by speakers during this historical time period. This third person correlation is the only instance in which the proverb is applied to another African-American. An aspect of the social meaning found in some of the other examples—the expression of hostility toward another— also pertains here. The situational meaning, however—that a member of the community who has engaged in some socially disapproved behavior will experience misfortune—is quite different.

In reviewing the examples of this proverb, several observations can be made. The various uses certainly illustrate that the same proverb was applied to different recurrent situations and that in each new situation different meanings were present. The examples also demonstrate that, while a proverb may have been used in a very particular immediate context, commenting only on the behaviors of particular community members— e.g., example #12—it could also be applied at a larger social or political level, commenting upon groups or types of people, e.g., examples #6, #7, and #8. Finally, as examples #10 and #11 indicate, the same proverb could be used to support opposite sides of an argument, even when applied to the same recurrent issue. All of these observations suggest the immense range of meaning that a given proverb can have within a given cultural group at any point in time, as well as the dangers inherent in attempts to extrapolate meaning without a careful investigation of the particular context in which a proverb speech act occurs.

As we have seen in examples #7, #8 and #9, proverbs are sometimes used by speakers as a form of social commentary or criticism, capitalizing on the social level(s) of meaning. This kind of application occurs in the uses of three other proverbs, two of which are used by the same speaker, with another occurring a number of different times in the narratives of different speakers.

The speech event in which the first two of these proverbs occur is very different from most of the discourse in these collections of interviews. The speaker, unlike many of those who express criticism in their comments, does not assume any postures or make any effort to disguise his message, other than that afforded by the anonymous character of the proverbs. Neither does he refer to the biblical canon in introductory or closing formulas (a common strategy of most speakers). And finally, the construction of his discourse, including the placement of the proverb in that construction, is divergent from that in many other cases in which proverbs are used. Instead of using the proverb as an established truth, as a symbolic referent to collective and societal wisdom supporting his position, he poses the item as a symbol of societal rhetoric, and then deconstructs its logic and truth value. In doing so, he casts the very society that the item symbolizes into a hypocritical and cruel light, undermining its foundation by foregrounding the inherent irony contained in its canonical wisdom and social rhetoric. The strategy here is also different from that of other proverb speech acts that have been discussed in that it locates the social meaning in the context of the dominant society, and dismisses rather than reinterprets it.

Example #13
They say a rollin' stone gathers no moss, but I tell you if I wasn't so old I'd be rollin' right now. This is no place for colored people. (Rawick 1972: S. S. 2, v. 7, Tex., 2593)

One of the critical components of the proverb here is the introductory formula "They say," which indicates not only an ambiguous number of past generations, but also those who are currently alive, and who in some way represent the conventional beliefs of community and society. The "they" here becomes the object of bitterness and irony and the proverb the symbol of "their" propaganda. The social meaning alluded to in the use of proverb is the positive value of a stable life and the negative value of a wandering one.7 "Stone" is applied to the person and the "moss" corresponds to the accruements of a stable life, e.g., family and property. The speaker's message is that such proverbial wisdom is only applicable to certain classes and ethnic groups. Efforts made by African-Americans to obtain stability are thwarted by the forces of racism. The only aspect of the message that is unclear is what is meant by "place." Does he mean America? Does he mean the southern United States? Or is he referring to a particular locale within a particular state?

The speaker's usage of the second proverb is just as poignant:

Example #14
The trouble with people here is they don't know how to treat humanity, white or black. **I know the sayin' when you're in Rome do as Rome do**. But the Romans got the best of it. (Rawick 1972: S. S. 2, v. 7, Tex., 2593)

Again the proverb points to the irony inherent in the traditional "truths" of a society in which those truths are not applicable to everyone, and again the speaker's anger and bitterness are apparent. As in example #13, the proverb is posed and then discredited in a particular case, thereby undermining the canon from which the proverb comes. This is accomplished not only through the logical framing of the proverb in the speech event, but also by the employment of a subtle, sardonic humor. "Rome" becomes a metaphor for American society, and, as such, is a rich and interesting reference, one which captures the very real position of people who found themselves in a western and alien world based conceptually on classical thinking. More than any other metaphor that the speaker could have chosen, this one emphasizes the cultural dilemma of African-Americans. This performance further parodies the conventional social meaning of the proverb—that one should adopt the behavioral norms of the groups in which one finds oneself in order to fit in—by drawing a picture of dark-skinned people of a very different cultural tradition attempting to blend into a very white world. Finally, it underscores the political reality that the behaviors of an oppressed group can do little to ensure their integration into a society that has no real motivation to avail itself to members of that group. In other words, "Romans got the best of it" means that Euro-Americans form the power base of the society, in contrast to African-Americans and others who are barred from significant entrance into that society. It is also possible that the speaker is equally annoyed with African-Americans who are abusive, as he refers to "white or black." This could, on the other hand, be interpreted to mean that both "white" and "black" are victims of oppression. In both proverb speech acts, this speaker is able to communicate his anger and hostility not only toward the system but perhaps toward any individuals whom he might perceive as abusive or toward those implicated by association, such as the interviewer. Although he does not make as much effort to disguise his feelings as some other speakers might, the nature of proverbs affords him some degree of personal distance from the sentiments expressed in them.

The third proverb that is applied at the social level is the biblical adage "Every man has to serve God under his own vine and fig tree". In both instances in which this proverb is used, the speaker is conveying the sentiments that African-Americans, like other ethnic groups, should have personal and social autonomy; however, there are significant variations in the applications that indicate differences in the social and situational meanings from one speaker to another. (We might ponder whether the proverb was used by Euro-Americans and, if so, what social meanings it might have carried for them.) In example #15, the speaker, Mr. Jim Allen, uses the proverb to support his contention that slavery was morally wrong, and that the wrongness of the institution is spoken of in the Bible.

Example #15
Abraham Lincoln worked by 'pinions of de Bible. He got his meanings from the Bible. "**Every man should live under his own vine and fig tree.**" Dis Abraham's 'mandments. Dis is where Lincoln started-"No man should work for another." (Rawick 1972: S. S. v. 6, Miss., 13)

The proverb in this instance actually conveys more than the idea that African-Americans should not be enslaved; it suggests an independence that would allow persons to be self-employed, self-supporting, self-reliant, and immune to the intrusion of state or federal interest into their personal and private lives. Implicitly, this suggestion, which reflects not only a sentiment that is strongly American but also one which was commonly held by enslaved Africans brought to the shores of America, involves the fair distribution of land to those who had rights to land, specifically vis-à-vis the promise of "40 acres and a mule," which was a popular element of the emancipation proclamation among African-Americans. The application of the proverb by this speaker, then, is extremely political in nature.

Example #16 is, in many regards, inconsistent with the sentiments of Example #15.

Example #16
Even with my good treatment, I spent most of my time planning and thinking of running away. I could have done it easy, but my old father used to say, "**No use running from bad to worse, hunting better.**" Lots of colored boys did escape and joined the Union army, and there are plenty of them drawing a pension today. My father was always counseling me. He said, "**Every man has to serve God under his own vine and fig tree.**" He kept pointing out that the War wasn't going to last forever, but that our forever was going to be spent living among the Southerners, after they got licked. He'd cite examples of how the whites would stand flat-footed and fight for the blacks and the same as for members of their own family. I knew that all was true, but still rebelled, from inside of me. I think I really was afraid to run away because I thought my conscience would haunt me. My father knew I felt this way and he'd rub my fears in deeper. One of his remarks still rings in my ears: "**A clear conscience opens bowels, and when you have a guilty soul it ties you up and**

death will not for long desert you." (Rawick 1972: S. 1, v. 4, Tex., pts.
1 and 2, 189–190)

Instead of prescribing social and political autonomy, the proverb here seems
to be used to encourage an attitude of compliance with the established
order. It is used in close connection with another expression that sounds
proverbial, and is a part of the father's argument that his son should not
attempt to leave the South because the North would not be any better. He
seemed to feel that dreams of leaving were unrealistic, and the meaning
of the proverb at the social level is that one should be satisfied with one's
lot in life. "His own vine and fig tree" in this application is correlated
to the circumstances in which one finds oneself or to the resources that
one has been given. The situational meaning is that the man's son should
be realistic and prepare for spending the rest of his life where he was.
This preparation invariably involved adopting a less rebellious attitude.
Throughout the passage, strong sentiments of loyalty and belonging to the
present environment are exposed; in fact, all of the maxims that the speaker
attributes to his father emphasize this point of view. Though the speaker is
not completely in agreement with his father's sentiments, he has complied,
and the passage indicates that proverbs could be used to intimidate and
discourage flight or rebellion. A noteworthy aspect of that intimidation
here is that it is applied by an African-American father to his son. This
is significant not only because of the glimpse of information that we can
obtain about the function of proverbs within the enslaved community, but
also because there is rarely any information available on the transmission
process of proverbs from one generation to another. For this reason, it
is not feasible to ascertain the particulars of proverb transmission among
the enslaved population in general. These considerations aside, example
#16 demonstrates how a proverb that, on one hand, could reflect the most
profound nationalistic sentiments could also on the other hand reflect a
compliance with the insidious but established social order.

It is difficult to determine what underlying messages the speakers in these
last two examples might have been intending to convey to the interviewers.
In example #15, the obvious meaning is likely the one that was intended, and
is supported not only with biblical authority, but with political sanction as
well. In order for the interviewer to disagree with the speaker's sentiments,
he would have had to disparage the Bible and the president. Quite possibly,
the second speaker relates the anecdote about his father to suggest that his

present views are less incendiary than they really are, and, in this case, the social meaning of the proverb may be that which is found in example #15.

Proverbs and the Supernatural

Aside from contexts in which topics of social import are central, several examples of discourse in which supernatural phenomena are being discussed also contain proverbs. With "Seeing is believing," a number of the previous points that have been made about the functions of proverbs are also applicable. The most notable is the use of the item in two separate examples to argue opposite sides of the same issue. As with some of the other topics that proverbs are applied to, belief in the supernatural is one of the areas that interviewers routinely questioned the speakers about, and that frequently elicited segments of elaborate, fictive discourse either describing or relating personal-experience narratives involving such phenomena. For obvious reasons, questions about the supernatural were less likely to evoke statements of political or social content.

In example #17 Mrs. Manda Boggan is stating her belief in ghosts and in voodoo, and uses the proverb to support her conviction.

Example #17
I believe in ghos'. **Seein' is believin'** an' Ise seed hants all my life. I knows folks can be hoodooed, mighty curious things can be done. One nite I wuz gwine to a dance. We had toer go through thick woods. Hit wiz one o' dem nites dat yo' feels lak deir is somethin' somewhars, yo' feels quir lack an' jumpy an' wants ter look ober yo' sholdier but scart to. Deys alwas' a hant 'round when hits lak dat. De fust thing us knowed deir wuz a ghos' right in front ob us what looked lak a cow. Hit jes stood deir, a gittin' bigger an' bigger, den hit disappeared. Us run lak something' wild. I went on ter dat dance but sho didn't dance none, I jes' set 'round an' look on, an' from dat nite I ain't neber gone to a frolic an' danced no mo'. (Rawick 1972: S. S. 1, v. 10, Miss., 4)

The narration takes the form of a ghost legend (one which chronicles the speaker's conversion from a party-goer to a non-party-goer), and the proverb provides the "moral" of the story, as well as the voice of authority that rhetorically adds validation and credibility to the tale. The tale, however, functions as much to validate the proverb. The strategy of the proverb is vastly different from that of some of the earlier examples in which the message of the proverb might be somehow applied to the interviewer. Here, the proverb becomes more a part of the performance of a legend, and may perhaps be a recurrent feature of the telling of the legend for this particular informant.

The second occasion of the proverb argues for the nonexistence of certain supernatural phenomena.

Example #18
The old folks told ghost stories to the children. They would think about them ghosts every time dark would come. That's how come folks grow up to believe in them. I am going to come clean and say straight out I got no faith in such as that. If them things could be seen I would run across one of them some time or other, but I ain't so I telling you I got no faith in it. I don't believe in them Hoo Doo doctors neither. I don't pay them no attention when I hears all this and that 'bout what they can do. I just says to myself, **"Seeing is believing**." And I ain't never seed. (Rawick 1972: S. S. 1, v.10, Miss., 5)

I suggest that, as in example #17, the speaker's discourse represents a social meaning of the proverb and a recurrent way in which this particular proverb was used: to argue the (non)existence of otherworldly phenomena. Of note is that the situational meaning is opposite in these two examples. In the former, the proverb is used to communicate the message "I believe in ghosts because I have seen them," but in the latter, the message is "I don't believe in them [or in similar extraordinary occurrences], because I have never seen them."

The other proverb that occurs in connection with the supernatural is "The straw that broke the camel's back." Once more the segment of discourse in which the item appears is a ghost legend. George Jackson, the speaker, is noted by the interviewer as a raconteur, a teller of "yarns and stories that took place in the distant past" (Rawick 1972: S. S. 1, v. 11, N. C. and S. C., 212), and he distinguishes himself as a skillful narrator, embellishing the tale with extended details and dramatic dialogue. The story is a lengthy one about a white man and his family who rented a haunted house in spite of warnings from his neighbors. The man is determined to prove himself "a real man" by confronting the ghosts and not giving in to possible fears. The "hant," however, creates so many intimidating disruptions that the family finally flees the house.

Example #19
By dis time de hant had reached de room above them. Over went a table. After de table noise, he heard a rattle of a tin bucket and footsteps going

toward de top of de stairsteps. When de footsteps reached de top of de steps, he heard de bucket set down with a heavy bump, like it was full of water. But de bucket didn't set dere long, for dat was turned over too and down de steps come water and bucket both. Dis last curious noise was too much; **it was de straw dat broke de camel's back**. Business picked up right now. He started for the front door but it was so full of his wife and Jimmie, he was obliged to make himself a door through a side window, glass, sash, blinds, and all. (Rawick 1972: S. S. 1, v. 11, N. C. and S. C., 212)

While the example represents the only one in which a proverb (expression) is applied humorously, there may also be a serious side to its usage. We cannot overlook the fact that the speaker has chosen to tell a tale that parodies the skepticism and machismo of a white man to a white interviewer. This facet of the legend is highlighted by some of the speaker's comments, e.g., "I'se a brave man and has a wife and son to 'tect. I'se gwine in de house and be at home wid my family, like a man, hant or no hant," and "He thought it wa sho' good to be a real man and scared of nothing." In essence, it is a tale of a skeptical man who, in efforts to live beyond his means, is humbled by supernatural forces. Although there is no way to be certain of the speaker's motivations for choosing this particular legend, the dynamics of ethnicity and social class are probably significant factors in the encoding and decoding of the message. It could easily be a tale poking fun at and mocking the interviewer through its derision of Euro-American hubris and arrogance. To know with certainty the social application of the proverb at that time in history would help to ascertain the extent to which this is actually a component of the speech event. If, for example, the proverb is one that was used primarily by European-Americans and that was associated in the minds of African-Americans with Euro-American society, mockery in its most biting form would likely be at the heart of this performance. In such a case, the use of the proverb would be the equivalent of the use of "proper English" by an African-American to mock European-American behavior.

The Symbolism of Objects and Animals

A discussion of the proverb in example #19 leads to a consideration of yet another category of proverbs that are found in the narratives—proverbs that contain images of objects or animals, and that correlate these images with people in actual social contexts. Seitel has noted in his discussion of

Yoruba proverbs that items containing images of animals are often applied
in a negative fashion or to criticize the character or behavior of those to
whom the items are applied (1969: 153). This tendency seems to hold true
in the proverbial speech of African-Americans, at least in the texts of these
narratives. There are five such proverbs, and, although the applications of
all of them are not clear, the ones that are conform to Seitel's observation.
With all of these, the grammatical level is crucial because the impact of
the metaphorical meaning relies so heavily on the proverb picture or image
that is created in the mind.

In "The straw dat broke de camel's back," the camel is correlated to the
white man who has already been parodied in the text and performance of the
legend. By way of this correlation, he is portrayed as a comic and somewhat
tragic figure, one who has honorably and haplessly borne as much weight
as was possible and is now falling beneath the strain. The proverb is even
more effective because the narrator has previously emphasized the man's
sense of responsibility for the care, protection and well-being of his family.
(It is also possible that the speaker is correlating the proverb more loosely,
applying the "camel" to the tenseness of the situation by the time the water
bucket is turned over. But even then, the association of the "camel" with
the man is still made in the listener's mind.) This proverbial expression is
humorous first at the grammatical level, in the image of a camel so loaded
down that a single straw is able to break his back. What compounds this
humor is the situational application of the metaphor, depicting the man as
a metaphorical camel, carrying the burden of his machismo, arrogance, and
perhaps whiteness.

Example #20 is recorded by the same interviewer, Mrs. Genevieve W.
Chandler, who recorded example #12, and the speaker is the same, Mrs.
Hager Brown. Mrs. Brown is relating more about the young man who was
found drunk the day of his mother's funeral.

Example #20
He jest wuz lying there drunk. They say half the people were coming
by the house and he had two guns (Ben did). Held 'em up! Wouldn't let
'em pass! Say he gwine kill 'em all! Say he Daddy kill his Mother. Say he
murder her and he going to get him! Held up he Ma funeral procession!
Some run through the woods! I hear 'em on church grounds. They say,
"Ben drunk!"

When we all come by, he jest laying there on the poarch. Some say
"Call him! Let him come on and see the last o' his mother!" I say, "No,

man! **Let sleeping dog lie!**" (Rawick 1972: S. S. 1, v. 11, N. C. and
S. C., 234)

In choosing this particular proverb, the speaker in the story is able to
accomplish two rhetorical goals simultaneously: to instruct the members
of the funeral procession that they would be better off not to disturb the
boy and to criticize the boy by referring to him as a dog. The proverb, then,
amounts to name calling, or a curse, resembling in function the strategies of
signifying that are used within the African-American community (Mitchell-
Kernan 1972a, 1972b; Gates 1988). By using the proverb as she does, the
speaker characterizes the boy as lazy, dirty, irresponsible, and out of touch
with socially approved community norms and behaviors. Again, there is an
important link between the situational application of the proverb and the
grammatical picture presented.

In example #21 an animal image is also employed critically. The speaker,
Mrs. Sarah Ford, is reminiscing about some of the people she remembers
from the plantation.

Example #21
Massa Kit has two brother, Massa Charles and Massa Matt, what lives at
West Columbia. Massa Kit on one side Varney's Creek and Massa Charles
on de other side. Massa Kit have a African woman from Kentucky for he
wife, and dat's de truth. I ain't sayin' iffen she a real wife or not, but all de
slaves has to call her 'Miss Rachel.' **But iffen a bird fly up in de sky it
mus' come down sometimes**, and Rachel jus like dat bird, 'cause Mass
Kit go crasy and die and Massa Charles take over de plantation and he
takes Rachel and puts her to work in de field. But she don't stay in de field
long, 'cause Massa Charles puts her in a house by herself and she don't
work no more. (Rawick 1972: S. 1, v. 4, Tex., pts. 1 and 2, 42)

Like the proverb in example #20, this one functions to characterize and
comment negatively on the person to whom it is applied. Underlying
the proverbial application is the malice that one would expect from a
member of the enslaved community toward another member who was
given special treatment or status and who had to be addressed in the same
manner as slaveowners and their family members; in this instance, the
resentment is felt by members of the slave community toward concubines
of slaveowners. At the situational level, an analogy is drawn between the
enviable characteristics of a bird (its ability to fly and associations with
freedom) and Rachel's social status, but then also between the limitation

of the bird (that it cannot *live* in the air) and the inevitability of Rachel's
social demise. The proverb not only dramatically depicts Rachel's dilemma
but also characterizes her, fixing an image of her in the listener's mind.
She is portrayed as experiencing a temporary and false sense of freedom
and an attitudinal break with her own culture. "De sky" is correlated to a
high rank of social status and assimilation, and "coming down" refers to
the socioeconomic status from which she sprang and to her cultural roots.
A similarity between this and the previous proverb is the way in which
the correlation of the person and the animal separates the person from
the community, drawing attention to characteristics that are asocial and
condemned. Regarding the intended communication from the speaker to
the interviewer, it must be considered once again that there may have been
some intent to comment negatively on the behavior of slaveowners and,
by association, on the character of the interviewer. More specifically, the
proverb may have carried some situational meaning that implicated the
interviewer's similarity either to Rachel or to one of the plantation owners.

Two other examples of proverbs also illustrate some of these features,
although their applications are not quite as clear. In the first, the speaker is
commenting on religion, arguing his case that he has always been a good
Christian, and then criticizing the efforts of missionaries in Africa to convert
Africans to Christianity.

> Example #22
> I went to church always and am a good Christian, and I hope to see
> my Maker and both my Masters because they was both good, kind men.
> Everybody should have religion, but **you got to go slow and not try
> to change the leopard spots quick**, like them people done in Africa. I
> don't think they done a bit of good. (Rawick 1972: S. S. 1, v. 3, S. C., 43)

While it is unclear exactly to what he refers, we can surmise that the speaker
is concerned with the zealous campaigns of European missionaries in Africa.
His use of the proverb is actually an allusion to "A leopard doesn't change
his spots," and as such communicates more in this speech event than is
readily apparent. The situational implication is that it might not be possible
for Africans to be converted to Christianity, and that if it is possible, the
process would have to occur over a period of time, not suddenly. The use of
the animal image here also serves to distance the speaker and his referential
group from the Africans about whom he is speaking, not unlike the way
in which the images in examples #20 and #21 functioned. I suggest that

this is one of the primary functions of this allusion, and that the speaker in some way seeks to impress the interviewer with his religiousness by juxtaposing it with the popular image of less developed people, as well as by juxtaposing his rewards with those of slaveowners. To what degree this is simply a rhetorical strategy is difficult to determine; however, at the same time that this juxtaposition is achieved, a criticism of European interference in the lives of Africans is also registered. Again, the grammatical level is highly significant, for the speaker is referring to Africans as "leopards," which connotes wildness and savagery and effectively locates them outside of the behavioral norms that identify the speaker's own group as human and civilized. "Spots" is thus correlated to cultural attributes that conflict with Anglicized values, beliefs, and behaviors.

A fourth example in this category of proverbs contains the image of an object instead of an animal, but some of the same features pertain. In one of the most self-deprecating instances of discourse found in the narratives, the proverb operates to crystalize and magnify the negative characteristics of African-Americans that the speaker expresses.

Example #23
Many niggers have gone north to live, since freedom, but de most of them either comes back south again or they wants to come back. De north don't suit de nigger. Cold climate lak they has up dere is too hard on him. He has thin blood and you knows dat **a thin pan gwine to git hot quicker than a thick one** and cold de same way. You see a heap of niggers is lak wild animals, in a way. He laks to eat a heap, sleep a heap, and move 'bout slow. When he goes up north he has to step 'round fas', 'cause if he don't, he gits in de way of them Yankees dat move 'bout quick. (Rawick 1972: S. 1, v. 3, S. C., 43)

The proverb image objectifies the nature of human beings, not only reflecting superstitious belief (the relative thickness of blood), but making it easier to view the people to whom the proverb is applied as other than human. The speaker amplifies this sentiment with remarks such as "a heap of niggers is lak wild animals." Again we can observe that the proverb functions to emphasize the separateness of the speaker from others and to comment negatively on those others.

One of the most common proverbial expressions that further illustrates the features under consideration is "Root, hog, or die."[8] The expression occurs in the discourse of numerous speakers and is generally used to refer to the philosophy of the slaveowners and the plantation system rather than to express the personal philosophy of the speakers. The speakers, in fact, usually mention the expression in a contemptuous fashion, pointing to the cruel and inhuman treatment of newly freed men and women at the end of the Civil War. Contained in the expression, as in the above proverbs, is the image of an animal that serves to dehumanize the persons to whom the expression is directed. The application of the expression to Africana people emphasized their status as less-than-human laborers, depicting them as property that existed for the consumption of the slaveowners. Indications are that the expression was used by slaveowners in their speeches to newly freed African-Americans at the end of the Civil War. Typically, plantation owners gathered the freed people together and informed them that they had the choice either to continue working on the plantation or to leave. Should they leave, they would be on their own, receiving no support; they would have to "root, hawg, or die."

> Example #24
> Massa John call all de niggers on de plantation 'round him at de big house and he say to 'em "Now you all jes' as free as I is. I ain't your marster no mo'. I'se tried to be good to you and take keer of all of you. You is all welcome to stay and we'll all wuk togedder and make a livin' somehow. Ef you don' want to stay, dem dat go will jes' have to **root, pig, or die**."
> (Rawick 1972: S. 1, v. 5, Ala. and Ind., 41)

Mrs. Ruby Witt, also from Texas, relates the same story: "I come back to the Witts and master calls up all the slaves and says we was free, but if we stayed and worked for him we'd have plenty to eat and wear, and if we left, it'd be **root, hawg or die**" (Rawick 1972: S. 1, v. 5, Tex., pts. 3 and 4, 209). Though it is uncertain to what extent this became a popular story in oral tradition, its social association is obvious, as is the dehumanizing quality of the expression. It is altogether possible that a social dimension of this item was its connection with a tale that functioned to celebrate the strength and perseverance present in the African-American culture in spite of such horrendous treatment. This has historically been one of the functions of African-American legends and memorates that on the surface might seem only to recall painful memories (Morgan 1980). If so, the telling of the tale in this speech event and the performance of the proverb speech act would be a proud and defiant declaration to the interviewer, communicating not only the positive element of African-American culture, but mocking and decrying the inhumane behavior of Euro-Americans and, by implication, the interviewer.

Personal and Other Proverbs

A number of proverbs in the narratives seem to fall into no clearly defined category, and some of these items are surrounded by too little contextual information to permit a detailed discussion of their possible meanings or functions in speech events where they occur. Other aspects of proverb function are suggested, however, in some cases. As illustrated with "Charity begins at home," there is the strong possibility that there was sometimes a connection between images in proverbs and personal naming, a practice common in parts of Africa (Finnegan 1970: 392; Omijeh 1973; Nwachukwu-Agbada 1991).

Example #25
Dey named me Charity, 'kase dey said **"Charity begins at home"** an' I recken I sho' stay at home mos' of de time. (Rawick 1972: S. S. 1, v. 8, Miss., 1193)

In example #26, we discover that proverbs were sometimes considered personal mottos. This is also a practice found in some African societies in a more elaborate form, and, at least among one group, proverb names or aliases are chosen by individuals to express their personal mottos or other elements of their life's philosophy (Nwachukwu-Agbada 1991). We have no further information on how such mottos functioned in slave or ex-slave communities. It is not clear, for instance, whether the individual chose the motto or had it bestowed upon him or her by others.

Example #26
In 1926, at the age of 111 years, he died, leaving a large family. His motto was **"A stitch in Time saves Nine"**; all his life he was law-abiding citizen. (Rawick 1972: S. S. 1, v. 8, Miss., 1)

Example #27 provides us with at least a minimal context and application of the proverb. The speaker, Mrs. Malindy Smith, applies the item to her experience as a young girl taking care of her niece. Even with this small segment of discourse, a rather vivid picture is painted, poignantly capturing the sadness of the situation. We can easily picture the speaker attempting to fill the parental role for which she is seemingly so unprepared.

Example #27
The only job I did 'fo de surrender was nursin' one my sister's chillun. I was so small **'twas like de blind leadin' de blind**. (Rawick 1972: S. S. 1, v. 10, Miss., 1994)

The next example is interesting in that the interviewer engages in an examination of the informant's application of the proverb. What is not mentioned in this interviewer's short discussion is that the proverb was sometimes used jokingly, either to parody the motif of the promiscuous and seductive preacher or to poke fun at the rationalizations of promiscuous members of the community (see appendix). At the social level this proverb means that as long as two people are Christian (two clean sheets), engaging in sex with each other cannot be a sin (can't smut).

> Example #28
> Sin, according to Uncle Rias, is anything and everything one does and says "not in the Name of the Master." The holy command, "Whatever ye do, do it in my name," is subjected to a very elastic interpretation by this aged Negro and by others in his community. For instance, he firmly maintained that "**two clean sheets can't smut**" which means that a devout man and woman may indulge in the primal passion without being guilty of sin. (Rawick 1972: S. S. 1, v. 3, Ga., pt. 1, 74)

A proverbial expression found in the narratives, "to smut the sheets up," seems to be generically related to the above item. At the very least, the expression appears to connote sexual relations; in contrast to the proverb, however, a negative quality is implied. A situation similar to that in example #21 pertains here: the Africana woman is a concubine of the white plantation owner. The speaker cites the expression as the woman's statement on intimate relationships with Africana men, and in this context it takes on the meaning of an undesirable or repulsive sexual liaison. It furthermore reflects the internalized racism of an Africana woman who sees herself as socially superior to other Africana people.

> Example #29
> So, when old Mistress died he wouldn't let this cullud woman leave, and he gave her a swell home right there on the place, and she is still there I guess. They say she say sometime, she didn't want no Negro man **smutting her sheets up**. (Rawick 1972: S. 1, v. 7, Okla. and Miss., 23)

Proverb #30 is given by the speaker as an item used by European-Americans, though it is unclear if it was ever parodied or used by African-Americans. It is a variant of "A dead man tells no tales," and gives an idea of a possible context that was associated with the proverb—the secret murder of Africana people who persisted in attempting to escape.

Example #30
After he had sol' ole John some lot of times, he coaxed ole John off in de swamp one day and ole John foun' dead sev'ral days later. De white folks said dat de owner kilt him, 'cause **"a dead nigger won't tell no tales."** (Rawick 1972: S. 1, v. 4, Tex., pts. 1 and 2, 230)

Item #31 reflects the common belief that Africans were especially attracted to red colors, a belief that found its way into American folklore in the form of a tale "motif." The speaker is explaining why African-Americans joined one group of soldiers and not the other.

Example #31
Then come Hampton and de Red Shirts. Had they been a black shirt I don't believe niggers would ever have took to it. '**Dog for bread, nigger for red**', they likes dat color. (Rawick 1972: S. 1, v. 3, S. C., 194)

Several other proverbs are also used to endorse a particular folk belief. Example #32 is, like #31, a rhyming proverb (although the version given by the speaker does not rhyme).

Example #32
My old Miss give me a brown dress and hat. Well dat dress put me in de country, **if you mahie in brown you'll live in de country**.

"Marry in brown you'll live out of town?" I quoted. "Dats it, my remembrance ain't so good and I fergits." (Rawick 1972: S. 1, v. 6, Ala. and Ind., 45)

A second proverb is given by the same speaker in response to an inquiry about children. Usually associated with a male perspective on marriage and relationship, it is applied here by a female, and is somewhat self-deprecating in that it supports the belief that women "nag" men. It argues that this speaker's deceased husband might have been better off had he not married so many times. Another possible shade of meaning includes an expression of resentment toward her husband or his former wives.

Example #33
No ma'am, I ain't got no chillun, but Bradfield had plenty un um, I was his fouf wife. He died 'bout three years ago and he done well to live dat long wid all dem wimmens to nag him. De Bible say **It's better to climb on top of the house and sat, den to live inside wid a naggin' 'oman**. (Rawick 1972: S. 1, v. 6, Ala. and Ind., 45)

Example #34 occurs in response to a question about belief in superstitions, but there is little surrounding discourse to indicate very much about the meaning and application of the item. Generally, the speaker seems to discredit practices aimed at predicting or influencing the future.

Example #34
When asked if he believed in a number of signs, he shook his head and replied: **What's goin' to be, s'goin to be**. (Rawick 1972: S. S. 1, v. 4, Ga., pt. 2, 392)

Proverbs without Contextual Discourse, Biblical Sayings, and Proverbial Expressions

A number of items in the texts simply do not have enough contextual discourse to permit a discussion of their applications, or their placement in the texts leaves ambiguous what exactly the proverbs refer to. These (all following citations are Rawick 1972) include "What God go lot out for a man he'll get it" [If it's for you, you'll get it] (S. 1, v. 3, S. C., 63), "Ways of woman and ways of snake deeper than the sea!" (S. 1, v. 3, S. C., 212), and "De truth makes you free and runs de devil" (S. 1, v. 3, S. C., 43). There are also numerous biblical quotations, some of which are applied proverbially, while others are not. These include "Lub thy neighbor as theyself" (S. S. 1, v. 11, N. C. and S. C., 224) and "Do unto others as you desire others to do unto you" (S. 1, v. 6, Ala. and Ind., 335).

In addition to the proverbs in the texts, there is a considerable number of proverbial expressions, some of which occur more than once. These seem specifically to reflect the realities of the slavery experience, and, although they do not function as true proverbs do to propose solutions, they do have associations with recurrent situations that arose in the lives of members of the enslaved community. Because the data on the proverbial speech of Euro-Americans in the context of the slavery period and even in periods afterward is so lacking, it is difficult to determine to what extent these expressions were shared by the European-American community, or to what extent the situations with which they were associated might have been identical for both ethnic groups.

These expressions reflect concerns with three basic areas: work, religious worship, and freedom. "Whip to a nub" (S. S. 1, v. 11, N. C. and S. C., 222), to do something "to death" (S. S. 1, v. 6, Miss., 5; S. S. 2, v. 2, Tex., pt. 1, 441), "from sun to sun" (S. S. 2, v. 9, Tex., pt. 8, 3514, 3530, 3537), and "within an inch of his life" (S. S. 1, v. 4, Ga., pt. 2, 480) reflect some of the harsher aspects of labor during the period of enslavement. The expression "to hoe your row," which Taylor has suggested may be of African origin (1969–70), seems also to mean that one should mind one's own business and "carry one's weight" in a general sense—"Just trust in God and **hoe your row** and sidestep away from the great temptation, that's what I say" (S. S. 1, v. 12, Okla., 111, 118). Already, the expression that is currently applied by African-Americans to discriminatory practices in hiring was existent, occurring in a shortened version, "Last hired" (S. S. 1, v. 4, Ga. pt. 2, 405). Expressions associated with freedom include "free as a frog" (S. 1, v. 3, S. C., 191), "from pillar to post," and "root, hog, or die." "From pillar to post," like "root, hog, or die," seems to be particularly connected with the antebellum period, at least as one speaker uses it: "If we hadn't er had ter work and slave foer nothin' we might have had somethin' ter show foer what we did do and wouldn't have to live **from piller ter post** now" (S. S. 1, v. 1, Ala., 411). The expression is used to indicate a disenfranchised condition of poverty and bare survival.

Another expression grew out of the secretive, nocturnal religious meetings of enslaved people, reflecting a belief that the noises of their meetings would be muted by turning large pots upside down (S. 1, v. 1, 39–42; Levine 1977: 42). Because of its close association with a context in which enslaved people could drop their masks and engage in forms of behavior that were more culturally affirming, cathartic, and empowering, the expression came to connote these dimensions. "To turn the wash bottom down" came to mean much the same thing as "to get down" does in contemporary idiom— that is, to "let go" and be completely oneself. Ironically, the same expression could be used to indicate suppression of such behaviors, as the secrecy of these religious meetings also testified to the oppressed condition of Africana people. Not only African-Americans but also European-Americans used the phrase, and there were two divergent social levels of meaning, one connoting freedom of expression and the other restriction and inhibition. As one speaker indicates, "Massa John quick put a stop to dat. He say, 'if you gwine to preach and sing you must **turn de wash pot bottom up**'; meanin', no shoutin'. Dem Baptis' at Big Creek was sho' tight wid dere rules too" (S. 1, v. 6, Ala. and Ind., 40). Two final expressions that are used in these texts are in current use among African-Americans today. One of these is "to come clean" (S. S. 1, v. 10, Miss., 5), which is used rhetorically to mean "to tell the real truth" or to stop withholding information. The second is "to be slack" (S. S. 1, v. 11, N. C. and S. C., 222), which means either to show a degree of leniency toward an issue or a person or to fail somehow to come up to standards.

In concluding, I would like to call attention to several facets of these speech events from the ex-slave narratives, including the frequency of items and their concentration. Although I surveyed most of the many volumes of narratives, proverbs tended to be clustered in the texts from only a few states. Even more significant is that the speakers who used proverbs tended to use many of them. While these trends may have to do with the predilection of collectors, it may also reveal something valuable about proverbial usage in African-American communities. Perhaps proverbs are used more in certain regions and by certain individuals. The question of proverb frequency has been addressed by Taft (1994), who resolves that there is no formula for measuring such an element. Does the number that I have found in the narratives represent a more infrequent use of proverbs than might be found in other natural contexts? There is really no way of answering the question. In any event, we will now consider examples of proverbial speech in more recent contexts, with the analysis here having provided important background information on some of the functions and ways in which particular proverbs can mean.

THREE

Proverbs in Blues Lyrics: Creativity and Innovation

Texts that illustrate the use of proverbs in context are almost as difficult to locate for the decades following the Federal Works Projects as they are for the years before the 1920s and 1930s. In this regard we are fortunate to have texts and recordings of blues music that contain numerous genres of folklore, including the proverb. But the study of proverbs in blues lyrics poses special kinds of problems that are not found in the study of proverbs in day-to-day speech events, and which were not encountered in the examination of items in the previous chapter. The investigation of these problems, however, promises to illuminate important facets of proverb use in the African-American community—for example, relationships between popular culture and folk tradition as well as between proverb and song, emic perspectives on proverbs, and changing cultural attitudes toward proverbial wisdom. It can also facilitate the consideration of "what counts as a proverb" (Arewa and Dundes 1978) alongside what scholars might recognize as such. Thus, it is fortuitous that these issues present themselves at this juncture, for one of the most interesting issues concerning African-American proverbial speech is innovation in performance and form.

For this chapter I have looked at the texts of over three thousand blues songs and listened to more than a thousand others. This corpus includes country and urban blues, traditions from all major regions of the United States, and songs from the earliest period of blues recordings through the 1970s. The corpus of proverbs dovetails with that from the previous chapter, for, as Taft notes, the first generation of blues singers and composers "represented a generation of men and women born between the years 1885 and 1915" (1994: 228). As our discussion will show, however, this context of proverbs offers different sets of functions and meanings.

Among the problems encountered in the study of proverbs in blues is determining to what degree blues should be considered "natural" and to what degree "fictive" discourse. Ultimately, these songs may be viewed as fictive or mimetic in spite of the obvious base in oral tradition.[1] They are primarily authored, representational texts, and the audience is a hypothetical one. This suggestion does not ignore the performance of blues music in venues from early juke joints to concert halls and the characteristic interaction between entertainer and audience that might at times change the nature of these songs from fictive to natural discourse. But a key consideration here is that no immediate audience is necessary for the performance. This means that proverbs occurring in blues are evoked not by an immediate historical event but by the formulaic content and context within the song. Hence the examination of proverbs in blues shares fundamental concerns with studies of proverbs in lyric poetry and other song traditions.

The use of proverbs in poetry and song is certainly not a recent phenomenon. Many scholars have written on this aspect of the poetic traditions of many nations and time periods, focusing on such authors as Shakespeare (Donker 1992), Donne (Pitts 1966), and Chaucer (MacDonald 1966; Whiting 1934a), and noting a number of functions that proverbs have served. Mieder observes that in American society proverbs have been "abundant in traditional ballads and folk songs, in the librettos of the ever popular musicals, and above all in the lyrics of mood music, country western tunes and even the latest hits of rock 'n' roll" (1988: 85). He further discusses some of the characteristics of proverbs that make them so well-suited for song lyrics and observes that they "are definitely more popular in the lyrics of 20th century songs than in earlier folk songs." He goes on:

> A strong case can be made for the fact that vocalized music in particular attempts to communicate certain basic human experiences and emotions, and we know only too well that the strength of proverbs lies exactly in being able to generalize universal rites of passages into a generally accepted statement. No matter what problem might be touched upon in a particular song—be it a broken heart, a declaration of love, an explanation of a feeling, the expression of a wish, or whatever—a proverb often will

come to mind as a ready made cliché which can summarize the complex nature of our thoughts and feelings. (85)

An element that tends to mark the use of proverbs in songs and poetry is innovation, and different authors have altered proverb texts and functions in a variety of ways. For example, Emily Dickinson consciously deconstructs traditional proverb form and meaning in her poems (Barnes 1979), and Shakespeare uses many traditional proverbs in a comic fashion (Donker 1993). Mieder observes that innovation is especially evident in modern American songs (85).

Proverbs have also played important roles in song and poetic traditions of African and New World African societies. Ogede (1993) discusses the use of proverbs in praise songs of traditional African poet Micah Ichegbeh, and another study focuses on the importance of proverbs in the work of formal poet Okot' Bitek (Okumu 1992). Proverbs are also one of the most important and extensively used genres in Jamaican reggae music, in which they serve numerous functions. They provide mechanisms for social critique, support spiritual and philosophical ideas, and contribute to the religious authority of the singers (Prahlad 1995). Innovation of meaning, owing largely to the personas and philosophies of the singers, is also an important feature of proverb use in reggae.

Elements That Influence the Application of Proverbs

A number of components have significant impact on the structure, meanings, and functions of proverbs in blues lyrics. One of these is the attitudes and worldview reflected in blues culture that are fundamentally different from those found in earlier periods. Philosophically, blues represents subversive attitudes, behaviors, and beliefs within an emergent African-American culture, and reflects the movement away from a sacred vision of life toward a secular (Levine 1977, chapters 1, 3). Whereas the church continued to represent the conservative, moral, and institutionalized religious center of the black community, blues culture represented an emergent alternative, replete with its own philosophical and religious base. As Levine observes, "Blues was threatening because its spokesmen and its ritual too frequently provided the expressive communal channels of relief that had been largely the province of religion in the past" (237). To some extent, this subversion was a response to the perceived association between doctrines of the church and the canons and policies of white society, and such a voice had historically always been present within the community. Ironically, the church community was also undergoing transformation during this period, becoming in many ways more conservative in its philosophical vision (Levine 1977), and was perhaps less able to accommodate or nurture certain forms of expression that might be considered more extrinsically African. Undoubtedly, there was some connection between the emergent blues culture's philosophy and the reclamation and reaffirmation of cultural identity (Jones 1963). This period, in which African-Americans were moving beyond the shadows of slave plantations, is distinguished by a number of social constituents, including large-scale migration out of the South, the rise of industrialization, continued economic and political disfranchisement, and urbanization. Researchers have suggested that, along with obvious societal changes occurring in this period, a shift in the consciousness of Americans—especially African-Americans—also took place (Levine 1977; Deetz 1977; Glassie 1969, 1975; Jones 1963). Besides the movement away from a religious focus toward a secular one, there was also a shift in emphasis from the communal to the individual that helped to facilitate the development of blues music as we know it (Levine 1977; Jones 1963).

These changes, notwithstanding the utter reliance of blues on religious performance styles, ensured an attitude toward proverbial maxims in blues lyrics different from those found in the core community. Though proverbial structure remained important and certain traditional items became a part of traditional verses, these items are often given different social meanings than they may have had or are applied in innovative ways to new situations. Certainly these factors must have influenced the limited frequency of traditional proverbs in blues, an issue considered in some depth by Taft (1994). Many instances of invented proverbs also occur. All of these developments are only logical, given the social forces at work within the Africana community at the time, in combination with external pressures. Taft mentions the pressures for innovation placed on singers by record companies and the creative balance achieved by artists who had synthesized commercial demands and community traditions (228–229). These components give rise to important questions concerning the nature of proverbs, particularly the criteria of traditionality and currency in oral circulation that have been commonly cited by proverb scholars (Arora 1984). Should, for example, items that clearly have a proverb structure and function proverbially within the song but that are not found elsewhere be considered proverbs? To what extent did such items ever gain currency within the community? If that currency was only short-lived, reflecting the temporary popularity of a song in which the item was found, should the item be considered as much a proverb as those that were current for longer periods of time? These questions are best answered from the perspective of the contextual analysis, which emphasizes the dynamics of function and process rather than the age of items in defining and analyzing folklore. Ben-Amos writes:

> In both cases the traditional character of folklore is an analytical construct. It is a scholarly and not a cultural fact. . . . Therefore, tradition should not be a criterion for the definition of folklore in its context. . . . The artistic forms that are part of the communicative processes of small groups are significant, without regard to the time they have been in circulation.
>
> The notion of folklore as a process may provide a way out of this dilemma. Accordingly, it is not the life history of the text that determines its folkloristic quality but its present mode of existence. On the one hand, a popular melody, a current joke, or a political anecdote that has been incorporated into the artistic process in small group situations is folklore, no matter how long it has existed in that context. (1972: 13–14)

This perspective allows us to consider invented items along with traditional ones, especially in a context such as blues lyrics that are infused with so many recognizable elements of folklore process and texts. Perhaps the tendency to invent items, often from necessity and usually in response to changing social circumstances, accounts in part for the lack of continuity over time from one African-American proverb collection to another and may suggest a fairly short currency of many items.

It is also noteworthy that conversational items in the African-American tradition, especially those with similar structures, such as superstitions, proverbs, and rhymes, seem to routinely cross genre boundaries.[2] Indeed, the attitude toward proverbial speech is marked by the same playfulness and improvisation that pertains to speech behavior in African-American culture in general. For this reason, the same texts may function proverbially in one context and not in another, which reinforces the contention that the meaning of items is context-bound. This also supports the suggestion that a recognition and appreciation for the form or structure of proverbs in many cases is more primary than a focus on the meaning per se. A look at "traditional children's autograph album rhymes" collected by Brewer (1965) illustrates these points. Some of these rhymes might have been adopted from blues lyrics, but might also have come from other sources within the larger society or within African-American culture. It is also possible and likely that blues singers might have taken expressions from sources as diverse as children's rhymes and the dozens. The possibilities for cross-fertilization of genres are vast.

Brewer lists as one of these rhymes, for example, "**Beauty is only skin deep and ugly is to the bone**;/ Beauty fades away, but ugly hangs on" (163), which is used in other contexts either in whole or in part as a proverb. Other rhymes that include proverbs are "Love all, trust few;/ Learn **to paddle your own canoe**" (163), and "**You never miss your water till your well runs dry**,/You never miss your baby till he says goodbye" (168). Parts of other rhymes might, at one time or another, have also functioned proverbially, for they have proverbial structures, e.g., "Be humble enough to always obey;/You will be giving orders yourself some day" (165), "Milk is milk, cheese is cheese" (167), "If a man makes a mistake, the world forgives;/A woman has to suffer as long as she lives" (169), and "When in the line of business/And you don't have a business of your own/Make it your business/To leave other people's business alone" (165). Moreover, many of the rhymes are lines that are also traditional in blues lyrics, e.g., "If you want your man, better keep him by your side;/If he flags my train, I'm sure gonna let him ride" (166), "You're my morning milk, my evening cream/My all-day study, and my midnight dream" (167), "If you don't like my apples, don't shake my tree/I ain't after your man, he's after me" (171) and, of course, the aforementioned "You don't miss your water." Such proverbial turns of phrases might easily have found their way also into the dozens, signifying, jump-rope rhymes or other genres. Brewer also lists under the category of "Behavior and Etiquette" (which includes short philosophical statements made about various aspects of behavior) some items that *could* be proverbial and at least one that can be substantiated as proverbial in other contexts—"I always kept my head up and my dress down" (Brewer 138; Barnes-Harden 1980: 70). It becomes evident from these few examples that the conventional tools for identifying and analyzing proverbs may not always be useful for doing so in the blues and in other areas of African-American life and culture. Keeping this possibility in mind, as well as the understanding that the scholar's concept of a proverb may be more limited than the emic category that includes these items and the suggestion that, in addition to the older and more traditional proverbs found in the blues, there are frequently invented items that also function proverbially, I will move ahead with my discussion.

Audience is another significant element in the use of proverbs in blues. In contrast to the speech events discussed in chapter 2, blues have traditionally been directed to the Africana community (Levine 1977: 190–197; Taft 1994: 227); hence, the need to use indirect speech as a strategy for protection from whites is lessened, as is the need to refer to sanctioned sources of authority in expressing thoughts and sentiments or presenting arguments. Certainly there was some degree of coding and discretion necessary, considering that the record company officials were present at recording sessions. In some instances, messages were no doubt directed to some of those officials, but blues primarily involves communications from African-American artists to an audience of other African-Americans. The difference in audience affected such features as introductory formulas, for example, which are less frequent and function differently from how they did in the speech events discussed in chapter 1. Performers are less concerned with the social levels of meaning that pertain outside of their own cultural group, and, consequently, a level of meaning that was often present or emphasized in the applications of previous items is not present or emphasized in these. When singers do use formulas such as "The Good Book says," they are not referring to the social meaning current in European-American society as much as to the meaning obtained from religious teachings within the black church, home, and community. In fact, whereas it has generally been assumed that proverbs serve to distance the speakers from the messages of particular utterances by ascribing the utterance to the voice of tradition, elders, or some respected and removed source, in blues proverbial statements often operate to further identify the speakers and add to their personal appeal as wordsmiths and innovators. This facet of proverbial lines in blues is sometimes overlooked (for example, Taft 1994: 247).

Critical in examining proverbs in blues is a consideration of the personas that are popularly found in the music. A further element of the changes occurring during the period in which blues developed had to do with fictionalized personas and voice, by which I mean those characters depicted in various genres of folklore and the speech behavior attributed to them. There may be correlations between the changes in such personas in folktales (Levine 1977, chapters 2, 6; Roberts 1989), for example, and the use of proverbs in blues, as these changes play a significant role in the range of voices that become a part of the blues tradition and, therefore, influence the way in which proverbial speech is actualized. Characters like the "bad man" in folktales are drawn upon in the development of personas in blues, affecting the attitude of the speaker toward thematic and structural aspects of the lyrics. Other personas that develop include the mistreated lover and the incessant wanderer and troubadour. These personas are overwhelm-

ingly male but can also be female. Undoubtedly, many of the applications
of proverbs reflect gender-centered concerns and perspectives. Considering
that the primary topic in blues is love or relationship, quite naturally many
proverbs are applied to these issues.

The structural element of proverbs in blues is also critical, so much
so that one could easily posit that proverb structure is one of the basic
building blocks of the lyrics, although traditional proverbs seldom occur. In
arguing that proverbial expressions, both traditional and invented, appear
much more frequently in blues than do true proverbs, Taft supports this
contention (1994). I am further suggesting that many blues lines are based
on the structure of traditional proverbs, an observation that others seem to
agree with. Ferris states that "[t]ight phrasing of blues verses encourages
their use as proverbs, for the blues verse sums up life for both singer and
audience and offers a handle for their experiences" (1978: 73). Evans also
comments on this aspect of blues lyrics: "Metaphor, simile, irony, and exaggeration abound, and many of the traditional verses have the sententious
quality of proverbs" (1982: 30). Moreover, the structural application of
proverbs in these lyrics reflects a recurrent, interactional dynamic found
widely in African-American culture, often involving proverbs. While the
root of this dynamic may predate the evolution of the black Baptist Church,
its stylized performance and most highly ritualized form is certainly found
there; specifically, the performance of these traditional religious forms
include formulaic, wise statements that function as intensifiers. These intensifiers utilize metaphor and vivid imagery, are often proverbial, and elicit
formulized responses from the audience, e.g., "amen," "tell the truth,"
"you're certainly telling it now," etc. As many researchers have observed
(Smitherman 1986; Hurston 1969), the intensity of the responses routinely depends on the intensity and creativity reflected in the imagery and
creative application of metaphor contained in a particular utterance. This
interactional dynamic is recurrent throughout African-American culture in
everyday speaking situations as well as in contexts of performed speech. To
this extent, the blues structure emulates patterns of speech dynamics found
within the culture, with certain blues artists showing a preference for verses
that more strongly evoke the religious, ritualized context.

The influence of religious forms is reflected not only in textual components and in elements of live performances but also in sociolinguistic
features of recordings. Countless singers have compared their performance
of songs to "preaching," the performance style associated with Baptist

ministers, and it is generally recognized that singers represent parallel figures of prominence in the world of the "street" (Abrahams 1963). One essential element of this style is a no-holds-barred intensity, and another is the telling of "the truth." It might not be taking the analogy too far to suggest that blues performances be considered secular sermons. Considering them as such, we can note the importance of vocal nuances that key the audience to the coming of particular intensifiers, such as proverbial statements, and the use of intonations and other verbal nuances to cue shades of meanings for given utterances. Just as preachers are known for their skill in manipulating audiences, heating them up to feverish pitches of emotion and taking them over terrains of peaks and valleys, carefully pacing the journey to make it all the more engaging, exciting, and enjoyable, bluesmen too have traditionally enjoyed such a reputation. In fact, blues singers have always credited the church—and, in particular, preachers—with being a dominant influence on their vocal and performance styles. At the same time, quite a number of blues singers turned away from "the devil's music" and became preachers, one example being Ruben Lacy (Rosenberg 1970). Many of these reformed singers maintained a healthy respect not only for the affective power of blues performances but for the mastery of the formulaic phrasing, which can be compared to the formulaic nature of sermons (Rosenberg 1970).

This brings us to another structural aspect of proverb use in blues: proverbs are consistently paired with lines that explain or elaborate on their application, a device that reflects the way in which proverbs are often used in everyday speech events. Furthermore, these explanatory lines typically mirror the structure of the proverb they pertain to, and this pattern holds true in verses that have invented or traditional proverbs in them. Scholars have noted that blues utilizes a verse form that introduces an idea and follows or concludes with lines that comment further on that idea, acting as emotional "punchlines" (Ferris 1978: 73). Such a pattern exemplifies the use of rhetorical strategies that are drawn from the performance style of sermons and that function to excite the audience. The initial lines cue the audience to expect the lines that deliver the punch for particular stanzas, and proverbs play a pivotal role in this form, acting either as the initial lines or as the lines that deliver the concluding punch. An important component of such lines is the vocal intonation, which assists in keying the audience and in adding dimensions of meaning to utterances. Simply the way in which the first lines are vocalized can indicate that elaborative lines are to follow and what the attitude of the singer is toward the topic being considered. Even in cases in which the concluding lines are not sung, they reverberate in the minds of the audience, often sung only by the voice of an instrument. In this way, the common rhetorical strategy found in sermons and in everyday speech events—whereby only the beginning of a thought or even of a proverbial expression is spoken, with the listener being left to complete it either verbally or silently—is evoked. This strategy serves to add emphasis to the unspoken portion of the speech act, as if the speaker had shouted it. Consider the following random verses that illustrate the pattern of proverb and accompanying elaborative lines:

> **Yes, you never miss your water water water**
>   **baby till your well's gone dry.** (2x)
> Yes, you never miss your loved one
>   son, until she says goodbye.
> (Sackheim 1969: 126)

> Yeh Yeh **what you want with a rooster rooster or banty**
>   **who won't crow for day** (2x)
> Yeh, what you want with a woman
>   she always want to have her way.
> (Sackheim 1969: 126)

> **You mix ink with water, bound to turn it**
>   **black.** (2x)
> You run around with funny people, you get
>   a streak of it up your back. (Taft 1994: 242)

Neither of the proverb-like lines in the second and third verses above can be identified as traditional[3]; however, each is used as if it were and is followed by a concluding line that provides a literal explanation for the application of the invented proverb. In performance, these concluding lines were likely to evoke the same kinds of responses from the audience that the emphatic portions of a sermon might elicit from a congregation. By utilizing conventional proverb structure, these invented lines appear traditional and seem to embody the voice of communal and ancient wisdom just as effectively as a well-known proverb might; in fact, audiences were highly appreciative of the creativity of artists who were able to invent effective items, this being a much-prized ability in all areas of Africana speech behavior.[4] It is probable that some such lines may have actually passed into oral currency, but this is a difficult point to test (and is beyond the scope of the present study), just as it is difficult to say with absolute certainty that every such line is invented on the basis of its absence from any printed collection. One point should be obvious from these representational examples, however: proverbs play a major role in the structure and poetry of blues lyrics. Another salient point is that, in contrast to the traditional function of proverbs—to distance the speaker from the utterance—these invented proverbs have the capacity to do just the opposite. There is a presumed knowledge on the part of the artists that the audience will recognize and appreciate their ability to invent proverbs based on traditional models and will associate these innovations with the voice of a particular artist. The artist is thus combining tradition and originality, improvising in a manner that comments on both the old and the new, and there is potential in this creative milieu for proverbial statements to be regarded as authored, a practice discussed by Yankah in his study of Akan proverbs (1989: 183–213). Arora (1984) comments on the question of new proverbs and the recognition of them by an audience:

> It may also happen that a listener will realize that what he is hearing is a saying new to him, but because its pattern resembles that of a known proverb he will accept it as proverbial also. . . . The proliferation of certain "families" of proverbs derives from precisely these kinds of cognitive processes, which facilitate the hearer's acceptance of unfamiliar sayings and encourage the invention of new sayings or variants by allowing speakers to rely on the proverbiality of the pattern to bring about the (erroneous) identification of the utterance as a proverb. (8–9)

The location of proverbs in lyrics is also related to the overall structure and theme of the particular song. Evans states, as many blues scholars have, that blues often tell a story, especially blues associated with commercial recordings. He writes further of "thematic texts" and "story-songs" (1982: 27), and notes that the idea of telling a story is important to blues singers: "A number of blues singers have expressed the opinion that blues lyrics ought to 'tell a story,' by which they mean that they should be thematic throughout the song" (131–132). As this chapter's discussion will demonstrate, the proverb is often the focal point or even the "moral" of the particular story being told. In most cases, these stories tend to be traditional and even formulaic, and so the proverbs are commonly used to comment on certain recurrent situations and are found in close connection with certain, traditional blues "motifs." The idea of telling stories is closely connected with the notion of telling the "truth," which is so frequently alluded to by blues musicians and audiences, and which shares profound similarities with "testifyin'," another genre that evolved out of the church. Evans cites the importance placed on telling the "truth" as "one overriding standard for all of the early blues and for later folk blues as well." He quotes a Mississippi blues singer regarding this standard:

> Sometimes I preach now, and I get up and tell the people now that I used to be a famous blues singer, and I told more truth in my blues than the average person tells in his church songs. . . . If you're playing the blues, you say, **"I never missed my water 'til my well went dry."** That's the truth. If you got a well where you get your water, when it go dry, you miss it. You got to go somewhere else and hunt a well, ain't you? You got a wife and she quit you, you may not miss her 'til she quit you. She quit you and you want her back or some other one, don't you? Well, that's the truth. (53)

Continuing his discussion, Evans gives an example of a stanza from the singer's repertoire: "I never missed my water 'til my well went dry/I never missed my rider 'til she said good-bye" (54). Considering the singer's explanation and the traditionality of the stanza and its social meaning within African-American culture, it seems that the song can clearly be considered to tell a story, though the story is more accurately an allusion to an implied narrative than the actual narrative itself. Here the song tells about someone who, over time, takes his partner for granted. Eventually, his partner leaves him and he is lonely. The "story" is evoked for African-American listeners by the formulaic lines, as is the moral that one should not take a partner for granted. Based on such stories, blues can almost be considered a catalogue of recurrent, dramatic situations. In many ways, the function of blues was often similar to that of memorates, inasmuch as the songs utilized traditional motifs to relate events and experiences within the singers' purview. Consequently, blues singers have sometimes been compared to African griots who disseminated information and maintained commentary on current and historical events, as well as on interactions among individuals in the society.[5] Of course, the performance context of blues songs influenced the kind of "stories" that may have been conveyed. Contexts such as house parties, for example, encouraged and sometimes demanded a more fluid, less "packaged" presentation of songs. In such situations, songs commonly lasted much longer than on recordings, and many more related verses could be added to a basic set of stanzas. These live performances also gave singers the opportunity to interact with the audience, add ongoing spoken commentary, and integrate themes or stories that might have been triggered by events going on during the performance. Hypothetically, then, live performances provided an opportunity for a more involved narrative than did the somewhat limited studio recording format. Unfortunately, there is not an abundance of published transcriptions of live performances, although a few are available (Ferris 1978: 115–154).

Some of the elements that I have discussed can be seen in the following song by T. B. Walker:

Example #35
Put your wig on mama,
    let's have a natural ball. (2X)
If you ain't happy,
    it ain't no fun at all.
You can't take it with you,
    that's one thing for sure. (2X)
There ain't nothing
    a little T. Bone shuffle won't cure.
Have fun while you can
    fate's an awful thing. (2X)
And that's why,
    I love the same. (Walker 1970)

Here, lines such as those in bold in stanzas one and three function as invented proverbs within the song (those in stanza two are traditional); however, their social and situational meanings promote a value system that is contrary to tradition. Whereas traditional values encourage frugality, perseverance, abstinence, etc., the message of these lines is that one should live spontaneously, intensely in the moment, fully enjoying the pleasures of drink, sex, dance, and good times, a sentiment that becomes a central value of blues culture. One can also see the importance of the persona and the structural components of the proverb lines. The persona is very male and located in the boasting, tough tradition. The use of proverbial lines accompanied by elaborative lines of the same structure is evident.

A blues by Muddy Waters further demonstrates these aspects:

Example #36
I might be getting old
    But I got young fashioned ways. (2X)

You know I'm go' love a good woman
   The rest of my natural days.

If my hair is turnin' grey
   You think it knows the way I feel.(2X)
There may be snow up in the mountain
   But there's fire down under the hill.
   (Spoken: Right down there, right down there!)

I may be gettin old
   But I got young fashioned ways.(2X)
If good women kill me,
   Then come on ahead and dig my grave.

A young horse is fast,
   But a old horse know what's going on. (2X)
You know a young horse may win the race,
   But a old horse kick out so long. (Waters 1972)

Again, there is the strong flavor of the male bravado in relating a dramatic
situation (or "story") that centers on the virility and sexual prowess of the
speaker in spite of his age. Such a persona and perspective is in sharp contrast
to the religious, family-oriented values found in much of African-American
culture. The coupling of proverbial lines with explanatory ones is also
reflected here, for example, in stanza two; however, the elaborative lines
are found in stanzas one and three, with the proverbial lines comprising all
of stanza four. Because the proverbial lines are apparently invented, they do
not necessarily carry social meaning, but rather depend upon the creativity
of the singer to invest them with situational meaning that will communicate
and move the audience. (It may be valuable here to distinguish between
invented lines that are used on one occasion by one singer and lines that,
although not traditional in the culture, become formulaic in blues lyrics. It
is in the former case that lines will not carry social meaning.) This example
is a good one to illustrate the importance of proverbial structure even when
there are no traditional proverbs used.

Discussion of Proverbs

It is no coincidence that a large percentage of the proverbs found in blues
are used in the context of female/male relationships (Evans 1982: 28). Many
scholars have suggested that proverbs can sometimes be an index to areas of
social tensions within particular groups (Abrahams 1972a; Daniel 1973), and

although no scholar has gone so far as to investigate the parameters of this suggestion, it is certainly a plausible one. In this regard, we would expect to find proverbs frequently applied to family and cross-gender relationships, for undoubtedly these are among the cultural areas that were most severely disrupted by colonization and slavery. Add to these considerations the fact that relationship is the most frequent topic of blues verses, and the frequency of proverbs that are thus applied is not surprising.

"You reap what you sow" is the most common proverb found in blues lyrics (Taft 1994: 235), as it was in the narratives of ex-slaves. Its frequency suggests that it remained the most popular proverb among African-American speakers into the second half of the twentieth century, but its applications are significantly different in the contexts of blues from what they were in the narratives, which suggests the secularization of this item. Though we must allow for the possibility that the religious meaning of this proverb found among speakers in the previous chapter continued alongside its secularization, we must wonder why it occurs only once in a spiritual and not in gospel lyrics at all.[6] Nor is it found in any of the few texts of sermons that are available from this period.[7] Whereas almost all of the examples from the narratives are different applications and versions, most of the seven examples from blues lyrics are the same version, with several illustrating the same application. The particular social problems that the proverb addresses also become less varied in the context of song lyrics.

In blues, the proverb is often used by a speaker or persona to another persona who he/she feels has hurt or betrayed him/her to vindictively state that the partner will in time also be abused, hurt, or betrayed. These cases all reveal a profound sense of victimization, and the proverb becomes, in effect, a curse, the intensity of which is masked by its religious connotation and its impersonal nature. The proverb's religious connotations, which are a component of the social level of meaning, are not dismissed but are subverted and manipulated to add new dimensions of meaning to the proverb and to the entire song. Peetie Wheatstraw's "Ice and Snow Blues," recorded in the early 1930s, illustrates these points:

Example #37

This winter, baby, in the ice and snow,
You know, my little momma gon' be sleeping on
her floor.

> **Baby, now, you know you got to reap, baby,**
> **Just what,**
> **What you sow.**

You remember last winter, you drove me from your door,
Now, little mama, it was in the ice and snow.
    (refrain)

You left me, baby because I was cold in hand
You taken my money, and spent it on your other man.
    (refrain)
I did more for you than you understand,
You can tell by the bullet-holes, mama, now,
here in my hand. (Garon 1971: 30)

In stanzas one through three the singer points to specific instances in which his partner has treated him cruelly, adding the proverb as a refrain to imply that the same kinds of experiences are going to befall her. There are strong undercurrents of anger and resentment, and the motif of victimization carries throughout, becoming even more accentuated in the last stanza. Stanza four casts the singer in the role of "savior," implicitly drawing parallels between himself and Jesus. Most obvious is the image of bullet holes in his hands (reminiscent of nail holes), but the stanza also suggests that he, like Jesus, has in some way sacrificed himself for his partner, and that she not only does not comprehend the extent of his sacrifice but (like Judas) has betrayed him. Unlike Jesus, however, he is not forgiving but angry, and is expressing his desire that his partner will suffer the same kind of betrayal and pain that he has.

An almost identical use of the proverb can be observed in Guitar Slim's "Reap What You Sow." The basic motif of betrayal or mistreatment constitutes the core of the song, although there are minor differences in the events. Here the singer alludes to his partner as perhaps his first important, romantic relationship. Having manipulated him in his innocence, turned him against his parents and teachers and taken him away from home, she then abandons him.

Example #38

They say you got to reap baby
You got to reap-just what you sow.(2x)
You treated me so bad honey
When you drove me-from your door.

I met you baby honey
When I was a kid at home in school. (2x)
You made me mistreat my parents baby,
And I broke all my teacher's rules.

That's alright baby
I know-**you gonna reap what you sow**. (2x)
I be done left you baby,
And you won't mistreat me no more. (Slim [1950]1972)

The theme of reciprocity is echoed again in one of Bobby "Blue" Bland's most popular hits, "Farther Up the Road," in which much the same social and situational meanings are conveyed as in the previous two examples. The difference lies in the degree to which Bland seems to be concerned with stating a general maxim as well as applying it to the particular situation in the song. His usage of the proverb contains a philosophical dimension that is absent from the others and a momentary distance from the emotional wound. Unlike the other singers, he portrays himself not so much as a victim as a partner with equal power who has simply been "wronged." Also evident here is the influence of the proverb's structure on the lines of the stanzas—almost all of the lines mirror it, as in "Farther on up the road/ someone's gonna hurt you like you hurt me" and "Now you laughin' pretty baby,/someday you gonna be cryin'"—and the explanatory nature of lines commenting on the application of the proverb.

Example #39
Farther on up the road
Someone's gonna hurt you like you hurt me.
Farther on up the road
Baby you just wait and see.

You got to reap just what you sow,
That old saying is true. (2x)
Like you mistreat someone
Someone's gonna mistreat you.

Now you laughin' pretty baby,
Someday you gonna be cryin', (2x)
Farther on up the road
You'll find out I wasn't lyin'.

Yeah, baby
Farther on up the road
You'll find out I wasn't lyin'.

Farther on up the road,
When you're all alone and blue. (2x)
You gonna ax me to take you back baby
But I'll have somebody new.
Ummmmmmmmm baby
Farther on up the road
Ummmmmmmmm baby.
Farther on up the road
You'll get yours. (Bland 1964)

In addition to the theme of reciprocity in relationship, in several songs the proverb also has an association with imprisonment. Curley Weaver, a rural bluesman recording in the 1930s and 1940s, connects both of these themes in his song "Dirty Mistreater." Contained in these lyrics is a combination of anger directed toward his lover and a longing for her because she is imprisoned. Romance is presented in a lighthearted fashion, as a game in which one partner must inevitably lose to the other. Becoming romantically involved and being hurt becomes a kind of initiation or rite of passage into a world of cynicism in which love is a sign of weakness and a threat to one's survival; this is a persistent and dominant perspective in blues. Despite the language of the song, the singer's tone of voice coupled with our knowledge of the actual sociohistorical context of the blues lets us know that the light-heartedness is a defense mechanism and that behind it lies an intense grief and longing. The proverb concentrates the expression of these emotions.

The context of the studio recording gives a further indication of the tension of these emotions in this song. As was a common practice on early blues recordings, the musicians engage in a call-and-response dynamic as the recording is being made. One of the musicians responds to the singer's line "What a fool I used to be" with "Yeah you was a big fool!" Within the larger process of the studio recording and the dissemination of the record to listeners, the two men form an interactional context, joined in camaraderie in their attitudes toward relationships and women. Such an example indicates that song lyrics, while offered to the general public, were also at times composite images of speech events occurring among groups of musicians, and that the aesthetics that influenced those lyrics in such speech events must also have influenced the use of proverbs.

Example #40

And you a dirty mistreater
You don't mean no one man no good. (2x)

I don't blame you mama
I'd do the same thing if I could.

Ummmmmmm the woman I love
She stays 'hind the cold iron bars
Ain't it hard, ain't it hard,
She stays 'hind the cold iron bars.
I ain't got nobody
To get my ashes hauled.

Ummmmmmmmm
Ummmmmmmmm
Ummmmmmmmm
Ummmmmmmmmmmmm

And you mistreat me baby,
You drove me from your door. (2x)
And the Good Book tell you baby
Ummm, you bound to reap just what you sow.

When I used to love baby,
What a fool I used to be.
When I used to love baby,
What a fool I used to be,
[Another voice: "Yeah you was a big fool."]
I don't love nobody That the fool do love me. (Weaver 1979)

That the proverb stanza in three of the previous examples is basically the same alerts us to the formulaic nature and traditionality not only of the stanza but of the particular proverb application in blues music. This stanza, like many, was woven by different artists into the context of numerous varieties of other stanzas and songs and is associated with the metaphor of being "driven from your door." This phrase, on the grammatical level, usually depicts an innocent male figure who becomes tragically mythic, being turned away by an insensitive, cruel, sometimes gloating female figure who holds power over him. It is possible to recognize multiple levels of proverb meaning here, connections among them, and a multiplicity of meanings at a given level and the connections also among them. For example, the grammatical picture conveyed by the proverb interacts with that conveyed by the companion phrase "driven from your door." On the grammatical levels, sowing and reaping seem to have nothing to do with being turned away from a door, but once the social and situational meanings are understood, these images take on new significance and beauty, separately and in conjunction with each other.

The proverb is concerned with a perceived abuse of a less powerful figure by a more dominant one, and the speaker's wish fulfillment is expressed in depicting the reciprocal maltreatment of that preeminent person. Once these components are clear, then the connection between the grammatical and social levels of meaning becomes evident, as do the multiplicity of meanings on each level. The cruelty of slavery and the subsequent wish for the demise of the oppressor and the simultaneous acquisition of long-denied goods and rights is one component of the social level of meaning of this item among African-Americans. This relates to the abusive and cruel lover and suggests, from a sociological perspective, that the slavery experience and the negotiation of power inherent in it becomes a part of romantic relationships for subsequent generations of African-Americans. One gender takes the place of the white oppressor while the other continues in the role of victim, and a new level of social meaning emerges, focused on the negotiation of power and issues of fairness and control between individuals, particularly between women and men. There is some associative correlation between being "driven from your door" and being racially oppressed and discriminated against, and between the pleasures of sex and security of relationship and opportunities for freedom and self-determination. "Sowing" becomes a metaphor for the misuse of power, abuse, or oppression and "reaping" for incurring abuse from others in return. "Driven from your door" also becomes metaphorical for being abused or unfairly mistreated. At the grammatical level both images are concerned with economic stability—the first with an investment of labor for food, the second with housing and family security. On the social level, both images suggest the vulnerability and disenfranchisement of the Africana male or female speaker. The situational meaning varies minimally with each song, depending on the innovations in the story or stories of the songs in which this stanza is found, but in all cases are informed by the social level of meaning.

As we have noted, the religious connotations, which are a social level of meaning, continue to echo. That the words are taken from the Bible moves the traditionality of the proverb beyond the realm of ancient wisdom to associations of mythological proportions. In this way, the singer is not simply evoking the voice of the elders, but of God: he dons momentarily the mask of preacher, becoming "holier than thou," and this strategy reflects some of the ambiguity that often characterized the lives and lyrics of blues singers. On one hand the singer is espousing a philosophy contrary to that of the religious community, but, on the other, he utilizes facets of that community's doctrine when it is convenient. To put it another way, the singer frames his performance within the context of a world-wise persona, but interjects the authority of a religious persona into that context. Certainly one effect of this strategy is to suggest the innocence of the speaker and to gain sympathy from the listener. Another function of the proverb here is to add credibility to the speaker's assertion, bolstering his argument and disguising the very negative tone of the message directed toward the partner in question.

Thus far we have focused on the meaning of the proverb as it is directed by the persona in the song to a character of the opposite gender. But another dimension must also be considered—the meaning communicated by the performer to the audience. This latter component of meaning is more difficult to ascertain without a record of specific performances, for in live contexts a variety of interactional dynamics may have influenced the encoding of particular stanzas and lines, and recordings were also influenced by social and personal forces prevalent at the time. Although these factors pose serious obstacles to the interpretation of meaning at this level, the issue generates significant questions to which general suggestions may be offered. For example, did women and men respond in the same way to this traditional proverbial stanza? Did audiences respond differently to the use of the proverb by male or female singers? Were singers consciously or otherwise utilizing the social meanings discussed in chapter 2, and expressing veiled hostility toward European-American society? A clue to addressing this latter question is found in the vocal nuances of these sung stanzas and, in fact, in blues in general, and demonstrates the importance of paralinguistic features in the encoding of proverb meaning. These nuances pose a contradiction to the grammatical message of the lyrics, for, in contrast to the victim portrayed in the lyrics, a very strong, determined, aggressive, and angry speaker emerges from the way in which the lyrics are sung. The speaker discovered in the voice is one who is wounded but tough, resilient, defiant, and who refuses to allow the situation to rob him/her of his/her dignity. The irony of this contradiction is an aspect of blues that makes it profound and enduring and raises it above exercises in self-pity that casual observers have often taken it for. The impact of the vocal nuances on the proverb meaning is immense, for in addition to the social meaning conveyed by the persona to the female character—a wish for revenge— the proverb also conveys another social meaning to the audience—the strength, determination, and resilience of the singer in the face of abuse and exploitation. At this level, the gender of the characters in the song is not very significant, and the female audience would be just as likely to identify with it as would males. Moreover, one would expect that, at the situational level, listeners would relate the song's experience to their own, putting the opposite gender in the respective roles. It may not, in the final analysis, be important that the singer is not directly confronting the issue of racism and oppression, for if there is a shared understanding that feelings about that oppression influence all other aspects of Africana lives, and if many of the situations presented in the lyrics are taken in the light of this larger context, then certainly the political, social level of meaning would continue to resonate in the use of such items as this popular proverb. The degree to which this is the case for particular listeners is a question that would have to be asked of individuals.

The first question raised above has not been answered conclusively, however, and there is no accurate way to do so. Blues singers often directed stanzas, lines, and even entire songs more to one gender than to the other, and this occurred in both live performances and on recordings. Such directed speech is often signalled very overtly, in phrases such as "Well, now boys" or "Now all you girls" and just as often more subtly. But the address of stanzas to a particular gender was usually a device of signification, for the singers had to be aware that the audience was composed of men and women. The analysis of this phenomenon and its impact on proverbial meaning would be extremely valuable, but without descriptive accounts of live performances of blues and some ethnographic data on participants in the performance, such a discussion cannot be undertaken.

While most of the examples from the Taft study (1994) reflect this basic application of the proverb, in a few it is indicated that the proverb could also be applied by the speaker to himself/herself. In these cases the speaker's mistreatment of his/her partner is blamed for present misfortune. The social meaning of these examples is closer to the religious meanings discussed in chapter 2 than to the political. The following stanzas exemplify this application: "Lord, Lord can't rest no place I go/Because the Good Book says **you going to reap just what you sow**" (235), and a stanza sung by Bessie Smith, "I want to take a journey to the devil down below/I done killed my man; **I want to reap just what I sow**" (235–236).

Several other examples of this proverb reveal a similar social meaning, one that was found in several instances in chapter 2. In songs by Bill

Gaither and by an anonymous, incarcerated prisoner, the singers apply the proverb to themselves regarding their criminal behaviors and subsequent imprisonments. The applications are distinct from earlier examples in that there is no persona addressing a second character in the songs, and the songs themselves are much more direct communications or stories told to the audience. Gaither sings:

Example #41

On my way to Sing Sing, there was only one thing
    could say, (2x)
Stone walls will be my home for five years and a day.

Early one morning, long between nine and ten, (2x)
I thought about that woman and wished I could see
    her face again.
My mother told me, **"Son, you've got to reap just what you sow,"** (2x)
Now I'm behind these hard stone walls, may never
    see the streets no more. (Oliver 1960a: 248)

The second song includes a use of the proverb with the same social level of meaning but also with another.

Example #42

Now the day's been a long, lonesome day,
    D'ya heah me talkin' to ya, did ya
    heah what I say?
Lord, the day has been a long, old, lonesome day,
And now 'morrow eeeh, Lord, will be the same old way.

I been to the Nation, 'round the Territo',
    You heah me talkin' to ya, **gotta reap**
    what ya sow,
I been all round the Nation, and round the Territo',
But I found no heaven on earth, Lord, nowhere I go.

I'm goin' t' the Big House, and I don't even care,
    Don't ya heah me talkin' to ya, scoldin' to ma death!
I'm goin' in the mawnin', an' I don't even care,
I might get four or five years, Lord, and I might
    get the chair.

I don't stop an' listen, see what t'morrow bring.
    You heah me talkin' to ya, start to prayin'
You better stop n' listen, an' see what t'morrow bring.

It might bring you sunshine, Lawd, an' it may bring
rain.

Some got six months, some got a solid year,
   You heah me talkin' to ya, buddy, what made
   ya stop by heah?
Some of them got six months, pardner, and some got
a solid year.
But I believe my pardner, Lawd, got lifetime heah.
(Oliver 1960b: 257–258)

The proverb here carries the social level of meaning that if one breaks the law, one is punished. Its message, however, may be more complex than this. A number of components invite us to speculate that the speaker is not only applying the proverb to himself but perhaps also criticizing the social order. Whereas Oliver interprets the song as the voice of a "spirit without hope" (257), I interpret it as a song of protest, anger, and resignation about the opportunities for positive life experience within a discriminatory social system. Undoubtedly, the second verse chronicles the singer's efforts to find a place within the United States characterized by social equality.[8] He is not only angry that no such place exists, but also suggests that his crime and incarceration are a result of the social situation. In this context, the proverb is an indictment of the social order and expresses a desire that the perpetrators of that order will "reap" all of the "harvest" they have coming to them; this is the same social meaning that occurs in example #6 in chapter 2.

"The woman who rocks the cradle rules the home" is another proverb that is applied to a familial situation.[9] Found in song verses of at least two artists, it has an association with the perceived power balance within a relationship, as did the previous item in numerous examples. Again, the male persona portrays himself as victimized, powerless, and resigned to this state of affairs. The following stanzas of Blind Lemon Jefferson's "That Growling Baby Blues" demonstrate these characteristics and also contain the use of the proverb to convey other levels of social meaning.

Example #43
Well the baby crying
   on up to his mama's knee (2X)
He's crying about his sweet milk
   and she won't feed him just that cream.

Crawled from the fireplace
   and he stopped in the middle of the floor. (2X)
Said, Mama ain't that your second daddy
   standing back there in the door.

Well she grabbed my baby and spanked him
   I tried to make her leave him alone. (2X)
I tried my best to stop her and she said
   the baby ain't none of mine.

Some woman rocks the cradle and
I declare she rules her home
Many man rocks some other man's baby
   and the fool thinks he's rocking his own.

Went out late last night
   when I learned the crawling baby blues. (2X)
My woman threw my clothes out doors
   and now I got those crawling baby blues. (Sackheim 1969: 87)

The story told here is about a man who discovers that his son is not "his." Implicit in his partner's communication is a defiant admission of infidelity and a disregard for his feelings or dignity that leaves him shocked, wounded, and deflated. As a result he abandons the home for a night out, and she dissolves the relationship. The social meaning of the proverb—that the woman who mothers the child has the control or power within the home—contains various components: that the mother is responsible for the discipline of the child, that the space of the home is ultimately hers, and that she has ultimate control over her own body and network of relationships. The situational meaning also contains several components, one of which is the suggestion that one's partner cannot be trusted to be loyal or to care about one's pride or dignity. A second is that the power to maintain a stable family environment rests with the mother. In Herman Johnson's "Crawlin' Baby Blues," which is almost identical to Jefferson's, similar characteristics are found (Oster 1969: 385). It would be interesting to examine the use of this proverb by women blues singers, to see if the nuances significantly differ. However, I have been unable to locate such an example.

A third proverb that has been applied to relationships is "You never miss your water until your well runs dry," which has been noted as one of the oldest traditional items in folk blues (Evans 1982: 54). It occurs here in L. C. Williams's "You Never Miss the Water" blues:

Example #44

Yes **you never miss your water water water
baby till your well's gone dry,** (2X)
Yes you never miss your loved one
son, until she says goodbye.

Yeh yeh what you want with a rooster or banty
who won't crow for day, (2X)
Yeh, what you want with a woman
she always want to have her way.

Yeh don't you know your house look lonesome
you know, when your baby gone. (2X)
Yeh, and you have the blues so bad
that you can't stay at home.

Yeh, my little woman she don left me lord, lord,
please tell me what I'm gonna do
Yeh, she's a good little girl
but she just won't be true. (Sackheim 1969: 126)

This song provides an illustration of how the interpretation and meaning of the proverb can be altered by the song "story" in which it is placed. The story here is about a man whose partner was independent and promiscuous and eventually left him. Contained in the song is the belief that one "has" a woman to fulfill certain domestic and other duties, just as one has roosters to wake one up and to fertilize eggs. The woman here has frustrated the speaker's expectations. In this context, the social meaning of the proverb is that one does not realize how important a relationship may be until it is over. Situationally, the proverb means for this speaker that he underestimated the importance of this relationship because he was so focused on ways in which it did not measure up to his traditional image of gender roles and behavioral norms. Even a relationship that was frustrating was better than being alone. The proverb is applied in basically this same way in four other songs (Taft 1994: 238; Evans 1982: 54).

"Seeing is believing," an item that was discussed in the preceding chapter, is also found in blues lyrics and applied to relationships. The strategy of its application is similar to that found in examples #13 and #14: a traditional maxim that represents the voice of the community is presented and then discredited, symbolically invalidating the perspectives of the community. Sonny Terry sings, in "Night and Day":

Example #45

Every since I was 11 years old
  You know bad luck stays in my way. (2X)
But 16 years with only one eye now
  You know I can't see nothing but night and day.

People people people
  I don't want nobody to beat me.
I got a sweet lil' girl in my corner
  And I'm just as happy as a man can be.

If I had a dog,
  You know I'd know him if I heard 'im bark.(2X)
I want to let you know I know my woman,
  If I touch her in the dark.

Seeing is believing,
  That's what the old folks always told me.
I can't see love but I can feel it,
  And you know that's good enough for me. (Terry and McGhee 1969)

Terry's use of the proverb is quite creative here, containing an element of irony and perhaps mockery, and providing an example of how the grammatical level of meaning interacts with the social, situational, and speculatively, the symbolic. At the grammatical level the proverb becomes a pun, reminding us of the Wellerism " 'I see' said the blind man, as he picked up his hammer and saw," for Terry is a blind musician. At the symbolic level, his use of the proverb with the closing formula "that's what the old folks always told me" points to an insensitivity on the part of those older members of the community who may have used the expression to and around him. Since the proverb suggests that the final test for validating reality and belief rests upon what one literally sees, it would preclude those such as Terry from ever knowing conclusively the nature of things or having any validation for their beliefs. We can speculate that a component of the symbolic meaning for the singer is a sense of exclusion, and though the proverb explicitly speaks of sight, implicitly suggested by its image is the horror of blindness or partial blindness, of being able only to distinguish "night and day." Hearing Terry sing the stanza and noting some of the other allusions to his vulnerability, e.g., "I don't want nobody to beat me," one can sense some of the pain associated with his impairment. Therefore, the use of the proverb assists in the expression of bitterness toward a community that so greatly values literal sight, and that is insensitive toward those who are physically blind.

The social level of meaning—that physical reality is the ultimate proof or evidence to substantiate one's beliefs—becomes suspect, as do those who accept that meaning. The situational meaning that emerges is that objective reality can somehow validate or answer doubts that occur at the subjective and emotional levels. The singer's conclusion is that it cannot; the invisible reality must be substantiated by the invisible, and intuitive reality is far more fundamental than the logical, objective one condoned by the community. In fact, there is a sense of triumph on the part of the speaker regarding his ability to validate his relationship without reliance on external sight. Thus, the message to the community is that they are wrong, not only in their belief in the social meaning of the proverb, but in the behavior implied in their application of it to him, and in the insistence on a literal or grammatical application of the item. In this way, the singer is commenting as much on the grammatical level of meaning as on the social and situational, reminding the audience that a literal interpretation of "seeing" is tragically limited. The beauty of this example is in the degree to which all of the levels of proverb meaning are woven together and commented upon.

"Every goodbye ain't gone, every shut eye sure ain't sleep" is yet another item that is applied to relationship and, like others, its social meaning and application reflect a profound distrust and antagonism. The story here is a very basic and simple one: the speaker's partner, who has told him that she is going to work each day but who has really been having relationships with other men, is finally discovered. There is some of the same sense of pleasure taken in the contemplation of revenge here as in examples of "you reap what you sow," and the song is essentially an expression of the satisfaction of gaining the upper hand by catching the partner in the act of betrayal. Whereas in some cases the proverb might function to warn the other person, here it has more of a gloating quality. Situationally, "Every goodbye ain't gone" (which is sometimes used as a single item) reminds the partner that being able to leave does not mean that she will be able to "stay gone," and "every shut eye ain't sleep" (which is also used sometimes as a single item) reminds her that his apparent unawareness or good-natured attitude does not mean that he is, in fact, ignorant or deceived.

Example #46

Every goodbye ain't gone
  Every shut eye sure ain't sleep.
Came home this morning
  Saw what I've been trying to see.

Tell me baby
  What made you come back home?
I say **every shut eye ain't sleep woman,**
  Every goodbye ain't gone.

Tell me baby
  Thought you was working from 7 to 3.
I say every goodbye ain't gone,
  Every shut eye sure ain't sleep. (Peterson and Peterson 1972)

Objects and Animal Images

Many items containing images of animals and objects are also applied to relationships in blues lyrics and are commonly symbolic of particular character traits found in human beings and of particular kinds of people. It is logical, considering that proverbs often contain animal imagery, that such proverbs would occur in these lyrics and relate to some of the other animal images and metaphors found therein. We have previously noted that proverbs containing images of animals are often applied quite negatively to targeted persons. Often, this is true in blues proverbs, but these images reflect more complex elements than simply a derogatory implication about given characters.

One stanza in which a negative depiction is obvious occurs in Roosevelt Sykes's "Ups and Downs Blues," and concludes the song. The basic topic of the song is the uncertainty of outcomes in life, regardless of how well intentioned one is or how well one plans. The song begins on a positive note, with the singer's hopes that his plans for a good relationship will be realized, and ends on a cynical note, with the singer reminding himself that he should not be too optimistic. The proverbial expression used is "like buying a pig in a sack."

Example #47
But women are so tricky, they'll try to tell
  you white is black. (2X)
To get a woman nowadays, is just **like buying**
  a pig in a sack. (Oliver 1960a: 99)

One cannot help but imagine that the intent and meaning of the expression here go beyond the social or group level and contain significant situational meaning. The social level of meaning might be simply that one can never be sure of the true character of his partner until sometime after the relationship is already formed. At this level the proverb meaning ranges from a note of caution to an extreme cynicism about women and relationships. At the situational level the expression may be comparable to signifying or capping, inasmuch as it refers to women as pigs, an insult that carries with it a number of distasteful connotations. Thus, a component of the situational meaning is likely a reflection of anger and disillusionment and an intent to degrade women by implying that they are fat, sloppy, and "pieces of meat."

A use of preexistent social meanings of a metaphor is also demonstrated by an invented proverb in Sara Martin's "Mean Tight Mama," which comments on the negative associations of a particular cultural image. Assuming that this is an invented proverb, based on the structure of "the blacker the berry the sweeter the juice," it illustrates a particular relationship between an existent cultural metaphor, invented proverbs, and social and situational levels of meaning. Specifically, the images of "cow" and "milk" can carry social meanings because they are already cultural metaphors, but the proverb itself can only carry situational meaning, for it presumably has no history either in natural or fictive speech events. So the singer is released from the burden of social meaning of the proverb, but takes on the burden of making the invented item understood at the situational level, a challenge routinely accepted by poets and authors. The social meaning that might be derived from the proverb is a function of the similarity in structure and application to "the blacker the berry the sweeter the juice."

Example #48

Now my hair is nappy and I don't wear no
   clothes of silk. (2X)
But **the cow that's black and ugly, has often
got the sweetest milk.** (Oliver 1960a: 100)

In the first statement of the stanza, the singer establishes the conflict that the proverb then comments upon. She acknowledges that she is poor and African-American, that her socioeconomic status and physical features are not those considered most desirable in the context of American society, and, even more painful, in the eyes of many of her own people. For this reason, the use of the term "cow" in the subsequent statement becomes all the more significant. First, the term has often been applied negatively to women as a way of calling them ugly and slothful. Second, the image has important symbolic significance in blues lyrics, frequently being used as a double entendre designating a sexual partner: the image of "milk" has traditionally referred literally to the sexual juices or figuratively to the sexual energies of women. The extension of this sexual metaphor becomes at times the entire focus of songs, as in, for example, Robert Johnson's "Milkcow's Calf Blues" (1934). The phrase "But the cow that's black and ugly" can be taken as a rhetorical strategy that makes use of sarcasm by referring to and commenting upon a well-established, cultural metaphor that reflects racial self-hatred. It is an acknowledgment of the painful depth of a battered self-image. "Has got the sweetest milk" can be interpreted, then, as a statement of toughness and pride, arguing against the popular, negative attitude toward dark skin and African attributes. The image of "milk" is enlarged to include not only sex, but holistic qualities of being.

A stanza in a song by Ida Cox also contains a proverb with an animal image and utilizes preexistent cultural metaphor:

Example #49

When I was down South I wouldn't take no
   one's advice. (2X)
But I won't **let that same bee sting me twice**.
(Charters 1963: 102)

The proverb is generically related to "don't let the same dog bite you twice," and it is difficult to determine whether or not the version in the song was in currency in the African-American speech community or if it is an example of an invented version. The use of the bee imagery, in any case, illustrates the weaving together of meanings on the social level and the connection between the social and grammatical. Literally, the image depicts an unsuspecting woman being stung, then becoming defensive and taking precautions against another sting. "Stinging" (or being stung) already exists as a double entendre in blues parlance, the stinger being recognized as a male or female labidic symbol, and there are numerous songs offering various depictions of it, for example, "Honey Bee," "Queen Bee," and "King Bee." In addition to these dimensions of meaning, the proverb also relates to the proverbial expression "to be stung," meaning to be taken advantage of. So the singer's meaning here might easily extend beyond the simple resolution not to be further exploited by men on to a resolution not to allow the pleasure of sex to induce her to lose her resolve, for the bee not only represents the "other," but also her own desires. None of these aspects of meaning would have been present had the singer chosen the version of the proverb with the image "to let the same dog bite you twice." On the grammatical level, being bitten by a dog is a much more ominous and violent image. Being stung is painful but more surprising than threatening. On the social level, the metaphor of "dogs" in African-American culture has a completely different and more negative connotation than that of the "bees." So the entire complex of associative meanings would be radically altered had the "dog" metaphor been employed: the stanza and proverbial expression would have taken on the name-calling, "signifying" quality that is found in the previous item. The meanings carried in one version cannot be completely divorced from those found in another, if an audience is familiar with both; an invented item based on a traditional one will ultimately evoke associations with the latter. However, an audience can recognize that one or the other meaning is being emphasized. To look at the differences between the two from another perspective is to see that the chief rhetorical power of the "sting" rests in the metaphorical realm, on the social level, whereas that of the "bite" rests more on the literal, the grammatical.

Another example of a proverb that utilizes animal imagery occurs in Dr. Clayton's "Pearl Harbor Blues," which comments on the beginning of World War II.

Example #50
December the seventh, nineteen and forty-one, (2X)
The Japanese flew over Pearl Harbor and dropped
    them bombs by the ton.
The Japanese is so ungrateful, just like a stray dog
    in the street, (2X)
Well, **he bites the hand that feeds him** soon
    as he gets enough for to eat.
Some says the Japanese is hard fighters but any
    dummy ought to know, (2X)
Even a rattlesnake won't bite you in your back,
    he will warn you before he strikes his blow.
I turned to my radio and I heard Mr. Roosevelt say, (2X)
    "We wanted to stay out of Europe and Asia but now
    we all got a debt to pay."
We even sold the Japanese brass and scrap-iron
    and it makes my blood boil in my veins, (2X)
'Cause they made bombs and shells out of it and

they dropped them down on Pearl Harbor
just like rain. (Oliver 1960a: 129)

The verses here demonstrate the metaphorical application of an animal image to connote negative human qualities. The Japanese are referred to as a "stray dog" and are later said to be less honorable than "a rattlesnake." As I have mentioned, the dog is anything but a positive metaphor in African-American culture. Dogs are popularly equated with those who do not follow socially prescribed norms of behavior and decorum, and their image is used to designate the baser behaviors of both genders. Whereas in Euro-American society qualities such as loyalty are associated with "man's best friend," African-American culture tends to emphasize the dependence of dogs on humans and the animals' use of begging, stealing, or other actions that they engage in for survival or biological gratification; civil behaviors are seen to be manipulative strategies, not inherent or natural traits. These metaphorical associations influence the social and situational meaning of the proverbial expression. Although the situational application of meaning is distinct from that which might be found if the proverb were applied in the context of relationship, in a very fundamental way the social meaning is the same: the condemnation of a party who betrays the one by whom that party was previously supported. The same tone of bitterness is found when proverbs such as "You reap what you sow" are applied to former lovers. The proverb becomes a "cap," "signification," or put-down of those to whom it refers; in the present case, it gives expression to anti-Japanese sentiment, including an attack on the character of the Japanese and an indignant condemnation of the bombing of Pearl Harbor.

Though cultural metaphor beyond the actual proverb may not be as important in several other examples, the proverbial symbols carry significant weight among African-Americans. It would be surprising if "the blacker the berry, the sweeter the juice" were not found in blues lyrics. Racial identity and skin color in particular are common topics of concern, and a number of phrases reflecting this are found frequently, e.g., "my brown," "yaller gal," "chocolate to the bone," "brown skin woman," "coal black hair," and "brownie." Undoubtedly such formulaic expressions are often indicative of internalized values of the dominant society and reflect a caste system based on color tones. There are also countless sexual expressions referring to both men and women, many of which use food imagery, e.g., "pigmeat," "yams," "jellyroll," "peaches," "orchard," "ham," "sweet potato," "coffee," "oven" and "squeeze my lemon." The proverb contains both kinds of imagery. When applied to women, it graphically conveys the social meaning that dark-skinned women are better lovers than lighter-skinned ones and the situational meaning that a particular woman is a better lover and partner for this and other specific reasons: "**Blacker the berry, sweeter is the juice**/I got a good black woman, and I ain't going to turn her loose" (Taft 1994: 239). Fundamentally, this proverb has a function that is similar rhetorically to "**the cow that's black and ugly has often got the sweetest milk**."

Another common image is found in "a rolling stone gathers no moss." We noted one occasion on which this item was used by an ex-slave man, and a component of its social level of meaning includes feelings of exclusion and disenfranchisement. This component carries over into blues lyrics and adds an important dimension to lyrics in which the proverb is found. Taft gives two examples of this item in blues, and in both the proverb is applied by a male persona to a female character who has left him: "You quit me, pretty mama, because you couldn't be my boss/**But a rolling stone don't gather no moss**" (239). The second stanza is similar: "Louise got ways **like a rolling stone**/When she leave a man, he have to grieve and moan" (239). In both instances, the speaker is suggesting to the partner that it would be better if she didn't leave, for in leaving she forfeits the opportunity for stability. The latter example, however, reveals the tendency to alter the form of the proverb, and it is used more as a proverbial comparison, with the implied reference to "moss" omitted. This tendency is highlighted in Muddy Waters's "Rolling Stone" (1950), in which the singer artfully synthesizes the social meaning of the proverb with the loose-footed persona of the bluesman and the temporal philosophy associated with blues culture. In contrast to the previous examples, this one is a first-person correlation: the speaker applies the proverb to himself. He goes a step further and links the proverb to marginalized personas of power within the Africana community, e.g., the voodoo man and conjurer, and then boasts and celebrates these roles. There are rhetorical similarities between this and the use of "the blacker the berry": both take symbols of marginalized status and turn them into images of empowerment.

Proverbs That Are Not Applied to Relationships

A number of other proverbs in blues lyrics have no association with relationships, but offer observations about current events or general tendencies in human nature. "Fool's Blues" by "Funny Papa" Smith is centered around the proverb "God takes care of old folks and fools." The song utilizes a strategy that we have noted in examples from the ex-slave narratives: the proverb is presented and its truth discredited, thereby posing a subversive stance to the accepted wisdom of the group. Although this strategy is also found in example #45, it is uncommon in blues. In contrast to occurrences in the narratives, in blues it is illustrative of the disillusionment that members of African-American culture might feel with the beliefs and values of their own culture, and expresses the same cynicism toward traditional religious maxims that is conventionally found in blues culture but that is usually expressed in other ways. In this song (which can be considered by any standard a protest song), the singer makes the point that God's care seems to pertain only to some people and not to others, a contradiction that has often been articulated by African-Americans and an indictment of the system of institutionalized racism that brings about such inequity. The sarcasm is extreme here; for instance, in stanza five the singer suggests that, considering the way in which he (and, implicitly, others like him) is treated by God, he may as well be praying to the Devil, for instead of blessings he is given nothing but ills and misfortunes. The entire song can be considered a sarcastic exposition of the conventional social meaning of the proverb— that there are some special blessings or care bestowed upon the elderly and foolish—and an attempt to understand why the conventional relationship between God and humans does not pertain to him, as well as being an expression of feelings of betrayal and loss of trust in conventional wisdom and social institutions.

Example #51

Some people tell me
    God takes care of old folks and fools (2x).
But since I was born
    he must have changed his rules.

I need to ask a question
    then answer that question myself (2X).
'Bout when I was born
    wonder was there any mercy left.

Look like here of late
    I've been crying both day and night.
Everybody talks about me
    and nobody don't treat me right.

You know, until six months ago
  I hadn't prayed a prayer since God knows when (2X)
Now I'm asking God everyday
  to please forgive me for my sin.

You know, this must be the Devil I'm serving; I know
  it can't be Jesus Christ
'Cause I asked him to save me
  and he look like he's trying to take my life.

  Now I got TB's
  I got LT's
  I got third degrees
  and Polk's Disease

My health is gone now
  and left me with the sickness blues.
People, **it don't seem like to me
  that God takes care of old folks and fools.**
(Sackheim 1969: 121)

Didactic Uses

Only a few examples of proverbs that are used didactically can be found
in blues lyrics. These make generalized comments about the nature of
existence and human behavior. Unlike examples such as those we have been
considering, they do not employ innovation in meaning or application and
do not necessarily refer to someone with whom the speaker is in a close
relationship. The first of these is used by a somewhat unusual father and
son blues duo, James and Lucky Peterson, whose songs have a strong gospel
flavor and are generally more educative than most.

Example #52
You oughtta be careful
  All the wrong things you do. (2X)
If you don't mind
  All a catch up with you.

Talk about the preacher
  Haven't never been to church. (2X)
Shame, shame, shame,
  Child while you talk don't work.

Way a tree falls,
   that's the way it lie. (2X)
The way a man live,
   that's the way he die. (Peterson and Peterson 1972)

Although the recurrent issue of reciprocity is central here, the proverb is applied to a general type of person rather than to someone who is specifically identified. We can imagine that the "tree" is correlated to someone's life or to particular deeds; accordingly, "the way it lie" could refer to death or to some other kinds of consequences. In short, the song is a general criticism of hypocritical people and a reminder that one's deeds and manner of living will determine the timbre of their last days or lead to some undesirable consequences. As we have seen in other examples, the line that follows the proverb explains its application. "The way a man lives," however, is so broad and general, in contrast to the focus on a specific event found in the earlier examples that have been discussed, that it could mean almost anything.

The proverb "Everyone wants to go to heaven, but nobody wants to die" is used in a similar fashion by Albert King, as if he is sermonizing. He is, in fact, utilizing the strategy of signifying that is so salient in the African-American sermon. Once again, the proverb is coupled with elaborative and explanatory lines, and again there is no particular character to whom the proverb is being applied.

Example #53
Everybody wants to laugh,
   But nobody wants to cry. (2x)
Everybody wants to go to heaven,
   But nobody wants to die.

Everybody wants to hear the truth,
   Yet everybody wants to tell a lie. (2X)
Everybody wants to go to heaven
   But nobody wants to die.

Everybody wants to know the reason,
   without even asking why. (2X)
Everybody wants to go to heaven
   But nobody wants to die.
(King 1980)

The final proverb in this group is literal and is used to offer encouragement and inspiration to the audience. The stanza in which the proverb comes is the final one in a long, autobiographical song describing an experience of being struck by lightning and surviving. In this case the stanza functions as a moral for the story. The stanza, however, appears to be a traditional one that migrates from one song context to another: it is also found in a song by Gene Allison, whose title is taken from the proverb (Oster 1969: 152).

Example #54
You can make it if you try.
Now if yo' baby tell you
That you is goin' wrong,
Don't you go out singin' the blues,
An' feelin' kinda bad,
You know you can make it if you try.

These three examples are illustrative of possible reasons why this type of proverbial usage occurs less frequently than do others in blues lyrics. First, there are fewer levels of meaning. Although the very general application allows for a broader range of interpretations at the situational level, it insists upon a narrow interpretation at the social level. Even at that, the wide latitude possible at the situational level ironically lessens the impact of the proverb, inasmuch as the interpretations of it are fragmented and dispersed. Finally, this usage abandons the dramatic intensity that is created when a specific situation is referred to in the song and by the proverb. In effect, the proverb in these latter examples is decontextualized.

These examples are also important from another point of view: they reflect the manner in which proverbs are commonly used in urban blues and even in rhythm and blues and soul music. Thus far I have drawn no distinctions between the different regional styles of blues or styles popular during different time periods, largely because the corpus of proverbs is not large enough to make such a distinction of major consequence in discussing proverb meaning. Furthermore, a general survey of different styles, e.g., Piedmont, Texas, Delta, Atlanta, Chicago, Kansas City, or Oakland does not reveal any noteworthy distinctions in patterns or frequency of proverb usage. A survey of different time periods, e.g., country, folk, classic, urban 1940s, 1950s, or 1960s, however, does suggest some speculative differences. Generally speaking, urban blues is more formulized, emphasizing the performance dynamics mirroring those of the black church (Keil 1966), and contains more rigid proverbial structures than country blues. The musical structure of urban blues also becomes more formulized, and the voices of instruments more emphatic in their mimicry of audience vocal responses. For example, in "Everybody wants to go to heaven," the music swells to an intense pitch at the end of the stanza, taking over structurally for the heated vocal responses that might have occurred in live concert or after a particularly well-spoken line of a sermon in the church. These trends are carried over into rhythm and blues and soul music,[10] and the use of proverbs that occurs during this period (1960s and 1970s) reflects yet another emergent ethos in African-American culture, in many ways one that is more conservative and traditional than the one that precedes it. It is no accident that the giants of urban blues, such as Muddy Waters, B. B. King, Howlin' Wolf, Albert King, Bobby "Blue" Bland, etc., often utilize proverbs as focal, rhetorical devices in sermon-like performances to excite and rouse audiences. Nor is it incidental that Albert King, whose music is so closely connected with rhythm and blues and soul, is one of the most frequent users of traditional proverbs. Consider the following song, "Don't Burn Down the Bridge (Cause you Might Want to Come Back)," from his 1972 album *I'll Play the Blues for You*:

Example #55
You got your mind set on leaving
   to a house **down a one way street**.
You say you gonna lock all the doors
   and **throw away the key.**
Don't burn down the bridge
   cause you might want to come back,
Cause **the grass ain't no greener**
   on the other side of the track.

You counted me out
   Before I could get to bat
Today I'm driving a chevrolet
   Tomorrow might be cadillac.
Don't burn down the bridge
   cause you might want to come back.
Cause **the grass ain't no greener**
   on the other side of the track.

All of your so-called friends
   Learnt you how to cheat and lie.
Now it seems like **you gonna jump**

> **From the frying pan into the fire.**
> **Don't burn down the bridge**
> **cause you might want to come back.**
> **Cause the grass ain't no greener**
> **on the other side of the track.**
> (King 1972)

This kind of stacking of proverbial items (which happens as well in the earlier song by Albert King) simply did not occur in the rural or country traditions. It is also notable that the form of the stanzas is a departure from the conventional repetition of lines one and two, with lines three and four delivering the emotional "punch," and constitutes a more innovative poeticized approach to songwriting. A number of points can be made about the function of these proverbial items—how it differs from earlier traditions and how it relates to the social factors influencing Africana culture at the time. In contrast to the subversive thrust of lyrics and proverbs in the early development of blues, these validate traditional wisdom and attitudes toward the particular situations to which they are applied. Accordingly, there is a shift in the nature of the persona, from the victimized, dispossessed individual to a more inclusive voice, one that has aligned itself with convention and in which the communal echo is louder than the individual. One can hear the community speaking in the use of the proverbial items. There is less sense of desperation on the part of the speaker and less anger or condemnation toward the partner, and the proverbs tend to be applied more philosophically. Perhaps this accounts for the difference between the posture of the persona in Bland's use of "you reap what you sow" and the usage by earlier singers closer to the rural tradition. So the social level of meaning of all the proverbial items is more likely reinforced than challenged or altered.

Perhaps this shift in proverb usage reflects the increasing entrance of African-Americans into mainstream society and the consequent need to reaffirm rather than challenge the traditional values of their own culture. From this perspective the symbolic value of proverbial items increases as the symbolic level of meaning decreases, for choice of items in many of these penned songs is probably more related to writers' desire to evoke symbolic meaning for the listener than to personal attachment to particular items. As I have suggested, while there may be wider appeal because of the symbolic value of the proverbs used in this fashion, there are, on the other hand, less complex levels of meaning.

While this discussion has not exhausted all of the traditional or invented proverbs that occur in blues lyrics, it has served to uncover important facets of proverb application and meaning that will assist in interpreting meaning in other kinds of contexts. Some of the items that have not been discussed include, for example, "ashes to ashes, dust to dust" (Taft 1994: 136), "it's a bad wind that never change" (Oliver 1960a: 305), "live and let live" (Oliver 1960a: 109), "the best of friends have to part" (Taft 1994: 237), "the bigger they come, the harder they fall" (Taft 1994: 238), "the first shall be the last, and the last shall be the first" (Taft 1994: 239), "beauty is only skin deep" (Taft 1994: 240), "if you make your own bed hard, that's the way it lies" (Taft 1994: 240), "let your conscience be your guide" (Taft 1994: 240), "love is blind" (Taft 1994: 240), "let your money talk" (Taft 1994: 240–241), "don't let your left hand know what your right hand do" (Taft 1994: 240), "that's a long old road that has no end" (Taft 1994: 241), and "where there's a will there's a way" (Taft 1994: 241). In addition to proverbs, many proverbial phrases also recur in blues; some of these are "fattening frogs for snakes" (Oliver 1960a: 74; Taft 1994: 233), "drylongso" (Sackheim 1969: 215), "sugar for sugar, salt for salt" (Sackheim 1969: 143; Taft 1994: 242), "one foot in the grave" (Garon 1971: 95), "strong as a lion" (Oliver 1960a: 282), "to play no second fiddle" (Taft 1994: 233), and "just feed your daddy with a long-handled spoon" (Taft 1994: 239).

In summary, proverbs in blues lyrics illustrate a strong penchant for creativity and innovation in forms and meanings of traditional items, as well as exerting a great influence on formal structure of lines and stanzas. Sometimes this influence is seen as newly invented proverbial items and at other times in lines that mirror proverbial structures. Furthermore, the use of proverbs in these lyrics challenges some of the commonly described characteristics and functions of proverbial speech, for only a few researchers have emphasized components of both innovation and traditionality in the performance of proverbs (Mieder 1987; Yankah 1989a). In the blues, for example, speakers often assume responsibility for proverb messages instead of distancing themselves for the communications. And, as the evidence suggests, the structure may be the primary, traditional element of proverbs that makes them appealing to speakers, more so than either the customary social meanings or any behaviors traditionally associated with those meanings.

The materials and discussion in this chapter also make abundantly clear that proverb texts should not be the basis for conclusions about the values of a community. As we have seen, many proverbial items here (as in

Yankah's study) are used to argue against conventional wisdom and values. In some cases these arguments may be very personal positions on a particular situation; in other cases, they suggest perceptions of a larger group. In either case, one cannot assume that the position reflected in a given song performance would necessarily pertain in other situations. The group most reflected in the proverbs used in blues is not African-Americans, anyway, but certain performers in African-American culture at certain periods of their lives. It would, moreover, be a mistake to conclude that the popularity of blues indicates that the audience gave the proverbial items the same interpretations as did the performer, or that some direct correlation between the proverbs and values obtained.

Though we have not considered how the rituals of defense/attack and masking discussed in chapter 2 might pertain to proverbs in blues lyrics, the former at least does have application here. It is no overgeneralization to state that in most cases proverbs in the blues exemplify the ritual of defense/attack. The difference between this context and that of speech events with white interviewers is that here the speakers are relating primarily to other African-Americans. A similarity in the uses of proverbs discussed in both chapters is the recurrent issue of reciprocity that is addressed, or, we might say, "fairness." We will see, as our discussion continues, whether the issues that we have noted concerning form, meaning, and application arise in cases of proverbial usage in contemporary speech events.

PART TWO

Contemporary
Speech Acts

FOUR

Proverb Masters and Symbolic Meaning

The contexts of the proverbs we will look at in the next two chapters are significantly different from those in the previous ones. In all cases, the items considered here are used by African-Americans speaking to other African-Americans and are representative of the ways in which these proverbs are used in contexts of day-to-day natural discourse. Most of them are gathered from situations where I was either a participant or an observer, and the speakers belong to three general categories: (l) friends or family members in Virginia, (2) anonymous persons in public places, in Virginia and California, as well as in locations in between, and (3) staff or students at an elementary school in Oakland, California, where I worked as a sixth-grade teacher between 1984 and 1988.[1] To supplement these examples, I have gathered proverbs from the University of California, Berkeley, folklore archives, which are identified as collected from African-American speakers. Typically, these archival entries contain basic informant data, indicate when, where and from whom the proverb was learned, and provide examples of situations in which the informant had heard or would use the proverb.

The most striking aspect of this corpus of proverb speech events is the overwhelming percentage in which adults use proverbs to or about children. To some extent this statistic has to do with the kinds of contexts from which many of the speech events come—homes and an elementary school. This is, however, less reflective of a bias in my fieldwork than of the actual settings in which proverbs among African-American speakers are most likely to occur. In the process of my collecting, many kinds of settings were surveyed. For instance, I spent long hours (eventually totalling months and years) in pool halls, bars, auto-repair shops, retirement homes, medical offices, churches, and on basketball courts and football fields, waiting patiently for speakers to use proverbs. I can attest that proverbial speech in these contexts is infrequent and does not necessarily conform to what one might initially expect. Men are more likely to use proverbs in competitive situations, for example, than otherwise. Proverbs are not as frequently used in formal church settings, although this would seem to be an ideal setting. Whereas a number of traditional rhetorical maxims frequently occur, e.g., "God don't come when you need him, but he's always right on time," and "The spirit moves in mysterious ways," proverbs are more likely to appear in the informal conversation of men or women before or after the actual church service. Thus, it appears that the most important context is the small gathering and not the church-related activities or formal structures associated with the church. That the home and adult-children interactions are by far the most fertile context of proverb speech events is further suggested by the data from the U. C., Berkeley, archives, as well as by other researchers (Daniel 1979). When informants are asked where they learned the proverbs that they use, most of their examples involve a parent using the proverb to them.

I was tempted to schematize types of proverb speech acts along lines of style, function, and context, making a division between the two contexts of home and more public spheres and between functions of polarization and bonding.[2] Certainly such patterns are noticeable in the speech events that I have collected. However, such division might give the false impression of compartmentalization of items and obscure the complexity of relationship between the contrasting elements of context and function that often forms the art of proverbial usage in any given situation. It is obvious that basic proverb style, selection, and application are learned primarily in the home. Proverbs are used to children from an early age on. But this does not imply any one style or function of proverbial speech, for, just as proverbs may be used in the home to evoke laughter and diffuse potential arguments, they may also be used to criticize and humiliate. And insofar as contexts go, I have mentioned that small gatherings may be considered a context regardless of the particular setting, for the persons present are often more fundamental to the ensuing dynamics than the place in which they meet. For this reason the concept of context must be reconsidered. It is apparent that groups of speakers invoke the ambience of a desired setting or time, transforming the place in which they find themselves. In some way such transformation facilitates the occupation of traditional roles, even in situations where the outward structure might require conflicting roles and behaviors.

This transformation of a normative context into a ritualized one is, in fact, one function of proverb speech events among adult speakers. It is similar to the function that music often plays in African-American culture, and I refer here specifically to situations that on the surface might be viewed as normative but that, with the introduction of music into the setting, become ritualized—for example, when a person working in an office begins singing a gospel quietly to himself or herself or when a boombox is turned on during a lunch break, on the bus, or in an office. The term "ritualized" implies here that a sense of time and of one's place in it, as well as one's sense of being, is keyed by cultural symbols and referents so that participants feel more surrounded by their own cultural space than by some other. This can occur, for example, when two people are speaking in the hallway of a school building, in the office, or on the playground, and can contribute to the sense that when one is at work, one is not very far from home. It is not difficult to see why proverbs would be an effective form in this regard: more than any other, they signal the collective cultural voice.

The location of proverbs in speech events in contexts such as homes and schools might also seem to have some connection with the idea that proverbs are instrumental in teaching traditional values. I take issue with this notion, though, as I have throughout my discussion. One of my main criticisms of the value-focused approach to proverbs is that the very term "value" is a nebulous one, with different connotations for different people, and those who have discussed proverbs in this manner have not taken the time to examine and define the concept that is central to their discussions. What is meant, for instance, by saying that "cleanliness" is a value of a given group? Does this mean that everyone in the group considers "cleanliness" a desirable trait? But in what circumstances? For whom? And what does "cleanliness" mean? And how does this "value" translate into behavior? The issue of values is one that deserves critical examination and that should be thoroughly explored before being linked to other cultural phenomena. As my discussion will demonstrate, the use of proverbs is much more tied to issues of power and control, and to attitudes and dispositions, than to what are generally considered values. In fact, much of what proverb speakers attempt to transmit to children is "wisdom"—individual and cultural attitudes and perspectives that are relative to other dimensions of culture. This relativity is a crucial factor, for it suggests further the inappropriateness of considering isolated items lifted out of particular contexts as indexes to culture.

Proverb Masters

The collection of proverbs in context is a type of undertaking that is very different from the customary practice of eliciting items or of collecting performances of narrative genres. There are no cultural settings in which an audience comes together expressly for the purpose of hearing proverbs performed and no culturally prescribed settings in which proverbs are predictably a part of formal or informal social interactions. Therefore the process is necessarily long and often unrewarding. What I did find in my fieldwork experiences is that there are particular community members for whom proverbial speech is an important part of speech behavior, that these individuals are responsible for most of the proverbs that are used, and that this form of speech is closely connected to personal identity and tends to occur irrespective of the context. I have termed these particular kinds of individuals "proverb masters," and they seem to share certain social characteristics. They usually grew up in a home where there was a proverb master from whom they learned to interpret and apply proverbs, often an older relative such as a grandmother, but sometimes a mother or father. Often they turn out to have been raised by an older relative, or, because of geographical or social isolation or health problems, to have spent a great deal of time around adults. They tend to have been and remain very emotionally connected with that person, and the decision to become a user of proverbs carries with it a complex of psychological and cultural elements. Being a proverb master in African-American cultures seems to place one in the role of a conscious bearer and active guardian of cultural traditions, whether or not one intends to assume that role. Others have discussed the status accorded elderly proverb speakers in African-American culture (Daniel 1979). While members of a community may not regard the proverb master as "wise," they do regard such a person as thoughtful, contemplative, "deep," caring, and connected to the knowledge of past generations. To become a proverb master is to step into a cultural role in the same way that storytellers, musicians, teachers, preachers, or midwives do, and certain sets of expectations are projected onto those who assume the role. Unfortunately, not until recent years have scholars begun to recognize the similarities among such roles and the attitudes toward them in African and African-American culture and to see how closely they can be compared.3 It is my observation that the filling of the role of proverb master, in addition to what is provided to the community, plays an important part in the development of positive self-esteem, security, and status for the individual, just as being known for the mastery of any valued art within a group often does. A prominent element of this identity, however, is being known as a contemplative person who is in touch with past knowledge and, implicitly, as one who remembers those who have gone before and through whom they continue to live and speak.

Contrary to what many scholars have historically assumed about proverbial speech, proverb masters need not be older members of the community. If one were to think about it, this makes perfect sense, for how would a proverb master become such without practice, and when would the period of practice and apprenticeship be likely to occur? Scholars have begun to recognize that young people do use proverbs (Prahlad 1994; Bornstein 1991). I have known a number of budding proverb masters from childhood who began imitating the proverbs of their parents or grandparents to other children on the playground or in other contexts of play. Very often the lives of these children fit the pattern of literary characters such as Ned in *The Autobiography of Miss Jane Pittman* (Gaines 1971), Janie in *Their Eyes Were Watching God* (Hurston 1937), Cocoa in *Mama Day* (Naylor 1988), or even of Denver in *Beloved* (Morrison 1987): either they were consciously "groomed" for roles of community responsibility or were simply much closer to older people than to peers. That such children would engage in proverbial speech is logical if we consider that to some extent it represents simply the imitation of adult role models by children. Such imitation of speech behavior on the part of children is natural and to be expected. As Bornstein notes in her study of proverbs in her own family, "[T]he use and parroting of proverbs is an integral part of the learning process and the beginning of a child's understanding of the family social hierarchy" (1991: 27). As much as the gross level of imitation is implied here, I also posit that artistic elements and constituents of style and technique are learned as well through this process. Any master proverb user has developed a particular style that encompasses a range of rhetorical features, e.g., vocal intonations, pitch, introductory formulas, and even kinetic factors such as frowns, lifting of eyebrows, or hands placed on the hips.

In my initial discussion, I will focus on four older proverb masters from California and Virginia, and later look at some younger speakers. By its nature, the collecting of proverbs in context involved my concentrating on persons with whom I had, or was able to develop, some close relationship, and so all of these speakers are people around whom I spent considerable time and to whom I have been emotionally close. Overhearing a proverb used by a stranger on a bus, on the other hand, was valuable to my study, but posed a number of problems regarding the gaining of more information about the speaker and his or her thoughts on certain aspects of proverbial usage. In most cases, it did not seem appropriate to approach speakers who used proverbs in public places, unless I already knew them, of course. And even if I did approach them, there was usually very little time to talk, or they weren't interested in talking, or suggestions about meeting at some point in the future to talk were met with suspicion and distrust. One of the questions that did occur to me in these instances was whether or not the speaker was a master proverb user.

The present focus on particular proverb speakers will allow me not only to continue exploring social and situational levels of proverb meaning but also to more fully develop the notion of symbolic meaning, which requires close attention to personal uses of items and background information on speakers. In this chapter I will examine the proverbial speech of older speakers, particularly proverb speech acts directed by adults to children or spoken to other adults about children. By doing so, I hope to illuminate some of the components of meanings of proverb performances, many of which have not been touched on by previous scholars, while others have been discussed but have not been approached from the perspectives of my model.

Symbolic Meaning

It may help to remember that proverbs for most informants do not exist as written texts. They are units of oral language that are connected in some way to the specific contexts in which they were first learned, to general kinds of contexts that are similar to those original ones, and to persons and relationships from those original contexts. I hypothesize, therefore, that proverbs contain a symbolic meaning for specific speakers, which may include (1) a specific *frame of reference*, (2) an emotional or *psychological association*, or (3) an *associative relationship*. The frame of reference refers to the original context in which the proverb was learned and succeeding similar contexts. An emotional or psychological association refers to the basic psychological components of a former context that were deeply imprinted on the listener. An associative relationship refers to the kind of relationship that exists between agents within the proverb and the implied analogy to persons or situations in the concrete world.

This hypothesis suggests that proverbs are linked not only to the historical past on a societal level but also to the personal past, and, in addition, that the user is in some way mediating the link between the past and present as well as mediating the components of symbolic meaning each time a proverb is spoken. Rather than defining a particular meaning, the proverbial item carries symbolic meaning. That symbolic meaning is the sum of any of the connotative components that have just been listed.

I propose the term *symbolic value* to designate the degree of importance of the symbolic meaning for a given speaker of a given proverb. In other words, a proverb that was learned by someone whose parents used it repeatedly would have a greater symbolic value for that person than a proverb overheard incidentally in the conversation of coworkers.

It is through this process of symbolic meaning that proverbial items can also emically become folk belief, a "truth" to live by, or a personal motto. The idea of proverbs being "true" was touched upon in the previous chapter. I suggest that the nature of the "truth" that is referred to by informants is based on symbolic meaning. They are concerned with the symbolic "fit" of the item, not with its formal structure. In other words, it is not truth at the grammatical level that informants are referring to, nor is a proverb "truth" comparable to, for example, a scientific statement of truth, such as "leaves are green because they contain chlorophyll." It is not the actual words and grammatical message that are of concern, but the associations that accompany those words, including situations and types of situations that exist in the informant's mind in which the proverb has been or might be applied. This is another way of saying that proverbs that do not key situational applications in the mind of a listener are practically meaningless. In Armstrong's words, we might say that the proverb has "affecting presence" (1971; 1981), or that, unlike the scholar who may be concerned with " 'truth' of the text" (Briggs 1993: 396), these speakers are concerned with the real-ness of experience that the text symbolizes. It is expressly because of the components just described that an item recalled in conversation can have no less "truth" value to a listener than if it were applied. This evaluative concern with proverbs is expressed repeatedly by informants whom I interviewed. Informants will state, "That sure is a true saying" or "That one is really true," if the item appeals to them and seems to carry some meaning with which they can identify. In interviews with informants, a common response to my asking if they knew a certain proverb was "No, but that certainly is true," or "Yes, that sure is a true one, too." My findings in this area are corroborated by Daniel (1979).

This quality of "trueness" is one that is also traditionally measured in the appraisal of other genres of speaking and music. It is a common traditional response to sections of a minister's sermon ("Tell the truth!") and likewise at musical performances of blues and gospel. The quality is alluded to frequently not only by members of the audience but also by performers. The concept seems to mean "authentic," in the sense of being honest in the expression of one's personal experiences and encounters with life. The converse of "trueness" would be the dilution or falsification of one's experiences or observations about life in some way. At the core of this evaluation, however, are actual or hypothetical experiences in which the items are used or to which they are applied. The criterion of truth gives a clue as to how genres separated by folklorists might be grouped together by some speakers. I suggest that a concern with the truth value and other aspects of meaning overshadows concerns with the particular structure of an item, so that there may at times be an ambiguity in separating proverbs from other genres. This ambiguity is also related to the issues of texts and contexts and to the way in which proverbs "mean" for specific informants.

An excellent illustration of symbolic meaning is found in the discussion of the proverb "Different strokes for different folks" by one of my major informants, Mrs. Dorothy Bishop. I became acquainted with Mrs. Bishop while teaching at Golden Gate Elementary school in Oakland, California. I noticed that she used occasional proverbs to students or to other staff at the school, and asked her if she would consent to being interviewed.4 She not only agreed but also continued to talk with me about proverbs after the interviews, from time to time bringing me proverbial items that she had found in magazines or on greeting cards.

Example #56
[The speaker sometimes refers to her grandmother as "Momma."] I like "different strokes for different folks," you know. A lot of times I used to

talk to my grandma, you know, and tell her, "Momma, why you won't let me do," you know, certain things, you know, that I wanted to do, you know. And she'd say, "Well, you different, you're different from, you know, some of the other children in the family." And I'd say, "Momma, I don't understand why you make difference between me." She says, "Because there's something special about you, you're different than them." And then she'd always tell me **"different strokes for different folks"** and I'd look at her and I'd just wonder, Momma, I don't understand that, but as I grew older I began to understand because I knew that I was different from, you know, the other relatives in the family. And one thing about it I always had a mind of my own. Regardless of what anyone said, if I wanted to do something and they said no, I was still bullheaded, I said, "I'm going to do what I want to do." She said **"different strokes for different folks,"** so I'll be different.

I never conformed to rules. I just couldn't. I wanted to be my own person. I wanted to make a way for myself the way I felt was better for me. And so, that's the best one that I've ever, you know, tried to live by, because it was something that kept me going, you know, through all my problems and troubles having my children and everything and then I'd go back to thinking Momma said, you know, **"different strokes for different folks,"** and things would happen to me in my life and I'd think about, wonder what would Momma do, or Aunt Thelma, I just couldn't understand it. And finally look like I fell into a groove for myself, you know, and I didn't have to worry about having to follow a pattern like everyone else, you know, so I really like that one.

It is clear that the meaning of the proverb for this informant goes well beyond the social, situational, or grammatical levels, and, in fact, that the proverb has meaning beyond any isolated performance of it. That overriding meaning derives from the context in which the proverb was learned by Mrs. Bishop and the host of associations that she has with that context. In a manner of speaking, the proverb has become an "object" that triggers a memory not just of one occasion on which it was used to her by her grandmother (frame of reference) but of a particular dimension of their relationship and her grandmother's life in general (psychological association). More specifically, the relationship implied by the proverb refers to Mrs. Bishop's identity, personality, and relationship to others (associative relationship). It suggests that each person is different from every other, that one has to come to an understanding of what is best for him or her, and that this is particularly true of Mrs. Bishop because she is uniquely different from others. An important component here is the idea of "specialness" or "uniqueness" and the necessity of trusting one's own development and growth.5

The importance of the symbolic meaning of the proverb for the speaker is paramount. It is clear that the proverb serves as an inspirational item, one that she has held dear all of her life. It does not, however, prescribe a particular course of action or promote a "value" so much as suggest an attitude or disposition, and, for Mrs. Bishop, a complex of connotative elements and relationships are the most important component of the proverb's meaning. The belief that no two people are the same and that each individual should seek to develop his or her own ways of looking at the world and of doing things is a strong part of the situational meaning as the proverb was interpreted by Mrs. Bishop; however, her grandmother's support is another component that has become an important dimension of the situational and symbolic meaning in Mrs. Bishop's adult life. Of note is the difference between the situational meaning that seems to have been intended by the grandmother and that which the child interpreted. The grandmother's use of the proverb suggests that the reason for her tighter restraint was her belief that her granddaughter had more potential and, therefore, should be kept closer to home and more carefully supervised. As a child, Mrs. Bishop sometimes used this proverb as a way of justifying her defiance and breaking of rules, and it was not until later in life that she more fully understood what her grandmother had been saying to her.

The extreme degree of symbolic meaning that influences proverbial speech for Mrs. Bishop is further reflected in some of her other comments about proverbs. As is the case for many proverb masters, the recall or application of most proverbs triggers associative memories that are invariably linked to strong symbolic meanings, and these tend to color many of the proverbs in this speaker's repertoire and to inform the choice, use, and function of proverbs that she uses. It is also apparent that her *awareness* of the strong symbolic value of proverbs influences her conception of what proverbs are and how they function. These points will become clearer as we examine more of her thoughts on these issues.

> PRAHLAD: When you use the proverbs do you think of your grand-mother?
> BISHOP: All the time, all the time. Every time I say one I remember, I remember, and you know I kind of think this was her way, you know, because she really wasn't an educated person. All her life she had, ah,

worked, you know, in the houses of white people, cookin' and cleanin' and taking care of their babies and what have you, and I think this is all she knew except, you know, she knew these proverbs and she knew, you know, cookin' and cleanin' and church. And that's about it.

She continues:

And she raised her kids, she had six kids of her own. And I think what happened, she sort of lived by these because after her last child was born she, her husband, my grandfather walked off and left her and I think this is about all she had to live by, to survive, you know, to keep her going, you know, to raise those kids. She had four girls and two boys. It was tough. So I think this is really what her life was all about and this is why she was sort of, you know, so strict with me, trying to keep me in line. She wanted, you know, what she couldn't do for her kids.

I really appreciate that and, ah, between her and my mother I don't think I would have survived because it was a hard struggle at that time. It took a lot of doing and I think some of these (proverbs) is the only things that kept me going. Even in my life, raising my children. I still go back over and think about it. A lot of times I think "know what Momma would say."

Even at the age of fourteen, fifteen, sixteen, I think that's when, you know, I began to realize Momma was doin' what she felt was best. I was sent to live with her by my mother, because my mother and father separated, they broke up, and my mother felt like she wasn't able to raise me and keep me by herself, you know, she had to work every day and I was left alone, you know, so she said, "I can't work and see about your school and food and clothes and things like you need."

My grandmother was home all day. She took in laundry, and that way my mother felt like she had somebody to keep an eye on me; she wasn't worried about me.

Her understanding of her grandmother's life circumstances, personality, and relationship to proverbs is further revealed in these passages of the interview, as is her very strong awareness of proverbial speech as a part of a cultural tradition and heritage. It is clear from these comments that Mrs. Bishop feels that proverbs were a survival mechanism for her grandmother, one of the only "things" that she possessed that gave meaning and inspiration to her life and that she could pass on to her granddaughter. It is also clear that the informant adopts her grandmother's perspective on proverbs, and, from the opening statement of this segment of discourse, that the symbolic value of the proverbs is deeply felt and pervasive. The informant further supports this contention in another segment of the interview, as well as indicating more of the religious context that proverbs fell into for her grandmother and, by association, for herself. These comments also bring us back to an issue that cannot be developed here, the relationship between proverbs and behavior: how does the proverb translate into the way in which one responds behaviorally to certain situations?

> I think I've lived my life off my mother's proverbs and things. Seem like every day, all day long, it was either the singing of these hymns or proverbs all day long, you know, and if she wasn't doing this she was sitting up readin' that Bible or quotin' something from Solomon, you know.

Another aspect of Mrs. Bishop's concept of proverbs that grew out of her childhood has to do with the process of learning and understanding them. As the following passage indicates, the symbolic value in this regard also influences her ideas of context, speaker and listener, and the process of learning proverb meaning—therefore, her own use of proverbial items. She indicates that in her belief system, proverbs, if they are to be effective, must be pondered, and that children may naturally resist this process. In her words, the turning point for the child is the interpretation of the proverb speech act as, "I love you and am trying to give you good advice." This indicates a component of the symbolic meaning for this informant that I have already alluded to: her grandmother's love and concern and her own love for her grandmother. As such, each use of a proverb is a celebration of that love, a eulogy and a litany. Moreover, it is evident that the proverbs at the symbolic level represent process, a lifelong involvement with the meanings from many perspectives, and that any single proverb speech act, then, is a part of an ongoing process in which meanings are continually being negotiated, are changing and developing. The proverb is perceived as a doorway through which philosophical introspection, contemplation, and emotional growth and maturity lie, a reference marker containing layer upon layer of meaning. So one can never claim to understand "the meaning" of the proverb, but learns to appreciate the mysterious unfolding of life's events, its depths, and the relativity of things in life that proverbs call attention to.

> See these things you have to think about. You can't just say 'em and you know, think that's gonna help somebody. My momma used to tell me all these things, oh I get *so* mad. I be burnin' up inside. I'm sick a hearin'.

She don't have to tell me nothing. I'm grown. I'm gonna do what I wanna do. And then I go off and word for word that she said to me would flash in my mind, and I'd go back and I'd think about it. And I'd say "Wait a minute," maybe she has something, maybe she's right. Maybe, maybe it might work that way. So I'd do it sometimes. Sometimes I'd listen because, in other words, what she was sayin' is "I'm not go' steer you wrong. I'm not going to tell you anything to hurt you. I love you enough to give you good advice. Now it's up to you whether you take it. It's for your own good."

We can also see here how the proverb as a unit of language, of fictive discourse, can be so effective in the impression that it makes on the mind of the listener. Undoubtedly, this aspect of the proverb is invaluable in those situations in which a speaker wants to state something that will not only offer multiple levels of interpretative meaning but will also form a lasting impression in the mind of the listener.

The evolution away from the speaker's childhood rebellion and toward the acceptance of proverbial speech is reflected in the above comments. Another element found here is common among children whose parents use proverbs to them: a part of the symbolic meaning becomes the perceived criticism of their perspectives and behavior, resulting in a negative response to proverbs. Oftimes there is no transformation of the sort that Mrs. Bishop underwent, and the response remains negative throughout adulthood. For some reason, something did change for Mrs. Bishop, and she eventually moved from the acceptance of her grandmother's maxims to her own active use of proverbial speech. This choice implies the occupation of a cultural role, one understood by Mrs. Bishop because she had seen her grandmother as model. She is careful, however, to define the role as much as possible in her own terms. One function of proverbial speech indicated by Mrs. Bishop is that of emotional healing and inspiration, and her comments suggest that she conceives of proverbs as tools not only for advising courses of action, but also for addressing problems of negative psychological states— e.g., depression and anxiety.

P R A H L A D: What makes you like a proverb?
B I S H O P: Well, I like it because to me it's food for thought. It's something to, you know, keep you straight. You never hear a proverb that's negative. It's always something positive. It's no negative ideas and things to get you going all haywire. You know, in the wrong direction. It keeps you with a good mind. That's what I'm saying.

To me it's sort of like a medicine. It'll work, you know, if you think it works. You know how sometimes you take medicine and you say, ah, this didn't do me no good, and sometimes you take it and you feel so much better, and you don't know if the medicine did it or not. You know, so that's the way these are.

She then relates, as an example, the story of her son's girlfriend, who in a state of despair and depression attempted suicide, and whom she helped to regain a more positive attitude toward life. One of the tools that she used in helping her was proverbial speech expressions.

The speaker, in using proverbs, places herself in the role of a healer.[6] The proverbs become medicinal tools for addressing psychological and emotional problems of those around her and for nurturing and empowering those persons with the problems. Within this conceptual framework, functional and aesthetic components are considered and mediated by the speaker in her choice and application of particular items. For example, she would view the desired resolution of a fight between two persons in terms of "healing" the conflict. The process of choosing and applying a proverb would include a consideration of the particular aesthetic and functional characteristics that would best serve this end. We will see more specifically how these characteristics are mediated as our discussion continues.

Another important element that can be noted in the use of proverbs by Mrs. Bishop is the mediation between time periods and even worlds. To the extent that the symbolic meaning pertains to a given proverb speech act, the past is consciously being brought into the present moment.[7] Not only is Mrs. Bishop speaking, but her grandmother is also present and speaking. That proverbs seem to carry the voice of ancient wisdom has been noted by proverb scholars time and time again, and this voice operates on the social level of meaning; however, these examples indicate that they carry a much more specific voice on the symbolic level. Mrs. Bishop is aware of the two dimensions of voice when using a proverb and is also cognizant of the reverberations among the different voices and the dynamics of a situation to which she applies a proverb. Stylistic features sometimes reflect her considerations of the way in which levels of meaning pertain:

> P R A H L A D: When do you say "as the old folks used to say" before you say a proverb? Do you ever say that or do you say it certain times and you don't say it other times?
> B I S H O P: Well, I say it generally when the occasion arises. It depends on what the situation, you know, at the present time, you know, if I have a problem with kids or with family, neighbors, friends, whatever, you

know, then I'll come on strong and let 'em know, hey, well it's just like, you know, "as the old folks used to say," and then we go, and then we get off on that track.

P R A H L A D: So when you say it, it helps to make what you say stronger?

B I S H O P: Yea. It kinda highlights, you know, really what you mean.

P R A H L A D: Do you think they pay more attention to it [the proverb] when you say it [the formula]?

B I S H O P: Yes, and sometimes they take it as something negative to start with because they don't believe it like I do, you know. No one has the experiences, say, that I've had and then you know, my mother used to use it with me all the time and I felt the same way, you know, "Aw, forget it, that's past, this 19-whatever-the year-was, you know." And I felt the same way, so I know how other people feel. Oh, that's an ole corny line, that's how they come on, but really, it rings true sometimes.

P R A H L A D: Is there a time when you wouldn't say it?

B I S H O P: Yes, to some people I wouldn't, because some people, you know, they kinda look down on you because you wanna bring up the past or bring up what your ancestors or great-grandparents or someone has said. So some people you kind of careful and you don't say it to. You want to in the back of your mind, but you hold back because you know, well, they wouldn't accept it anyway; so I accept it with a grain of salt and go on about my business.

P R A H L A D: So you would say the proverb, but you wouldn't say "as the old people say" to those people?

B I S H O P: No. Not really.

For her, the use of traditional formulas adds impact and emphasis to her assertions, but they also create a certain contextual dimension that colors the ensuing conversation. She also states that traditional formulas may be negatively received by some listeners and that her assessment of this aspect of a speaking situation influences her decision to use or not to use them. Implicitly, this consideration involves the receptivity of the audience to the idea that the opinions of ancestors might have legitimate bearing on current and contemporary situations and the positive or negative disposition of that audience toward cultural identification. She states that she might also at times use other formulas—e.g., "well, like my Momma used to say," "like I always say," "like I used to hear my Momma say," "like my Momma used to tell me," and "as they say."

The following passage further emphasizes the notion that the ancestors are invoked with each proverb speech act, and also gives insight into another function of proverbs implicit in Mrs. Bishop's comments as well as in my discussion: that the speech acts provide psychological comfort and pleasure for the speaker. Arora has referred to this little-discussed aspect of proverbial speech as "the use of proverbs in inner speech" (1984).

> P R A H L A D: When you say some of the proverbs, you smile. Why are you smiling? Is it the words of the proverbs that are kind of funny? Is it something that is connected with it in the past that you're thinking about?
>
> B I S H O P: Well, sometimes it is connected with the past. Like I told you. Each time I say one, I remember, and I'm smiling, I can remember when someone told it to me. So that's how I learned them, from different people. And you know, from my grandmother, like I say, she was the master of all, and ah, my grandfather, you know, when I was a child. And let's see, teachers . . . I never will forget . . . So I mean, it's people I remember when, they're not here I mean, they're dead and gone but I still remember you know, the knowledge, and all the good information I received from them through the proverbs.
>
> P R A H L A D: So you're smiling because you have memories—
>
> B I S H O P: The memories, yes.
>
> P R A H L A D: More than just the picture in the proverb?
>
> B I S H O P: A lot of times it's the picture I still remember, and I remember what *help* I received from them, you know, and I'm hoping that someone will remember what I've said to them when I'm gone. The same way you know, as people inspired me. This is what I'm saying.

The enjoyment or amusement that she gets from thinking about a proverb is directly related to its symbolic meaning, and the above comments indicate that perhaps for her the grammatical image cannot be so readily separated from its symbolic associations.

The role she has assumed is more evident in comparison to the way in which her mother has chosen to use her grandmother's proverbs. The comparison underscores the element of individual choice in relating to the repertoire of a proverb master with whom one has lived. Not only might the symbolic meanings and associations be different for two persons raised by the same proverb master, but the individuals' responses to the style and function of proverbial speech can be dissimilar. As Brandes notes, "Even when several individuals, for example those of a single family, share the same roster of proverbs, they may very well employ them in distinct ways" (1974: 169). In this case, the art of one speaker is more colorful and innovative but less religious; conversely, that of the other is more serious and conservative.

While one speaker has adopted a worldly, secular, and bawdy role, the other has taken on that of healer and community pillar. The variations in the proverbs from the proverb master to those used by Mrs. Bishop and her mother range from the addition, deletion, or changing of a single word to changes in tense and overall wording. Tone is another important element of this variation, as the exact words might be used but the proverb altered considerably by changes in tone, pitch, and rhythm. Mrs. Bishop commented on her mother's use of proverbs that the two of them (Mrs. Bishop and her mother) had heard used by Mrs. Bishop's grandmother. The segment reveals to us an interaction between the two that focuses on their discussion of their "mother's" proverbs and demonstrates their awareness of her mastery and of their "apprenticeship" to her.

> Now a lot of these rubbed off on *my* mother. Now *my* mother would come up with her story, it'd be altogether different than what my grandmother had said. I'd say "Wait a minute, wait, hold it! Momma didn't say it like that!"—"Ahh, but it mean the same thing, you know." Me and my mother, now me and my mother battle about it all the time. "Now look, you know Momma didn't tell you like that, now you know my Momma would add her little four-letter bit. [Laughter] Naww, I know Momma told me but she didn't tell me like you said. She say 'Now look, you know I like to put the icing on the cake.'" And we'd just crack up. [Laughter]
>
> P R A H L A D: So she'd say it different, huh?
>
> B I S H O P: Oh yes, it's a *million* ways you can say these now. Don't think it's got to be just like this.
>
> P R A H L A D: Could you give me an example of how she would say one of them differently?
>
> B I S H O P: Ohhhh [hesitantly], oh no, no, no, no, no, not like my mother, oh no!

Having discussed more in detail some of the dimensions of symbolic meaning for Mrs. Bishop, let us examine several proverbs that are used by her in context. As previously mentioned, I knew her as a fellow staff member at Golden Gate Elementary School, but some description of the school environment is in order before looking at speech events that were collected there. Golden Gate, a small school of three hundred to four hundred students, is located in a predominantly African-American community in north Oakland. It is plagued by many of the same problems that affect inner city schools in general, and its students are considered a "high risk population," according to criteria established by the federal government. This designation reflects such factors as the income levels of parents whose children attend Golden Gate as well as the community environment. The school suffers from lack of adequate funding, negligence from the district administration, and problems from the community that spill over into the school, including drugs and alcohol. There are never enough basic supplies (paper, books, pencils), nor is there sufficient basic service personnel, such as speech therapists, counselors, and custodians. A large percentage of students are well below grade level in basic academic skills, and discipline is an ongoing and extreme problem. Students tend to have little or no respect for adults, regard for rules, or internalized concept of the principles of formal education. The "war zone" of the streets outside routinely encroaches on the school environment, and one often feels a sense of chaos and despair. Mrs. Bishop represents an older group of parents and community workers who can remember when the school was more effective and the community more stable, and who are struggling to maintain some of the respected and central values of the African-American community within the present situation.

Example #57
Two women, Mrs. Bishop and another woman approximately forty-five years old, were talking in the school library. The conversation turned, as it often did, to the severely disruptive behavior of many of the children. Unfortunately, most of the students did not come to school academically prepared and were uncooperative and often indifferent to the efforts of the staff to educate them. Mrs. Bishop, in a tone of exasperation said, **"Well, you can take a horse to water, but you can't make him drink."** "That's right," the other woman responded.

The social level of meaning here is that one cannot force someone to do something that he or she really does not want to do; specifically, the children cannot be forced to learn or to be receptive to learning even if they are sent to school. There is some negative component, as we have seen with other proverbs containing images of animals, in the correlation of the children with horses; the implication is that they are less than intelligent—noisy, wild, and stubborn. In spite of this critical element in the situational meaning—that these children are not able to do very simple things that will benefit them—what is pervasive in this speech event is a feeling of pathos and sadness. This feeling was conveyed strongly in the facial expressions and tone of voice of the speakers; they are lamenting the probable fate of children who do not obtain a good education. To consider the symbolic meaning of the proverb for the speaker adds a significant dimension to its application. She has stated that she focuses on her grandmother every time she uses a proverb. In this case, then, she is not only concerned with the apparent situation, but is in internal conversation with her grandmother, perhaps thinking how right her grandmother was or how sad she would be to see the situation that these children are in. The speech act not only brings her grandmother into the present but also helps to distance the speaker somewhat from the immediate situation by allowing her to move backward in time and to take solace in the memory of their relationship.[8] Although this function is similar to a much-cited aspect of proverbs—that they distance the speaker from the utterance—there is a fundamental difference. Proverbs are commonly discussed as having some inherent quality that facilitates the distancing of the speaker (Norrick 1985; Abrahams 1972b). Here, it is not some general quality of the proverb but the particular symbolic meaning that facilitates the distance. The effect is somewhat the same, for in both cases the speaker occupies a role that is not only apart from the audience but superior to it.

An aspect of the bonding that occurs between the two women is the sharing of a space that is both apart from and superior to that occupied by the children: a momentary "us" and "them" paradigm is created. Norrick has noted these characteristics of proverbial speech. He writes, "Proverbs are like clichés, jokes, especially inside jokes, allusions, quotes and ways of speaking generally, all of which can lead to bonding between people" and states that "proverbs tend to place the speaker in a one-up position *vis-à-vis* his hearer" (1985: 25, 29). This speech event functions to unite the two speakers at the point of their agreement on the criticism of the children. It becomes an affirmation of their common feelings toward the children in question and perhaps also toward the social climate that produced those children. The proverb acts descriptively and critically, comparing the children to horses and characterizing them as individuals who, even when given an opportunity for something that is good for them, will not take it. The correlation of the proverb here is third person.

Different speakers have used the same proverb with the same social meaning. For comparative purposes, let us take a look at one of these examples before going on to a second proverb used by Mrs. Bishop. A comparison demonstrates that the social level of meaning can remain consistent while the situational changes. Reported as "You can take a horse to water, but you can't make him drink, you can send a fool to college and you cannot

make him think," a second version demonstrates how speakers may alter
the original form of the proverb by use of an extended phrase that parallels
the proverbial structure. In this case the extended phrase not only adds
the element of rhyme, but also identifies the specific application of the
proverb. The proverb here is used again among two adult women who
are commenting on the failure of a student to take full advantage of his
educational opportunities.

Example #58
Mrs. Richardson first heard this proverb from her mother in Monroe,
Louisiana circa 1930. Her mother and a friend were discussing the failing
of a mutual friend's son in college. Mrs. Richardson was overhearing all
of the conversation from another room. At the time, she thought the
situation and the proverb [**You can take a horse to water, but you
can't make him drink, you can send a fool to college and you cannot
make him think**.] to be very funny. Mrs. Richardson has used this proverb
numerous times. She uses it when describing anyone in a position of
opportunity and who doesn't make good use of that opportunity. (U. C.
Berkeley Archives)

The speaker here is uttering the proverb out of anger or disgust rather
than out of sadness; it is the anger felt by someone who places a high
value on striving to gain advancement in American society toward someone
who apparently does not value an opportunity to progress. This attitude
is reflected in the extended phrase that specifically refers to the third
party as a "fool," and is a part of the situational meaning. This example
differs from the first one in that the speaker here does emphasize the
critical and negative component of the proverb metaphor, the stupidity
and stubbornness of the horse. While the social meaning is consistent with
the first example—that one can send children to school but cannot force
them to value the educational opportunity—the situational level takes on a
different significance, partially because of the differences in the situations
and the attitudes of the speakers. A part of the situational meaning in one
example is that children are unfortunate victims, and, in the other, that the
child is a "fool." It is impossible to determine the symbolic meaning of the
proverb for the speaker in this second example, but we can infer that some
of the symbolic meaning for the child overhearing the speech event will
involve her amusement at hearing the proverb used. While it is unclear
whether humor was an element of the speech event, it was undoubtedly an
element of the child's response to overhearing it.

In a second proverb performance by Mrs. Bishop, the item exemplifies a speech act directed toward a student instead of being about one, a second-person (rather than third-person) correlation:

Example #59

A class of third graders were in the library, and one of them came up to the librarian, Mrs. Bishop, and complained that another student was hitting or "bothering" him. The librarian remarked in a suspicious tone of voice, "**Yea, the pot calling the kettle black**. Just like you ain't never done nothing to him."

The social level of meaning of the proverb is the suggestion that one person is accusing another of something that he himself is guilty of. The situational meaning of the speech act here was the communication to the boy that the speaker was not fooled by his innocent facade, that she knew there was more to the story than he was telling. The speaker's attitude implied that the boy was mischievous, and, further, her tone of voice implied that *he* was a chronic behavior problem. There was little instructional emphasis as the proverb was used to the listener here. The speaker, in fact, seemed resigned to the boy's behavior and there appeared to be no expectation that the proverb would have any effect in terms of his learning from it and changing. The overriding problem or issue addressed is the boy's annoying presence at that moment, not the possibility that he might change his behavior. The use of the proverb is similar to a "cap," a rhetorical put-down of the person to whom it is directed. If we think in terms of the proverb proposing a solution, the solution would be for the boy to sit down and allow the speaker to continue with her duties. In Norrick's terms, there is no "syntactic cohesion" between the text of the discourse and the *implicature* or meaning of the speech act (1985: 25–26). The symbolic level is important here because it tempers the critical dimension of the speech act. Mrs. Bishop's conviction to pass on some of the experience symbolized by her grandmother's proverbs and her honest concern for the welfare of the students are components of the communication to the student. Although he may not have consciously understood this, he could perceive that what she was saying to him was said out of concern. Furthermore, the use of the proverb was a way of "leaving the door open" and "inviting" the student in, even if it was unlikely that he would enter. At least the possibility that he might understand some of what was being said to him and correct his behavior was left open.

A final comment regarding this particular case concerns the impact that such a proverbial speech act can have upon someone overhearing it. I did not know the student, but I immediately formed an impression of him. The speaker's use of the proverb combined with her facial expression and vocal intonations labeled the boy as being not only a behavior problem but also devious and incorrigible. As I discovered later, the student had many emotional and academic problems and was known for his disruptive behavior.

In two other examples this same proverb is spoken to children by another elderly proverb master. The speaker in these examples is Mrs. Clara Abrams, the great-grandmother of this researcher. Though slightly different circumstances led Mrs. Abrams to her acquisition of proverbs and her development into a proverb master, some of the same factors obtain. Raised on a farm in rural Virginia that was once part of a slave plantation, she grew up around her mother and many other community members who frequently used proverbs. Her sense of culture, history, and tradition were acute, as was her commitment to pass these on to succeeding generations, and she was considered "the mother" of the church, the elderly member of the community who held all of the information about persons and events from the past, who told stories, knew medicinal cures, and used proverbs. My grandmother, my mother and, in turn, my siblings and I grew up with my great-grandmother as one of the central people in our lives (see Folly 1982), and this relationship added considerably to the meanings of proverb speech events involving her. We had been told, for instance, many anecdotes of historical events detailing the lives of relatives going back for many generations, including events that occurred among relatives who had been slaves and interactions between relatives and Euro-American plantation owners and their relatives. Very often, we were informed about relatives who were fond of certain proverbial expressions or other folklore items. Consequently, when we heard these proverbs used, this knowledge was a part of our interpretations of their meanings. One of the most commonly mentioned characteristics of proverbs is their association with ancient voices of wisdom, but this notion has remained an abstraction. Scholars have not gone so far as to ask: Who are these ancient speakers in the minds of an audience? If we were to give them faces, personalities, cultural attributes, postures, what faces would they have? I suggest (and it is a suggestion that applies to proverb masters in general) that for this speaker and audience the voice of ancient wisdom is not an abstraction: it is the voice of their

African-American ancestors, and proverb speech acts are a way of bringing *particular*, envisioned voices to bear on given speech events. Contrary to the common scholarly thought on this issue (Smith 1978: 74), speakers do often relate to items as if they were authored by particular persons, and some sense of cultural and familial ownership is involved, especially with proverb masters.

Example #60
A family of five children, two parents and one great-grandmother had gathered at the dinner table for dinner and was waiting on one of the children to come and sit down. Another of the children impatiently criticized the one who was coming for being so slow. A third child agreed with the criticism. The great-grandmother at this point said, "**The kettle calling the pot black and the frying pan standing up for witness.** All of y'all contrary when you want to be."

The speech event here was a criticism of all of the grandchildren. The speaker was struggling with issues of aging and dependency. She had been accustomed to living alone and independently, but, due to poor health, had moved in with her granddaughter and family. While on one hand she longed to be taken care of, on the other, she feared having to be dependent. In the speech event, she was lashing out at the grandchildren and at the parents, venting her frustration. The speech event struck me as an expression of her powerlessness and loss of ability to control the environment around her. The proverb speech act had a bitter tone to it and functioned as a means of commenting negatively about the family members; it was, in essence, the equivalent of "signifying," or "capping." All of these factors obtained at the situational level, including a wish that the children would simply stop their bickering and get on with the meal. Also registered as a part of the communication was some sense of disappointment that no one of the children could be relied upon to be as receptive to the transmission of her values or as malleable as the speaker might have wished them to be. At the symbolic level, the children were aware that this was one of the speaker's favorite proverbs and that it reminded her of her own mother; they were aware of the symbolic meaning of the item for their great-grandmother. In some way this knowledge allowed them to interpret the speech event as an indication of her insecurity and sense of displacement and vulnerability, as well as her need to evoke memories of cherished and secure moments in her life. Furthermore, the images of kettles and pots have another shared dimension for the speaker and audience: these items were literally the ones that Mrs. Abrams had held onto from the time of her mother's tenure on the plantation and that had been shown to the children. So, the grammatical level informs the situational and symbolic, for the proverb contains images of actual objects that have symbolic meaning for speaker and audience, representing enslavement, struggle, and emancipation.

In another situation Mrs. Abrams used the same proverb to two of the great-granddaughters (see Folly 1982: 238).

Example #61
The two sisters were washing dishes, and one of them criticized the other for the way that she was stacking them. Mrs. Abrams rocked back in her chair and slid her feet across the floor. "Ah Lord, well there! **The kettle calling the pot black**," she said, laughing.

This speech event contains aspects of humor, ignited by the play already occurring between the two sisters. The proverb is applied to remind the critical party that they also have shortcomings *of some kind*. A difference between this example and the previous one is that here the proverb speech act functions to unite the speaker and listeners emotionally, whereas in the first example it functions to isolate them from each other. The speech act here has a light-hearted quality about it that the previous example obviously did not. Its social meaning remains relatively the same, but because of the nature of the interaction, the situational message becomes humorous. Here, the speaker is feeling close to and positive toward the listeners, and, at the symbolic level, the proverb evokes fond memories of ancestors that are being shared with the children. At the situational level, there is no directive here—there is no behavior or course of action that is being suggested—rather, the proverb speech act is intended as an act of bonding. Note that the speaker in this case does not actually say the proverb to anyone specifically. She says it aloud so that both of the girls can hear it, and they clearly understand how it is being applied and to whom it refers.

A second proverb used by Mrs. Abrams—"if you fool with trash, it'll get in your eyes"—also carries strong symbolic meanings for her, in this case reminding her of her grandfather.

Example #62
I often heard granddaddy say that about his son. You know, he had been married and he had a son and two daughters. He hadn't heard from Arthur for years and years, and he say Arthur wrote to him, "Papa, I'd like for you to help me, I'm in trouble."

He said, "Yes what you need?" He, "Need some money." So he said he sent him the money. But he wrote him a letter and told him, "**If you hadn't been fooling with that trash you wouldn't got, wouldn't got in that trouble**." Say "You wouldn't listen to me." I hear him say he told him, "you was fooling with trash, that's the reason you're in trouble." (Folly 1982: 239)

A characteristic of the use of the proverb in this anecdote is the way in which the literal or grammatical image is at once metaphorical and imbued with social meaning. Grammatically, the proverb states that if one handles trash, some speck of debris is bound to blow into one's eyes. But the term "trash" is also slang for people of low morals or unsavory character. Hence, the statement made to the man's son could be a deliberate mixing of the metaphorical and literal for rhetorical or poetic effect. As such, it could be interpreted humorously, the literal image adding emphasis to the metaphorical, colloquial use of the expression. Mrs. Abrams used the proverb in a similar context.

Example #63
Mrs. Abrams and Mrs. Folly were talking at the dining room table about the son of a relative who had been habitually in trouble and seemed to be getting into more and more serious kinds of situations, involving drugs and petty theft. "He didn't used to be like that. When he was growing up he was always such a good boy. So polite," said Mrs. Abrams. "Yeah, he sure was. I think it's that crowd he's been running with," replied Mrs. Folly. "**Well, they say you fool with trash it'll get in your eyes**. I remember granddaddy used to say that thing," Mrs. Abrams said, smiling. "He sure did," said Mrs. Folly, beginning to laugh. "Clara," Mrs. Abrams began, deepening her voice and changing her mannerisms to imitate her granddaddy. This led to a few minutes of intense laughter as the situation turned into a joking one.

The symbolic level of meaning of the proverb is apparent, as its performance keys the memory of the person from whom it was learned and evokes emotional associations with that person, leading to a joking interaction focused on his mannerisms. This kind of interaction was a common one within my family, and through it the children were educated not only about events involving particular relatives but about components of their personalities, mannerisms, and speech behavior, as well as being exposed to a variety of stylistic features in proverb performance. At the situational level, the proverb speech act here supports the opinion given by Mrs. Folly that the boy was not inherently bad but was influenced by peers. It is extremely critical of the peers, implying that they are of the lowest social character possible—"trash." The social meaning of the proverb involves the idea that the person in question is in pain as a result of his associations, and this level includes here an honest empathy and concern for that person.

Two further examples from two other speakers can help to illustrate the importance of symbolic meaning in proverb usage. The first comes from my mother, Mrs. Jean Folly, who was raised by my great-grandmother and became heir to her oral traditions. Mrs. Folly was raised not only by a proverb master but around other older people as well, many of whom were active bearers of traditions emerging out of the southern, African-American plantation community. Growing up in this environment made her privy to details of folklife, and I have noticed that many of the proverbs she uses contain images that relate to some aspect of life in a rural environment. To reiterate, a knowledge of the symbolic meaning of many of these items is understood not only by those in the immediate family, but by people in the community at large, for most of those people are aware of the same stories, anecdotes, and events, and are aware of various community members' attitudes toward particular ones.

> Example #64
> Mrs. Folly (approximately thirty-six years old) was talking about her son who had dropped out of college and seemed lost and regretful. "**Well, like the old folks used to say, you make your bed hard, nobody but you has to lay in it**," she said to her grandmother (who was approximately seventy-five years old). "That's right, Jean," the grandmother responded.

Before using the proverb, the mother had been talking for quite a while about her son's situation. Her voice was sad and mirrored her anxiety and concern. There was the sense that the proverb speech act functioned in some way as a consolation, a mechanism to prevent her from becoming tearful. There was also the sense that she wished that the wisdom of the proverb were not so, and that she longed to intervene in some way that would make her son's "bed" less hard. The use of the proverb lightened the mood of the conversation, if only for brief seconds, and allowed her and her grandmother an extra moment of sharing. This bonding was facilitated by the symbolic meaning of the proverb, the memories of the old people who had once used it and perhaps a shared recollection of particular instances in which they might have done so. A further dimension of the meaning here is that the speaker is practicing an art form learned from her grandmother in addressing her, as well as using a particular item learned from her and probably applied in a similar kind of situation to the speaker as a child. This becomes an element of the meaning conveyed by the speech act. Another component of the symbolic meaning relates to the grammatical level of the proverb's meaning and its literal images: there is a shared attitude toward the making of a bed. For both persons, making up a bed is nothing less than an art form, one that was preached to my mother by my grandmother, although she never mastered it to the degree that my great-grandmother did. The proverb, then, evokes a dynamic between the two of them at the same time that it makes a comment about the speaker's son. That I was present when it was spoken contributes yet another dimension of meaning, for I was able to observe the bonding process, which then became a part of the symbolic meaning of the proverb for me.

The social meaning of the proverb (which is one of the most common in African-American culture) is that one has to live with whatever situations his or her actions create. The symbol of the bed becomes a metaphor for the son's life and the making of it representational of his making choices that define the parameters of that life. The speech act represents the speaker's efforts to accept the fact that her son is now an adult and has the responsibility for making his own decisions and for bearing the consequences of those decisions. This effort is reflected in the phrasing "nobody but you has to lay in it," the situational meaning of which is that since he has dropped out of school, he now has to confront the consequences, and which is deepened by the symbolic meaning infusing the speech event.

Before examining another speech act by Folly, I cite two other examples of the same proverb from other informants, once again to demonstrate that current, popular items can have different situational and symbolic meanings in different contexts. In a second version of this proverb, the function and context are significantly different. The informant reports the proverb as "When you make your bed hard, you have to lay in it," and gives the following context for its usage:

Example #65
My mother used this quite a bit when I was growing up. She brought this . . . with her from Cleburne, Texas about 35 years ago. I would break a house rule and when I got punished would sulk and complain about it.

This was mom's retort [**When you make your bed hard, you have to lay in it**]. (U. C. Berkeley Archives)

Here the proverb speech act is spoken directly to the person to whom it refers, by mother to child. In contrast to the previous version, which is third person, the correlation here is second. The speaker is emphasizing the misbehavior of the child and "teaching her a lesson." The situational meaning of the proverb is that if the child breaks the rules of the house, her mother will punish her. Quite obviously, the symbolic meaning here, involving punitive connotations, is different than for Mrs. Abrams, Mrs. Folly, and me. It is also, in contrast to the first example, behaviorally directive, owing basically to its correlation.

The usage of a third version—"If you make your bed hard, you have to lay in it"—is identical to that of the previous example. It is clear in this example, however, that the situational meaning of the proverb speech act extends further than the immediate context in which it is used to serve as a warning about the dangers of future violations and the potential severity of future repercussions. The instructive level of the speech act emphasizes the general importance of acting responsibly and of avoiding actions that might have negative consequences. Specifically, the proverb may have been intended to apply to situations that could lead to altercations with legal authorities. Again, the symbolic meaning is specific to the case. For the informant, who learned the proverb from his mother in Des Moines, Iowa, it is likely going to include associations with this particular incident and his mother's reaction.

Example #66
On the way back from a football game given for the benefit of Cerebral Palsey victims he was egged on by a group of boys he was with, all of whom were older, to hit a "white boy." He did so and the Juvenile Authorities came and talked to his mother the next day. After talking to them, she went to his room and gave him a scolding and said the above proverb. (U. C. Berkeley Archives)

The examination of a second proverb used by Mrs. Folly is revealing of how shared knowledge and experiences can contribute to levels of meaning in a given speech event.

Example #67
A seventeen-year-old was sitting at the dining room table, anxious and overwrought about a girl in whom he was romantically interested. His

mother, who was ironing in the same room, began a sentence and then cut it short. A few minutes later she said, "**You know the saying, don't put all your eggs in one basket**. You know what I mean, I guess."

First, let us look closely at the speech event. The speaker here is concerned about her son becoming too "wrapped up" in a world of romance and forgetting himself and losing sight of pragmatic considerations. She is expressing her love and concern while encouraging him to balance his idealism with pragmatism. The proverb speech act is an instructional tool for pointing to the importance of maintaining a balance between investment in someone or something else and taking care of oneself. Its social meaning is that one should always have an alternative plan. The situational meaning is that one should not invest completely in one person or one relationship.

Poetically, the metaphor employed in the proverb captures the delicate nature of the challenge that the son faces. Just as a simple accident could potentially break all of the eggs in the metaphorical basket, leaving the carrier empty handed, investments in another person can just as suddenly go awry. It is also interesting that the speaker chose to use a proverb, after beginning a sentence and then deciding, presumably, to use a more indirect approach. The directness of the proverb's meaning is further softened by the introductory phrase "You know the saying," ascribing the message of the proverb (as is often done) to traditional sources. The proverb speech act is further colored by the speech act that immediately follows it. This second speech act underscores the parental impulse to go on at length about the situation and the speaker's restraint in not doing so. The voice intonation and shrug of the shoulders give additional emphasis to meaning and function of this secondary speech act.

A number of dimensions of symbolic meaning that are not readily apparent contribute to the situational meaning of the communication here. One is the shared experience of having had to gather eggs from the hen house and of having broken them at times. One incident in particular is a part of the family's store of anecdotes. At one point during the boy's childhood, the family owned a particularly aggressive rooster that would literally attack anyone who came into the hen house to gather eggs. The boy had once been attacked by the rooster and dropped the basket of eggs that he had just gathered, breaking most of them. The story was recalled and told periodically, evoking a great deal of laughter, and in some way had come to represent the boy's vulnerability. The grammatical level of meaning, intentionally or unintentionally, sparked memories of that incident. So the proverb speech act communicated on yet another level the speaker's awareness of how vulnerable she perceived the young man to be at that moment, as well as her concern for him and an acknowledgment of her understanding that a protective or intrusive action on her part was inappropriate at that point in her son's life. The symbolic meaning added to the situational in yet another way. Because of the common knowledge that this proverb, like others, was learned from Mrs. Abrams, the use of it suggested that it had been used to the speaker and, at some point, to Mrs. Abrams herself. It follows that they too would have been in similar situations, in which they experienced love and frustration. This level of meaning was nothing short of a revelation for the son. The proverb speech event conveyed on many levels the notion that life, relationships, and the heart are all delicate, and that, although this fragility gives life some of its beauty, it paradoxically magnifies the potential for disappointment.

Just as Mrs. Bishop has indicated that she continues to contemplate the meanings of proverbs used to her by her grandmother, I have continued to do so with this item and many others that were used to me by my great-grandmother and mother, and suggest that the meanings that might be prominent for someone overhearing the use of a proverb (and especially someone reading the text) are not the ones that necessarily strike the intended audience when the proverb is used with such an intensity of symbolic meaning.

Another proverb used by Mrs. Folly is applied to herself:

Example #68
Mrs. Folly is discussing the financial aspect of the construction of her new house, a project already underway. She is concerned about being able to meet the payments once the house is constructed and anxious that the undertaking will obligate her to work longer than she might wish to, forcing her to retire that much later. In the speech event, which takes place with her thirty-year-old son (myself), she communicates her anxiety. The proverb spoken is **"Well, I guess we'll have to cross that bridge when we get to it, huh?"**

The proverb is spoken as much to herself as it is to the listener, as if she is evoking the voice of ancestral wisdom to address the anxious child within herself. The social meaning is that the problems of the future will be handled when the time comes to handle them. Situationally, the proverb's meaning could be paraphrased as "Don't worry about the financial part of it now, it'll take care of itself. It'll all work out." It is the symbolic import that allows the speaker also to be the spoken to, to fill both roles—the wise, parental voice and the insecure child. When this speech event occurred, Mrs. Abrams had died, and her physical absence from the lives of the family was an overwhelming presence. One result of this was a change in the symbolic nature of proverb speech events, a change that will not be explored in detail here. This change, though, contributed to the meaning of such simple choices of wording in proverb speech events as the poetically suggestive use of "we'll have to" in this version, which evokes the image of the speaker being accompanied when she crosses the metaphorical bridge and adds to the consoling quality of the proverb.

I have found at least two other examples of this proverb in speech events that give some indication of contexts in which it is used. The following is given by an informant:

> Example #69
> I tend to be a worrier and I've always worried about what would happen if . . . and my mother told me this proverb [**"Don't cross the bridge before you get to it**."] and said that worrying about something before it's even happened is always a waste of time and energy. But still I find myself doing the same things. And my mother keeps trying to reach me through this proverb of the futility of wasting time thinking about something that you can't help or something that hasn't happened yet. My mother is from Monroe, Louisiana and first heard this proverb from her mother there. It seems that she too, as a child, used to worry about things prematurely. (U. C. Berkeley Archives)

The informant's comments about the proverb amplify the points that I have made concerning symbolic meaning, the awareness of specific proverb application over generations within families, and the long-term involvement that a person might have with proverbial speech that contains strong symbolic meaning for that individual. It is apparent that the symbolic level of meaning for the informant includes an awareness of her mother's tendency as a child to worry a lot and of her grandmother's use of the proverb to her mother. As in example #65, the proverb is used to console and relieve anxiety. The social meaning is identical, whereas the situational meaning varies; in this last example, the proverb is applied to a range of different situations that involve the problem of anxiety for the child. The informant's comments also give an indication of the extent to which a proverb can become a lifelong reference point in relation to a particular context or problem. The speaker obviously still relates problems of anxiety to her mother's proverb.

In a final example exactly like the first version, "We'll cross that bridge when we get to it," the informant gives a hypothetical context as follows:

Example #70
She might ask her mother, "Can I go to the movies Friday?" Her mother might answer, "I don't know, **we'll cross that bridge when we get to it**." (U. C. Berkeley Archives)

She states that this was a favorite proverb of her mother, who used it as a way to avoid answering questions. At least in the interpretation of the listener, the speaker is not concerned with an instructional function. The speech event communicates to the child that the speaker does not wish to be bothered at that particular time, and the proverb speech act contains the same message. If there is an instructional component in this example, it would be along the lines of "be patient" and would be closely connected with the message "don't bother me about it now" or "I don't want to answer you now." Unlike in the other examples, the proverb speech act does not reassure the listener, although it poses a similar solution to the listener's problem. The problem is different also, being one of curiosity rather than anxiety, and the proverb leaves the listener uncertain rather than consoled. Perhaps the ambiguity of correlation contributes to this anxiety. Does the speaker really mean "we," or is this simply a rhetorical device, with the proverb actually being applied to the listener?

Examination of a final informant and example of a proverb speech event gives yet another perspective from which to view symbolic meaning and how it is obtained. It is common for parents to use proverbs to children and to teach them about the background and associations of those proverbs that pertain within their own families and communities. This inscribes the proverbs with symbolic meanings that may never be apparent to outsiders and suggests just how complex the topic of meaning in proverb speech acts can really be. In the following example, a proverb provides the nucleus for a humorous speech event that occurs between a mother and her children. The mother is an informant with whom I worked at Golden Gate, Mrs. Laura Tallie. When I conducted the interview, Mrs. Tallie was approximately forty-five years old, the natural mother of three children and the adoptive mother of one. In this speech event, she is joking about her separation from her husband and the financial inconvenience that it has caused her and her family.

Example #71

A little while ago, me and the kids were talking and I was telling them about my separation from my husband. And ah, mainly we were saying that **"you don't miss your water 'til your well run dry."** I miss Ed, but not as far, not as far as for companionship, but as far as not having the money in the house that we usually have. But as far as missing him as a companion I don't miss him for that, but I miss him as far as having the responsibility of paying the bills, and stuff like that.

And I was just saying, you know, my mother, I was telling 'em I say, Momma always say **"you don't miss your water until your well runs dry,"** I say, my well is just about dry! I don't have no money [laughter]. I say, my well is just about dry. We had a big laugh off it and I was telling them, I say that's what it mean when you hear Momma say **"you don't miss your water until your well run dry."**

I say, **so my well is just dry**, I don't have no money but if your daddy was here I wouldn't have to worry about when the rent was gonna be paid or PG&E or telephone or was I go' have $150.00 this week to go make groceries and stuff, you know, so we was just having a big laugh off it. So I would use it in a statement like that or a sentence like that.

The proverb occurs in two separate speech events here. The first is the situation in which the speaker simply applies the proverb to her husband's absence. In this she makes a point of correlating the "well" to the financial support that he supplied, emphasizing that she does not miss his emotional support. The situational meaning is that she did not miss (fully appreciate) the economic support of her husband until he was no longer in the home. In the second speech event the proverb becomes the focal point of a humorous interaction between the speaker and her children. The main metaphor is taken out of the proverbial structure and personalized and extended as it is applied jokingly to paint a picture of the speaker's situation. The conversion of the proverb into a joke is apparent not only in the language but in the vocal tone and pitch and in the kinetic signals of the speaker as she says it. Her opening words, expression, and the gestures in her description of the speech event all signaled that something humorous was about to follow.

Even in this humorous speech event, the proverb obviously has a serious side, and perhaps the humor is a way of softening the reality of the situation. The main issue is the speaker's regret that her husband is no longer present to help support her and her family. One can see that the use of the proverb reveals the speaker at a vulnerable moment, openly expressing her feelings to her children. The similarity of social meaning here and in blues lyrics is also evident, as a central component in each context is the economic crises that intensify whatever emotional issues are caused by a partner's departure. Perhaps the use of humor allowed Mrs. Tallie and her children to share a possibly painful and somewhat frightening experience more comfortably. Aside from everything else, the speaker is consciously teaching her children one of her mother's proverbs, and a part of her dialogue is aimed specifically at explaining what the metaphor of the proverb means and giving them an example of how it functions. The proverb is taught to them with emphasis on its familial and generational component, which ensures that this will become a part of the symbolic meaning for them.

Story Proverbs: Interpretation of Meaning for Children

Abrahams suggests that one characteristic of proverbs is that they tell a story (1972a), and other scholars have noted the use of proverbs as parts of parables or tales (Finnegan 1970; Yankah 1989; Carnes 1991; Dolby-Stahl 1988). But some proverbs are more closely linked to stories than others, as central units of meaning within larger stories or as structural units of language containing images that suggest stories. A number of scholars have pursued the question of how children perceive proverbs and how the process of interpretation is related to the images in them (Pasamanick 1982, 1983, 1985; Brewer 1973; Chambers 1977). It is not my intention to fully engage this issue here, but to propose that there is a relationship between the images in proverbs and the symbolic meaning that pertains for given individuals. A further proposal is that some proverbs lend themselves to imaginative responses on the part of children more than do others. For the sake of convenience, I am referring to these as "story proverbs," and in the following discussion will explore briefly how the grammatical level of images in two of these contributes to the process by which proverbs come to have symbolic meanings for specific individuals. Some of the items that have already been discussed, of course, would also be considered "story proverbs," and some of the statements made concerning the following examples are pertinent in many cases.

Seitel has stated that in some African societies, proverbs are not used singularly to children below a certain age; instead, they are accompanied by stories explaining their meaning or they are literalized or otherwise made easier for children to understand (1969: 155–156). As our discussion has indicated, this is often true in African-American speech communities. For purposes of our discussion here we can note four different ways in which the relation of proverb to story is operative. First, the grammatical images of the proverb can convey a condensed story (Abrahams 1972a). Second, the proverb can be related to a particular story, e.g., Aesop's fables that end with particular proverbs (Dolby-Stahl 1988; Carnes 1988). Third, an event may unfold illustrating a proverb that has been applied to it so that a child comes to associate the proverb with an actual event (Bornstein 1991). Fourth, an event in which the child is an actor and to which a proverb has been applied may cause an association with the proverb and an anecdote involving that child (Bornstein 1991). All of these would influence the process of symbolic meaning for given individuals. Each of them would furthermore involve to varying degrees the three components of symbolic meaning that were discussed early in this chapter: frame of reference, psychological association, and associative relationship. It is not as likely, for example, that the symbolic *value* of a proverb would be as great in the case of the first type of story/proverb relationship given above as it would in the case of the fourth. More specific assertions, however, should form the basis for further investigation. How is, for example, the associative relationship affected by the different types of story/proverb dynamics? Or the frame of reference? These are broad issues that cannot be adequately addressed here although I will pose brief suggestions about them.

The proverb "Hard times will make a monkey eat cayenne pepper" is an especially good one to look at because it suggests at the grammatical level that there may be some story to which it refers. Certainly it creates a rather vivid picture in the mind and would be likely to impress a child to whom it was spoken. It is found on three different occasions in the U. C. Berkeley Archives, and, although the situational meanings vary, the social ones are consistent. Because these examples were obtained from archives, there was no possibility of questioning the informants about their responses to the actual images in the proverb when it was used by their mothers. We can point out, however, how the image of the proverb becomes permanently associated with a particular incident partially through the reinforcement of the mothers' responses to situations over a period of time; thus, the frame of reference is reinforced. In each case the psychological association and associative relationship vary and are influenced by the type of story/proverb dynamic that pertains. Furthermore, there is an indication that not just the proverb but the experiences they are connected to have taken on great symbolic meaning for the informants.

One informant gives a context in which he remembers his grandmother using this proverb:

Example #72
"In those days they fixed your plate and you ate everything on it or what you didn't eat then you ate the next morning for breakfast," the informant told me. The informant had objected to some food on his plate when his grandmother told him this proverb [**Hard times make a monkey eat red pepper when he don't care for black.**] It was usually told in the context of when there was an insufficiency of food or something considered basic to life. (U. C. Berkeley Archives)

The speech event, I conjecture from the data, is one in which the grandmother is stressing the importance of eating or utilizing whatever one has, of not being wasteful, and of having an appreciative attitude for what one has instead of complaining or indulging in fantasies about what one *could* have. I would imagine that another aspect of the dynamic in this context and of the situational meaning might be a sense of anger on the part of the speaker. She has probably had to work in less-than-pleasant circumstances to obtain the money to buy the food that the boy does not appreciate. As in the other examples, it carries a critical component. Here, however, the person to whom the proverb is being spoken is the object of the criticism and is also the person to whom the metaphorical "monkey" in the proverb refers. This draws this child into the proverb/story, exemplifying type four, and suggests a demeaning associative relationship and a negative psychological association. The monkey in the proverb—seen to be at an extreme level of deprivation, at the very edge of survival—is a somewhat pitiable character. He does not like *any* pepper, but must eat the hottest pepper in order to survive. This image emphasizes the severity of the family's economic situation. The notes of the collector indicate that the proverb was used in a wide range of contexts, but always related to food or to other basic items of survival.

Imagining, for a moment, the response of the child upon hearing the proverb used to him might give some insight into our central issues. Did the child focus at all on the images in the proverb? Probably. Did he detect and respond to being compared to a monkey? Probably. Did he wonder who the monkey was and what the rest of the story might be? Probably. Of course he also understood that the proverb was really an imperative, telling him that he'd better eat his food. But the images of the proverb must at some level have engaged him and contributed to whatever symbolic meaning he derived from the speech events in which it was used.

In a second example the meanings are drastically different. Here the symbolic monkey is an upper-class person who comes down, instead of a poor person who must live realistically within his means. In one, the child is the monkey; in the other, the child is the observer who watches the monkey grappling with his new station in life. This second case exemplifies the third type of story/proverb dynamic. The child watches the unfolding of a drama to which the proverb is applied but in which the child is not a character. Because of this difference (which essentially corresponds to correlation in Seitel's model) there is a vast difference in all components of the symbolic meaning.

Example #73
A friend of the family gave her mother a Persian cat whose name was Flossy, Circa 1942. Flossy had never had her feet on the ground, came with a box of toys, and ate certain foods "which had nothing to do with the way we lived, of course." Flossy's favorite food was calves' liver and she refused to eat the table scraps that Blackie, already a feline member of the family, ate. Some time passed and Flossy began to get scrawny and looked as if she were going to die. Mrs. Pollar said that she and her brothers and sisters begged her mother to buy liver for the cat, but their mother responded, "No-o-o-o, honey, she won't starve. **Hard times will make a monkey eat cayenne pepper.**" Flossy lived. (U. C. Berkeley Archives)

The proverb in this example can be considered from two perspectives: first, as it obtains in the recalled context in which the mother used it, and second, in the anecdotal speech event between the collector and the informant. As the mother uses the proverb, it is obviously intended to encapsulate a certain "lesson" that the children can learn from watching the drama of the new cat, observing the mother's attitude toward it, and, finally, hearing the proverb applied to the situation. The situational meaning of the proverb is that the cat would eventually eat the food even though it might not be her dietary preference. This level of meaning in the speech event carries a number of other implications. It is, to an extent, a criticism of the cat for having such specialized taste, an indication of being "better," more important, or more privileged than others. Taken to a larger application, this criticism would be applicable to anyone in the cat's situation, and this implication is a part of the "lesson" of the proverb. The cat is being criticized as well by use of the metaphorical referent, a monkey, which is anything but complimentary. An additional aspect of the meaning of the proverb speech act is the needlessness of worrying about an animal or person in the cat's position because the drive for self-preservation is so strong as to overcome socialization or acquired habit or taste. In the anecdotal context, the story becomes a parable in which the proverb is symbolic of the upper class who are brought low, with Flossy being the characterization of the upper class and the anecdote an illustration of the validity and application of the proverb.

The application of the proverb is even further extended in a third example, in which the components of the symbolic meaning are more varied. Notes of the collector read:

> Example #74
> My informant said that she heard this phrase used by her mother whenever someone would say very dogmatically what they would or would not do. She would always say, "Never say what you will or will not do. You never know when circumstances will change your fortunes and then **just like the monkey, who hated them, ate red peppers and cried his eyes out**." (U. C. Berkeley Archives)

Specifically, the proverb warns against making emphatic declarations about one's future actions. The major difference in the application here is that the mother and child do not seem to be facing any immediate issues of hardship or survival, and the mother is warning the child that one may unexpectedly find oneself in adverse circumstances of some kind. In such circumstances, the message advises, one may have to do things that he or she previously thought were beneath him or her. In contrast to the previous examples, the frame of reference here is varied and dispersed instead of concentrated on one kind of situation. Even the grammatical meaning here is distinct, relating to the story/proverb dynamic: the monkey's survival is not necessarily threatened. In this speech event, the proverb is not stated but is alluded to, with the allusion taking the form of a freely worded simile that is integrated into the utterance as a short parable. The allusion seems to refer to a particular folktale or anecdote and strongly suggests the second type of story/proverb dynamic, in which an emphasis is placed on a fictive, preexistent story.

Often the application of proverbs to children is less than kind, and there is no effort to aid the listener in understanding the proverb metaphor. In some cases there is a strong element of intimidation, with the proverb sharing many of the qualities of other confrontational speech genres in African-American culture (a topic that will be discussed in the next chapter). The quality that distinguishes these cases of proverbial speech from speech behavior with similar functions is the power imbalance between adult and child. Because of this quality, the spoken words tend to have much more impact on the listener, and, furthermore, the child is somewhat defenseless to respond. In many such instances, story proverbs are chosen, perhaps because the images in them have more impact on the young and impressionable. The following example is illustrative of these points. In addition, this example suggests more strongly than previous cases how the symbolic meaning of an item for a given individual might have extremely painful associations, and how the object of proverb use to children is not always positive or ultimately in their best interest. Finally, this example makes suggestions about the process of interpretation and understanding that a child might go through in response to the use of a proverb to them. Here, the speaker indicates that she did not understand the metaphor being used. This suggests that the poetic impact of the speech act—its eruption as fictive discourse in the context of natural discourse—can be effective on a functional level without the child's having an articulate understanding of its metaphorical application. This recognition tends to contradict one of Dundes's assertions about proverb structure relative to that of riddles. He states: "It is true that in riddles the referent of the descriptive element is to be guessed whereas in proverbs the referent is presumably known to both the speaker and the addressee(s). And that is one of the principal differences between proverbs and riddles" (1975: 108).

As we will see, the addressee obviously does not know the referent, and this would doubtless be the case in many speech acts involving children; in other words, proverbs are, for many children, riddles. In this first example the informant provides not only a context in which the proverb was used to her but her reactions to it at the time:

Example #75
My aunt, Mrs. W. L. Fredericks of Ellenboro, N. C. made this statement to me the year I lived with her, 1963. I was in the kitchen helping her with dinner and was whistling when she came in, looked at me, made that statement [**A whistling woman and a crowing hen will not come to good**.] and left me with it. When I later asked her what she meant she told me to think about it, then asked me if I ever heard a hen crow.

I said no to which she replied—"well then." Images of unnatural nature passed before my eyes as I tried to dissolve the fog, so to speak. She never did explain it to me but I gradually came to assume that it was simply unlady-like to whistle. The part about never coming to a good end still bothers me though; what horrible fate could befall a hen who behaved like a rooster or a woman who behaved like a man? I prefer not to go into any psychological considerations, further than I have already hinted. (U. C. Berkeley Archives)

Unlike the case in most situations we have seen, the speech event here is composed solely of the proverb speech act. The only additional communication in that event is made up of whatever paralinguistic signals the speaker may have encoded into her message. The very act of coming in, speaking the proverb, and then leaving is in itself an important part of the communicative act. Functionally the speech act is directive; it is intended to make the girl stop whistling, not simply in the immediate context, but as a future code of behavior. It is also teaching a rule of conduct and implying negative consequences if that rule is broken. Its ends are achieved through the effect of a warning, of intimidation, and the impact of the warning is amplified by the brevity of the speech event.

It is interesting to note the child's struggle to understand the grammatical and situational message of the proverb speech act. The element of the bizarre or of the unnatural is a strong component of the proverb's poetic impact, as is evident in the informant's comments. Her comments illustrate how the situational meaning of a proverb can be understood without any knowledge of the social level of meaning. I suspect that in cases where proverbs are used to children this might often be true; in fact, the impressionable nature of children as regards fictive speech acts in combination with the inability to comprehend the metaphorical context of many of these speech acts must certainly contribute to the long-term impact of such items. The speech act, though succinct, is complex, because it engages the child in all types of story/proverb dynamics. The speaker might as well have come in and told a tale about a hen and a woman who came to a bad end, implying that the child was the woman in the tale. The aunt's alluding to the end without providing more information to clarify her meaning makes the speech act into a puzzle for the child: the puzzle of metaphorical application to the present situation as well as the puzzle of why these actions should bring about such dire consequences. Of course, a child would ponder these issues, sensing that she had done something wrong but not really understanding what. The symbolic value of this item for this informant would have to be great, because of the intensity of the psychological association and the haunting quality of the associative relationship.

In a second example, the proverb is used in much the same manner. It is spoken by a parent to her daughter; however, in this case the daughter is presumably a young adult herself. There are also two other persons present when the proverb is spoken—the daughter's "prospective husband" and her father; thus the dynamics of the speech event are considerably different. This example also provides us with the informant's interpretation and evaluation of the proverb. The collector writes:

> Example #76
> Specifically, however, she recalled an incident when she and her prospective husband were sitting in the back seat of her parent's car with the parents in the front seat when a song she liked came on the radio. As soon as the informant started whistling along with the melody, her mother turned around, "Now Evelyn, **You know that a whistling woman and a crowing hen will not come to good**." (U. C. Berkeley Archives)

Here, as in the first example, the proverb speech act is directive, with a critical component. The speaker is advising the daughter to stop whistling, indicating that whistling is unladylike and may lead to undesirable consequences—e.g., disapproval or withdrawal of affection from her prospective husband. In the use of the proverb here, the aspect of intimidation is not as prominent as in the previous example, and the warning seems to have to do with concerns of social disapproval rather than the realm of the supernatural. An element that may have been present in this interaction is embarrassment, and, in fact, this element is salient. Without additional information we cannot know conclusively *how* the proverb was spoken, but it is reasonable to surmise that in such a situation the daughter must have experienced some degree of embarrassment. The daughter is being "put in her place" in the presence of her fiance, for an action that she apparently regarded as innocent. Additional comments do indicate the informant's understanding of the strong sense of cultural value attached to her mother's usage of the proverb and how that value was central in the proverb speech act:

> The informant claims that this proverb has to do with acting "feminine."
> She said that she believed the woman in the proverb was compared with

a hen because just as a "chicken is going in the pot to fry so will a woman if she don't act like a lady." (U. C. Berkeley Archives)

These comments reveal the same intensity of influence of the story/proverb dynamic as in the first example. The story is a frightening one, and succeeds in translating not only the parental and societal scorn for the girl's behaviors but the unnaturalness of such behaviors as well as the social right of the parent to humiliate her daughter. Certainly, such symbolic meanings connected to unpleasant memories can sometimes influence children to dislike or avoid using certain proverbs later in life (Prahlad 1994; Page and Washington 1987; Bornstein 1991: 22–23).

Rituals

In earlier chapters I discussed the connection between proverb performances and rituals of behavior engaged in by African-American speakers. To avoid confusion, I have chosen to explore the symbolic meanings of proverbs as thoroughly as possible before examining their relationship to rituals. There are some profound differences between the relationship to rituals found in this chapter and those discussed in earlier parts of the book. Whereas the ritual of "masking" played a prominent role in the speech events involving European and African-American participants discussed in chapter 2, it is not significant in the present chapter. In fact, the opposite behavior characterizes these speech events, and we can speak of the ritual of "bonding" instead. This "bonding" occurs in a number of ways. Sometimes the ritual is enacted between two adults who are speaking about children, as in examples 56, 57, 62, and 63. At other times it occurs when proverbs are directed to children by adults, as in examples 60, 66, 67, and 69. In many instances the "bonding" may not be easily apparent because of its occurrence over an extended period of time. This occurs with Mrs. Bishop and her grandmother. A facet of this ritual is the desire to reveal rather than conceal one's true self, including cultural and psychological dimensions. Through this revealing, elements of cultural and individual heritage are shared in hopes that they will be appreciated and preserved. This component is evident in the comments and attitudes of all of the proverb masters discussed in this chapter.

Another difference between speech acts in this and in previous chapters pertains to the ritual of "defense/attack." Because of the social status of participants in speech events in this chapter and their relationship with each other, this ritual becomes simply that of "attack." There is no customary need for adults to verbally defend themselves against children; however, examples such as #59 and #74 indicate that at times they do feel the need to lash out in attack. At least in my corpus of materials, this pattern is not a frequent one. A final point about rituals indicated in the speech events in this chapter emerges from the comments made by Mrs. Bishop and her perceived role as a master proverb user. Having heard those comments, we can suggest the ritual of "healing."

Summary

The symbolic level of proverb meaning is a critical one, however, and one that has been widely overlooked by proverb scholars. An examination of this level includes noting the multiplicity of meanings that may obtain in any given speech event as well as the possibility that interactants may be communicating on one level when a proverb is used but not on others. This model should also facilitate an appreciation for the art of proverb users and some of the dimensions of their art. Just as performances of musical or narrative traditions within the African-American community carry definitive cultural connotations and signal culturally recognized components of heritage, so do many proverb performances, even if those proverbs are not of African-American origin.

It is obvious that the *process* of symbolic meaning begins most often in childhood, and, therefore, that more scholarly attention should be given to the learning and interpretation of proverbs by children. By this I mean studies that actually consider individual children and their relationship to proverbs that they hear in their homes or in other environments. To date, most studies have focused on semantic or psychological understanding of proverb texts, omitting many important personal, cultural, and contextual elements. The acquisition of language skills and development of speaking behaviors are complex issues, and must include considerations of age and developmental processes, gender, ethnicity, and personal psychology. It is presumed, for instance, that children become capable of metaphorical thinking at certain ages (Chambers 1977; Pasamanick 1982, 1983, 1985); how do they interpret proverbs before that, and what effect does this have on the levels of meanings for particular children? My findings further suggest the poetic nature of proverbs. I am referring here not so much to the linguistic features as to the way in which meanings are engendered for proverb masters and audiences of children. Proverb speech acts evoke powerful associative memories. Memories of the kitchen. The picture of Jesus on the living room wall. The odor and taste of cornbread. Fields of cotton or tobacco. Fireflies. The scent of crepe myrtle, forsythia, or magnolia. Willows. Greens and pork chops. The fragrance of a grandmother. Her smile. Her glare. The veins in her hands. Her in her Sunday-go-to-meeting clothes. Her in her work clothes. Her kneeling beside the bed in her nightgown offering up prayers. The measurement of distance or closeness between these reflections and present moments in time. Undeniably, the psychology of nostalgia, self-esteem and security should be of interest to those who study the functions and meanings of proverbs.

It is also apparent that proverbs are often markers of power dynamics between speaker and addressee. One of the implicit lessons taught in some speech events is that parental and conventional opinions override those of children and that children are of lower social status than adults. Rarely do proverbs invite comments from children, but instead reinforce the traditional role of adult dominance. As Bornstein writes, a proverb "establishes a hierachy of authority . . ." (1991: 19). This aspect of proverbial speech acts is one that often encourages a negative response to such utterances, sometimes into adulthood. As we will see in the next chapter, this component can become ingrained in the symbolic meaning of proverbs and can influence the way in which they are used among peers.

FIVE

Proverb Speech Acts among Peers

In the last chapter, we discussed the use of proverbs by adults to children and the importance of symbolic meaning. This chapter will focus on speech events involving peers, which tend to have very different kinds of dynamics. As Norrick states, one of the functions of proverbs is to put the speaker in a position that is rhetorically superior to that of the spoken to (1985: 29). A natural response to this strategy is rebuttal, either direct or metaphorical. However, in speech events involving children and adults, there is little opportunity for socially appropriate rebuttal on the part of children. When the participants in the speech event are peers, this social restraint is removed, and, as examples in this chapter will demonstrate, duels often ensue. We will also see that the use of proverbs by younger people often includes components of other genres of speech behavior common in the African-American community and is often less linked to any conscious transmission of cultural heritage than to considerations that would inform the use of, for example, "caps," "talking shit," or other confrontational genres. I have already mentioned the similarities between aggressive speech genres and proverbs, and suggested parallels between certain African categories of speech behavior and ones that exist among African-Americans. These suggestions will also be more fully addressed in the following discussion.

Several of the speakers in this chapter can be considered examples of younger proverb masters, and their lives fit the pattern that I discussed in chapter 4. Unfortunately, I was not able to interview these speakers, for a number of reasons. Two of them are friends or acquaintances from Virginia from whom I collected proverbs before my graduate work in folklore. At that time, I had no reason to conduct formal interviews, and have not been able to do so since. A third speaker, J., worked at Golden Gate at the same time that I did. Although I approached him about interviews on numerous occasions, he was uncomfortable with the idea, and so a formal interview never materialized. I was able to informally gather bits and pieces about his background and some of his feelings concerning proverbial speech. I worked on a construction crew for several months with a fourth speaker, P., a carpenter who had moved to the Bay Area around the same time I did in 1976. All four individuals were speakers from whom one could expect to hear at least one proverb in the course of an hour's conversation and who were known by others for this component of their personality. While they did not have the status that an elderly proverb master would, they were somewhat set apart from their peers and considered mature or "serious" for their ages.

Proverbial Speech at Golden Gate

Because the Golden Gate community was one in which a number of proverb masters lived, and because proverbial expressions were fairly common not only among adults but also among children, it can be revealing from numerous perspectives to focus first on this speech group. A number of proverbial expressions were commonly used by children of all ages at Golden Gate and were picked up and used jokingly by adults who worked at the school. Traditional opening and closing formulas were sometimes replaced by such phrases as, "Well, like my kids are saying," when adults used these items. Some of these were taken from television commercials, some from popular recordings, and others from memorable statements made by one of the children. The active delight I witnessed in such expressions conforms to the observations of others who have written about speech behavior in African-American culture (e.g., Abrahams 1974; Hurston 1934; Smitherman 1986) and to the suggestions I have made throughout this study. In the words of Mrs. Tally, "These kids always have something going around." Whatever expression was popular at the time was inevitably going to be used in the context of verbal dueling and "capping." Though a number of scholars have written about "capping" among African-American speakers, none have come close to suggesting the proliferation of this speech behavior in Golden Gate and many other public elementary schools in Oakland and the Bay Area.[1]

Perhaps because of the community and home environments of most of the children, they were always on guard and routinely interpreted communications directed toward them as attempts to put them down. Consequently, they were always ready with retorts. It must be acknowledged that many of these children had never experienced the stability or security that is associated with childhood in the minds of most Americans. Many came from unstable homes and played on the same corners that prostitutes and drug dealers claimed for their own. There were many third graders, for example, who were responsible for getting their younger siblings up, dressed, and ready to walk to school in the morning, and many of all ages who returned home in the afternoon to empty houses and a television. The description of them here is in no way an indictment of the children but of the social system that created the situation in which they had to live and grow; indeed, they were wonderful spirits, and I felt fortunate to be able to work with them. Certainly these environmental factors exacerbated the existent tendency toward aggressive speech behavior found in many urban, African-American communities. At any rate, many innocent comments were taken as caps: one of the most common replies to some of my comments to individual students was "He's always trying to cap on people."

The degree to which a cap or other kind of put-down could emotionally wound one of these children cannot be overemphasized. When one considers their circumstances, this is only logical. Self-esteem is a major issue for any elementary school child, and sixth graders (with whom I worked) are especially sensitive to issues of self-presentation and the evaluations of peers. They felt so duty bound to reply to a perceived put-down that the possibility of punishment would not deter them. So expressions such as "Where's the beef?"[2], which was popular one year, could under certain circumstances provoke a confrontation. Another year a common saying was "All in the ice cream and don't even know the flavor," sometimes changed to "All in the ice and don't even know the cream." This, like other similar items, was said playfully most of the time and appreciated for its silliness and humor. In fact, it sometimes became a game to invent phrases that fit the verbal structure of such utterances or to change the wording around in creative ways, providing a source not only of amusement but of gratification for students who were learning and mastering different facets of language skills. Often, such expressions would be used in situations where students were playing at duels and teasing each other. This particular one was typically said to someone who was being "nosey" or "getting into business that didn't concern them." There were times, however, when its use signalled a possible confrontation, and teachers had to be alert so that any potential conflict could be diverted before it got too far along. When an expression was popular, it was heard frequently throughout the school and often elicited the equivalence of applause in reactions from other students. The same dynamic noted in chapter 2 as being present in interactions between ministers and congregations was practiced by children as early as elementary school. Specifically, those around the speaker might clap their hands together, turn their heads downward, pretend to walk away and then turn back, or respond with "ooohh, got your feelings hurt," "oops, she sure capped on you," or other such invectives (Holt 1972; Kochman 1970).

Abrahams, in discussing conversational genres, suggests that children "cannot be expected to have sufficient control over words to know the proverbs and to use them in establishing canons of conduct and social relationship," and that they therefore utilize simpler forms such as taunts or boasts (1968a: 55). There are two separate components of this suggestion that invite comment. First, my own research and that of others indicates that children do have sufficient mastery of language to use proverbs (Prahlad 1994; Bornstein 1991). The second point is more complex. Implicit in Abrahams's statement is the notion that proverbs function to establish and maintain behavioral norms and define relationships. As my study has shown, these are far from being the only functions of proverbial speech; however, according to my research, these can be operative functions in proverb speech acts by children. When Abrahams states, "Taunts are, in a very real way, the proverbs of children" (1968a: 55), he is on to something. There is, as my discussion of children's rhymes in chapter 3 demonstrated, an overlap between the etic genre of proverbs and emic categories of speech, and proverbial items are often included in categories of children's lore.3 But this does not mean that children are incapable of recognizing and using proverbs; it simply means that their use of them may have a wider range of rhetorical executions than that of many adults. Furthermore, children are aware that the use of proverbs involves symbolic meanings and the adoption of roles and responsibilities associated with the adult world. One of the components of symbolic meaning connected with proverbs for most children, as we have seen, is the submissive role and restrictions on behavior. Another element involved is that the use of proverbs might signal membership and identification with authority figures, which could be disastrous for one's acceptance among peers. While there are some adult properties and behaviors that children are anxious to adopt, the use of proverbs is not usually one of them. My suggestion is that most often children choose not to use proverbs for a number of reasons, not that they are incapable of doing so. Hence, speech events involving proverbial expressions among the children at Golden Gate took on characteristics very different from those that we have previously discussed. The following examples illustrate some of these points.

Example #77
The class consisted of approximately thirty-two students, an equal number of boys and girls, all of them African-American except for one Anglo and three Asian-American students. The speaker was an eleven-year-old girl who was one of the brightest students but who often had problems with her temper. In this case, she had gotten into an argument with one of the smaller boys and was angry enough to fight. Finally she said, hands on her hips, **"Don't let your mouth write a check that your behind can't cash!"** "Oh, I can cash it, don't you worry about that!", the boy responded. "You might think you can but you can't," the girl shot back, by which time the teacher was able to quiet them down and to get them seated again.

The proverb speech act was intended as a warning that the boy should not say anything more than he was able to physically defend. The value of the "check" was calculated in the ability to win in a physical battle. There was another implicit message understood by the two students and by others in the class: by using a proverb that the parents in this community often used to children (see appendix), the bigger and more mature girl was assuming the adult role and implying that the boy was an immature child. This aspect evoked a response from other students. They "ooooooohhed," laughed, and shot teasing looks at the boy who had been so badly put down. Because this was a common proverb in the community, most of the children understood its social meaning—that one should not say more with words than one can back up with action—and were aware that the situational meaning was often a warning that if the person kept talking he or she would be physically beaten. The proverb functioned as a taunt and as a "cap" or put-down. The boy was, in terms of the verbal duel, defeated, although he sought to bounce back and regain his esteem. A part of the verbal strategy was the choosing of a proverb that exposed the boy's inferior physical abilities and verbal skills and that implicitly cast him in the role of the child (a common tactic in antagonistic interactions among children in this age group). Another aspect of the interaction here is that the girl "wins" in front of a classroom of peers, making the defeat for the boy that much more painful.

It is also important that the proverb was used strategically as a retort in a verbal duel, the kind of speech act typical of students this age in that particular community. This speech act also challenges the idea that children do not understand more complex metaphorical proverbs. The proverb in question—"Don't let your mouth write a check your behind can't cash"—structurally consists of what Dundes calls multidescriptive elements, is oppositional, and contains contrasting pairs of features; in other words, it is one of the more structurally complex types (Dundes 1975). Its structure can be seen more clearly in the version "Your mouth is goin' to write a check your ass can't cash": mouth/ass, write/not cash. This example, as well as several others in which proverbs share functional characteristics of other genres, also raises the possibility that certain proverbs may have evolved from these other genres. Inasmuch as taunts (dozens, caps, sounding, etc.) were probably once highly original aphorisms spawned by very creative individuals, the best of these would likely be adopted by others until they became traditional utterances, viz., proverbs.

Other versions of the proverb collected elsewhere in Oakland indicate that, although it is most commonly used in the manners just described, and especially as a form of social control by adults to children, it can be used in other contexts. In each case, however, it maintains the taunting, warning quality. Its correlation in all cases is second person. It is generally a way of telling someone that he or she has overstepped certain boundaries and that unpleasant consequences are on the verge of materializing. For example, one informant gives the proverb as "Don't let your mouth write a ticket your ass can't cash" and explains it as "Don't take a position that you can't defend" (U. C. Berkeley Archives). This usage suggests the onset of an intellectual rather than a physical altercation, but the tone of the warning persists.

A final informant explains the meaning, giving a situation very similar to the first example. The version that he gives is "Don't let your mouth write a check that your ass can't chase."

Example #78
By this statement the informant means that a person or animal is causing some kind of distraction . . . and if he keeps it up he's going to pay this

check by getting his ass kick. The speaker is also telling the listener he has had it and look forward to getting his ass kicked if he doesn't hurry up and get in line. In other words shut up or put up. And it is left up to the lessoner to shut his mouth; and if the lessoner don't respect the speaker feelings, then the lessoner knows the fight is on. Sometimes physical features are altered from chase, to pay. (U. C. Berkeley Archives)

A similar example occurred on the playground during the morning recess. The dynamics involved were completely different from those in the previous example, however, demonstrating that expressions derived from other genres can become proverbial and that the children sometimes choose to use them playfully instead of in serious ways. This item, "Don't let your mouth overload your hips," was also found among archival entries and collected from an informant who stated that it is used as part of the dozens. In the situation in which I heard it, two male sixth-graders were coming toward the building because the bell had rung, indicating that the recess period was over. Lines had begun to form near the doorway of the school building. Just as they reached the line, the two boys began pushing each other and exchanging words. After they had been broken apart and were in line, the words continued, although they were more for the sake of the verbal battle than to incite a physical fight.

Example #79
"You just wait 'till lunch time, punk. You'll see," one of the boys said. "Nigger, you go' **let your lips overload your hips** if you keep on talking," responded the other, to which a female teacher then responded, "Boy! I know I didn't just hear what I think I heard, did I?" "No ma'am," the boy said. "I didn't think so," the teacher said, glaring at the boy, her look daring him to say any more.

A major difference between this and the previous speech event is that the boys did not really want to fight. Nor were they particularly concerned about the evaluations of onlookers. To some extent the exchange was a part of the ritual mock competitions that characterized much of the male interactions of fifth- and sixth-graders. The speaker was smiling when he used the proverb, taunting the other boy but enjoying the power of language and the beauty of verbalization. One could see that he was pleased with himself for coming up with the expression, and that, as was the case in example #77 for the female speaker, it held some symbolic meaning that had to do with adult behaviors. This association made him feel, if not in the eyes of others at least in his own eyes, more grown up.

A number of other proverb speech acts were performed by J., an instructional assistant (I.A.) and proverb master who worked at Golden Gate. About twenty-two years of age and a former student at Golden Gate, J. often seemed to identify more with the children than with the faculty or staff at the school. He worked closely with students on assemblies and other kinds of school programs, and the students regarded him more as a big brother than as anything else. J. lived only a few blocks away from the school and gave generously of his time and energy, spending as many hours working on after-school activities as he put in during the normal work day. In conversation with J., I learned that he had grown up feeling very close to his mother, who used proverbs frequently, and that he had experienced a great deal of isolation from his siblings. The circumstances that led to this isolation were never revealed. He fit the model of a young man who had avoided the temptations of the street and was devoting his life to helping educate and foster positive self-esteem in the children of the community.

In general, one of J.'s proverbs, "One monkey don't stop no show," is used less frequently as a taunt or cap than the previous one, and more as a way of signifying. It is used by adults to children, by adults to adults, and by children to each other. In some cases the proverb is used to the person being referred to, and in others it is said about a third party who may or may not be present. Its signification emerges out of the metaphorical referent "monkey," which, like other images of animals in proverbs, can be used to make indirect critical comments about the person to whom it is applied. Also, the impersonal nature inherent in proverbial utterances provides a smokescreen for the speaker. Because of this quality, insults can be readily made with proverbs without the speaker having to take responsibility for them. In the following example, the proverb is used by J. to a child.

Example #80
On the school playground, a group of boys were playing a game of kickball and J. was playing with them. A disagreement erupted and in the verbal squabbling one boy shouted that he was quitting. "If y'all go' play like that I ain't go' play no more!" the boy shouted as he walked away fuming. J. attempted to change the boy's mind by reasoning with him and encouraging him to be a good sport, but all efforts failed. Finally he said to the boy, "**Well, you know as they say, one monkey don't stop no show.**"

The function of the proverb speech act is critical and expressive. J. is criticizing the boy's behavior by comparing him to a monkey. This aspect of the proverb, however, was toned down so that the boy would not be as severely wounded as he might otherwise have been; the speaker accomplished this by shrugging his shoulders as if to make light of the situation and to indicate that he was not speaking out of anger. The situational meaning of the proverb could be translated into an interrogative: "Are you going to be like a monkey and be immature enough to quit because things aren't going your way?" The speaker's delivery therefore served to allow more room for the possible instructional value of the proverb. The social meaning was that no one person is so important that his or her absence will disrupt what is going on, and anyone who thinks that it will is childish and harms only himself or herself. That the child did, however, take offense at the proverb speech act showed in his demeanor as he walked away from the game. We can observe also that this is a story proverb, and evokes the possibility of some fictive story from which it might be drawn.

In a second example, the proverb was used by the same speaker, this time with a different tone and emphasis. J. was also in charge of a dance troupe at the school, a group that performed dances choreographed to popular songs. In rehearsals he encountered many of the same problems that teachers encountered in the classrooms: bickering, anger, defiance, and behavior generally disruptive to the task at hand.

Example #81
In this particular rehearsal one of the girls became angry because she didn't get a part that she wanted and began throwing a tantrum, com-plaining, crossing her arms and pouting, and glaring at J. Finally he told her to either "cut it out or to leave." She replied, "I ain't go' dance at all then, now!" J. responded, "Don't dance then, I don't care. **One monkey don't stop no show.**"

In this context, the proverb was spoken angrily. J. had been getting more and more annoyed, and, at the point when the proverb was spoken, he was exploding. There was no effort to spare the feelings of the student, and, in fact, the proverb speech act functioned as a severe reprimand, a way of implying that he was almost glad that the girl would no longer be involved with the project. There was also no sense of an instructional function of the proverb here. Situationally, it was a severe and critical dismissal of the student, emphasizing the negative component of the "monkey" in the proverb context in reference to the girl's behavior. Its situational meaning could be translated as "You are an extremely annoying and aggravating person who is making the rehearsal painful, and I'm glad that you're leaving. Good riddance!" Very aware of the name-calling component of the speech act, she muttered in response, "And I ain't no monkey, neither."

One can note in this example, as in the previous one, that the proverb speech act shared characteristics of caps or put-downs. It is obvious that in this example the proverb functions as a part of the ritual of "attack." A difference between this and most of the situations examined in chapter 4 is that students routinely engaged in verbal battles with J.; thus, rituals of "attack/defense" were often observed. It just so happened that on this occasion, the student had not directly attacked J., although some of her impudent comments would have qualified as offhanded signifying and marking. As is often the case with contexts where capping occurs, the presence of an audience was an important element of this speech event. Typically, in a capping duel, the audience evaluates the contest and the winner gains status, whereas the loser's status and esteem are diminished. Given the timbre of social relationships in this community and school environment, it is not surprising that proverbs would be used and interpreted in a manner consistent with a theory of language as aggressive and hostile behavior.

Two other examples, also from Oakland, illustrate the usage of this proverb among peers and demonstrate many of the same features found in the previous instances. It functions as a critical taunt in a confrontational speech event, and one speaker's comments indicate a common awareness of the derisive element of the proverb. Involved with the social meaning are the negative racial connotations of being called a monkey, since Western society from the beginning has sought to devalue and dehumanize Africans by calling them monkeys. Characteristics apparent at the social level carry over into the situational level; for example, monkeys are "ugly," "stupid," and "showoffs," who would naturally disrupt any organized, human social activity.

Example #82
In my neighborhood there was a playground where the kids hung out. There was swings for the younger children, a playing field for running and playing, and a basketball court where the older boys played. As an example of the context that I heard this saying . . . Say that the older boys were playing a game of basketball, and it starts to get rough (And there's no referees in playground basketball), then a fight starts. If someone gets mad and says that he is going to quit playing someone will pipe in and say, "Go on and quit, **one monkey don't stop no show.**" They are telling

him to go on and quit. They don't care, and that they will keep playing without him. Plus they add insult to injury by comparing him to a monkey. (U. C. Berkeley Archives)

In a final illustration, the proverb is worded "One monkey don't *spoil* the show," and it is used to criticize the disruptive behavior of young people at a dance. It is unclear whether the proverb is spoken to the disruptive persons or by one adult to another about those persons.

Example #83
When my grandmother was a young girl she attended Saturday night barn dances with her sisters. If anyone's temper flared up and a fight started, the person/persons would be put out and people often made the comment above and would continue with the dance. It means that one or someone's else's bad behavior wasn't going to ruin things for everybody else. (U. C. Berkeley Archives)

On another occasion J. used a second proverb in a speech event in which he was speaking to a fourth-grade class. He had been watching the class because their teacher was out ill and the substitute had not shown up. At the pleading of the students, he had agreed to take them outside to play for a while, but had gone next door to speak with another teacher before doing so. During the time that he was gone, the class became very rowdy and loud, disturbing other classes down the hall. Eventually, the principal showed up and reprimanded both the class and J.

Example #84
When the principal had gone, he angrily lectured the class on their behavior. "See, I can't let y'all do nothing! I should have just gone on and made you do schoolwork. I guess I'll learn one of these days. **You know they say, if you play with a puppy he will lick your mouth.** And it's true. Don't y'all ask me to do anything else for y'all, you hear?"

Just as in the previous proverb performance, there is a strong element of capping or putting down of the audience. Again, it amounts to name-calling, attributing to the children the characteristics of a young dog, which, however charming, is not able to show restraint and therefore must be handled with a stern hand. Rhetorically, J. lectured as if he were delivering a sermon, giving long pauses after each sentence so that the somber mood of his talk would be emphasized. The class remained absolutely silent during his discourse. One aspect of the situational meaning of this speech event is the topic of J.'s relationship to the students: on the one hand he wanted them to think of him as a "pal," but on the other, he wanted recognition of his status as a staff member. Such recognition would include respect for his authority in certain circumstances and concern for how he would be approached by other staff members; in this case, he wanted the children to refrain from behaving in ways that would make him seem irresponsible. The situational meaning also involved J.'s desire to retaliate for the trouble that he perceived the students to have caused him; thus, he attacked them by stressing their immaturity, which would wound any fifth- or sixth-grader.

A final proverb used by J. was spoken about the principal, who was not present at the time. The day's gossip was that the principal was going to be transferred to another school, an indication that the administration was dissatisfied with his performance. One of the sentiments expressed by faculty and staff was that he was getting what he deserved because he had routinely betrayed loyalties and turned against many of those who had supported his rise in the ranks from classroom teacher to administrator. This betrayal included a refusal to socialize with old friends and the replacement of those friends with other administrators and people of power and influence. J. was talking with this researcher about the rumors and made such comments as: "Well, nobody's go' feel sorry for him. He dissed all of his friends. And you know a lot of people did a lot to help him get where he's at, and then what did he turn around and do to them." The proverb came at the end of several minutes of such discourse:

Example #85
"Well, you know what they say, **never burn your bridges behind you**."

There is no syntactic cohesion between the grammatical and situational meanings of the proverb in this speech act. J.'s facial expression, a smile, indicated that he was happy to see the principal in difficulty. J. was one of those who felt betrayed and experienced some gratification from seeing the principal demoted and having no one to turn to for emotional support. Hypothetically, his administrative associates would no longer socialize with him, and he had alienated his former friends. The situational meaning of the proverb included the message "He hurt and betrayed me and I'm glad to see him finally get what's coming to him," and was a way of verbally retaliating, criticizing, and putting down the principal.

The Game Room and Competition

The aggressive use of proverbs among peers is also found in speech events involving older participants in contexts beyond the elementary school setting. I have mentioned that proverbs sometimes occur in competitive situations between males. This speech event was collected in the billiard room of the student union building at Virginia Commonwealth University in Richmond, Virginia. This was the most frequented room of the moderately sized building, which also contained pinball machines, a television lounge, and a study room. Most of the males who came into the union gathered in the room with the pool tables, even when checking out board games such as chess or checkers. I was employed there and was responsible for supervising the building on certain afternoons and evenings, including checking out game equipment.

The three men in the following examples were regulars, usually coming in on a daily basis, staying at least several hours, and moving from one kind of game to another. The proverb speech act occurred during a game of pool. S. was around twenty, D. and R. around thirty years old. R. was a proverb master who could easily be considered a "man-of-words" (Abrahams 1983), and whose speech behavior included frequent rhymes, jokes, raps, lines from the dozens, philosophy, and "talking shit." While D. was not by nature the talker that R. was, he adopted the role when he was around R., and their conversations often resembled the male interactions recorded by Hurston on numerous occasions (1934, 1942) and referred to often by Abrahams (1963, 1970, 1972b, 1974, 1976). Although D. did not use proverbs as often as R., he did on occasion use them. R.'s conversation was almost entirely about women, and, in fact, women were often the topic of conversation among the men in the billiard room. I had seen these three playing there on a regular basis and had often overheard their conversations; in fact, they often addressed their comments to me, attempting to get me involved in their interactions.

Example #86
The conversation turned to a particular woman, whom they all apparently knew. D. said, making a face as if he had eaten sour grapes, "You like her? Man, but she's so black. I mean she ain't just black, she blue black. And on top of that she's ugly!" Then he chuckled momentarily to himself and went back to shooting. R. said calmly, "Yea, well, you know what they say"—putting chalk on the tip of his cue stick—"**the blacker the berry, the sweeter the juice.**"

The proverb, spoken with the same expression that the man would have after beating his friend at a game of pool or making a particularly difficult shot, functioned expressively and critically. Expressively, the speaker is exalting the attributes of a dark-skinned woman. The social meaning of the proverb is that the more dark-skinned a person is, the more desirable she is. This level of meaning includes a concern with negative racial images of dark skin that exist in the popular Western mind and is often in a spirit of rebuttal to that sentiment. Therefore, the proverb has a cultural history as a part of the ritual of "defense/attack" and as a verbally astute "come back" in speech events resembling duels, both among children and adults. In this speech event, the proverb metaphor referred not only to the sexual characteristics of the woman but to the broad range of her personality, manners, and physical attractiveness. Obviously, the berry is a metaphor for the woman, and the "juice" refers to the range of her attributes. Critically, the proverb speech act occurs in the immediate and general context of the ongoing rivalry and competitiveness that existed between the two men. This competitiveness was acted out routinely on the billiard table and in conversational exchanges. D. was of a light complexion, whereas R. was darker, and a component of this interaction had to do not only with a general spirit of competition but with R.'s retaliation in the face of an attack on his choice in women *and* on dark skin in general. In this regard, the proverb speech act functioned as a cap, or a successful comeback and put-down of the first speaker. By using the proverb to assert the beauty of dark skin, the speaker puts the other man in a position where he cannot publicly argue without seeming racist. Note how the speech act becomes an integral part of the physical contest going on between the men, and how the impact of it becomes as prominent as the impact of what is happening on the billiard table. As such, the situational meaning includes the communications "I am better than you," and "I am a better pool player than you and can beat you any day."

On a similar occasion involving the same three men, R. used another proverb to D. S. had recently been dating an Anglo woman, and D. was expressing his belief that African-Americans should not date people of other ethnic groups. The idea was deeply disturbing to him, and he went on for some time (semihumorously) giving philosophical reasons why interracial relationships were wrong. D. and S. were playing a game of eight-ball, while R. looked on, waiting to play the winner.

Example #87
R: "Why don't you just leave the boy alone."
D: "Me? I'm not the one he has to worry about. Even if I don't believe in it, I'm not going to do anything. But what about all those dumb crackers

out there? Anyway, I'm halfway joking. Halfway. I'm not trying to make the man feel bad."

R: "Yeah, right, just like you not trying to beat him. I always say **different strokes**."

D: "I never heard you say that when I'm doing something you don't agree with. You always tell me straight up."

R: "Yeah but that's *you*."

The proverb speech act is a defense of S. by R., and a subtle attack on D. The attack occurs in the context of their ongoing rivalry. Elements of the situational meaning in this speech event include a positive position on interracial dating. That the speaker takes exception to D. is also an important, though subtle, component of the proverb's communication. It conveys his feelings that whatever people choose to do with their lives is all right with him, unless that person is D., in which case criticism is in order. So the application of the proverb is somewhat misleading, because it is equally a taunt directed toward D. that has little to do with the immediate context but relates to the ongoing dueling that characterizes their relationship. Another dimension of the speech event involves the pacing of it. The speech acts were regulated by the speed of the game being played; although transcribed the conversation might seem to have progressed at an even pace, it did not. There were considerable gaps of time (at least several minutes in length) between the responses, influenced by the time that it took the two players to study the table and shoot. D., for example, would not respond until after he had made a shot and was waiting for another turn. This tempo added to the tension of the interaction and to the weight of each speech act, and framed the proverb, at least on one side, by silence.

Additional proverbs occurred in the interactions between D. and R., although I did not make note of the exact situations in which they were used. Their usage in competitive exchanges, however, further supports my suggestion about the aggressive functions of proverbs in particular contexts. "Talk is cheap," was one of the common proverbs that was said in response to boasts during pool games. D. might say, for example, "When I get through running the table on you, you're gonna wish you never saw a pool table," to which R. might say, "Talk is cheap." Grammatically, this proverb is ideally suited for contexts of verbal dueling because its topic is conversation, speech, or talk. Situationally, it was usually the equivalent of a boast, and implied that R. was "cool" and not the least bit worried because D. did not have the skill to follow through on his boast. In this way, the proverb was a put-down of D.'s abilities. "Put your money where your mouth is," and "put up or shut up," occurred in the same kind of context. Topically, "put up or shut up" also addresses talk, particularly, "talking shit" or boasting. In this context it was a challenge to either demonstrate one's superior skills at the game or to stop boasting about them. On one occasion, R. used a version of one of the proverbs that I later found to be popular in Oakland, "You're letting your mouth overload your ass now." The performance of it signalled a more serious message than that conveyed by the previous items. The situational meaning included the message that D. had in the speech event touched on some sensitive area and had overstepped the boundaries of their friendship—one that did not in practice extend beyond the context of the pool room. Further, the proverb communicated that D. had better not pursue a particular direction in his speech, and that if he did a friendly game of pool could become a bitter rivalry. In fact, the transgression was not momentarily forgiven, and the proverb suggested that R. was going to do his best to retaliate by winning the game as decisively as possible. Another item that was used occasionally by R. during games of pool and cards was "Study long, study wrong," which seems to be particularly context bound. The tone of its usage ranged from the mildest possible offhand remark— sometimes the speaker would say the proverb almost musingly, while his concentration was focused on his own hand—to an irritated, almost angry response. The intensity of the response was incited by D.'s habit of taking an unusually long time at his turn and his sometimes deliberate exaggeration of the concentration needed to make a decision and execute it.

Working Construction: Curse and Insult

Proverb performances share characteristics with speech genres other than capping, and the proverb "What goes around comes around" is one that sometimes exhibits properties of the curse. Abrahams says of this genre: "And many curses do, in fact, work like taunts, consigning the spoken-to (cursed-at) to an inferior social position" (1968a: 52–53). He further discusses the association with many curses and the supernatural—e.g., "God damn you!"—noting that the spirit of the genre is "the wishing of evil upon a person," or "consign[ing] the cursed-at to a despised social realm" (1968a: 52–53). While there are traditional curses in African-American culture, some unique to African-Americans and some shared by Americans in general, it is also possible that items not traditionally recognized as such may function in this manner. We noted this with the proverb "You reap what you sow" in blues lyrics. This proverb, however, seems to have been replaced in the modern period by another that has similar social applications and often has similar situational uses: "What goes around comes around" has become one of the most popular among African-Americans contemporarily.

In our first example the immediate physical context was an old building that a group of carpenters were remodeling. The building had been badly damaged by fire, and the entire inside structure was being torn out and re-done. The context also included the general feelings of the workmen toward the job and toward the employer. While the majority of the workmen were young African-Americans struggling economically, drastically underpaid, and living in extremely modest apartments in the East Bay, the employer was an older, very wealthy, Jewish man who lived in Sausalito, a Bay Area community known for its lavish homes. When visiting the site, the employer always showed up in an expensive automobile, dressed immaculately in suit and tie, and walked into the dusty building as if he were afraid that he might get a speck of dirt on his clothes. The morale on the job was low and the resentment toward the employer high.

The proverb was used by one of the carpenters to no one in particular during a conversation in which everyone was criticizing the employer. P., the speaker, and his brother, M., were approximately twenty years old and had recently moved to the Bay Area from one of the southern states. P. was a proverb master who frequently used proverbs on the job. While M. was the more verbal of the two, his talking did not contain very many elements of traditional speech genres; he simply liked to talk a lot. P., on the other hand, spoke less often, but included proverbs, philosophical reflections, and sometimes anecdotes in his speech. Leading up to this proverb speech act, the men had been engaged in one of the complaint sessions that occurred daily, allowing a venting of frustration, promoting a feeling of camaraderie, and helping to pass the time. Comments included: "I wonder if he ever had to work for anything," "Next time he shows up, I'm go' demand more money," "That motherfucker would rather die than give you more money," "You wouldn't believe what Union carpenters get paid, and the benefits," and "Let's sneak out there and steal that car next time he comes."

Example #88
"Yea, you know what they say though, **what goes around comes around**," P. stated, to which everyone voiced their agreement.

The proverb speech act functioned first to unite the men by drawing attention to their common exploitation and articulating their bitterness, facilitating the ritual of bonding. Secondly, the proverb speech act functioned at the situational level to curse, or to wish ill will upon, the employer. All of the men were joined in their desire to see the employer one day know the suffering and powerlessness that they had to experience or to have some kind of misfortune come to him. Contained in the situational meaning was also the suggestion that the men did not need to do anything to harm the employer, that natural or divine law would ensure that he got what he deserved.

In a second speech event the same proverb was used by a student in referring to a professor whom she felt had betrayed her. It was her opinion that the professor, who was African-American, had betrayed the loyalties of African-American students in order to gain prestige among other professors. The speaker was approximately thirty years of age and a graduate student. The proverb was spoken to this researcher on a university campus, and there were no other persons present at the time.

Example #89
After spending close to twenty minutes expressing her anger and bitterness, the speaker said, "**Well, what goes around comes around, don't it?** It sure do, and I hope I get to see that one when it comes right on back around."

Functionally, the proverb speech act is identical to the previous example. Both are also correlated in the third person. The speaker is attempting to create a sympathetic bond between herself and the listener by articulating a commonly shared sense of injustice. She is also strongly stating a desire to see a third party suffer pain similar to that which she is experiencing, and the expression of this feeling in some way provides momentary consolation. The situational meaning contains a strong element of the curse; she was so angry that she would have liked to retaliate against the professor.

It is difficult to overlook the similarity in social meanings of this proverb and of "you reap what you sow." The comments of one speaker seem to sum up some of the common components of its social meaning.

Example #90
Walter used to always say this in reference to bad, or negative things that some people did to other people. He would look at the behavior and shake his head and say "**what comes around goes around.**" He meant

that all the bad things that were occurring would be the reverse in years to come, or in the near future. It meant that all those on top, and had got there illegally, would be on the bottom before it was over with. It meant that nature was in control, and she had control over the balance of nature and she does take care of her own. (U. C. Berkeley Archives)

In all of the examples collected from the archives, the issues of fairness and, one might say, the "laws of karma," are at the core of the proverb's social meaning. In most cases there is a desire to see the person to whom the proverb is referring experience a pain similar to that which his or her actions have inflicted on someone else, and this is where the element of the curse is found. The desire is most acute when the speaker is the one who has been wounded by the actions of that other person. Other examples of this proverb found in archival material provide us with more information about its application in various contexts and give an indication of its popularity and wide use by African-American speakers. There are seven other examples reported in the archives, a far greater number than with any other proverb. I will cite two of those here. In one the proverb application is reminiscent of "you reap what you sow" in blues lyrics:

Example #91
"If a man is unfaithful to a woman and later he finds out that she's been unfaithful to him, one might cite this [what goes around comes around] to explain it . . . in other words it means, what you do to someone, someone will do to you." (U. C. Berkeley Archives)

Another illustrates the same components as those that we have been discussing:

Example #92
"If a friend who has refused to help you with your homework asks to borrow money, clothes, etc., it would be appropriate to cite the proverb [what goes around comes around]." (U. C. Berkeley Archives)

The citing of the proverb in this context carries the situational meaning that includes the wishing of ill fortune upon the spoken to. There is an acknowledged satisfaction on the part of the speaker in seeing the addressee in need of help and refusing to give it. Implicitly, the speaker is retaliating (attacking the friend) for an earlier event in which the speaker was emotionally wounded (attacked). Figuratively, the speech act creates the wound and then "rubs salt into it."

On a separate occasion, P. used another proverb to criticize one of the fellow carpenters. The carpenter, L., was European-American and the foreman of the crew. His style of dress and demeanor were something of a joke to others on the job because he was extremely disheveled, rude and abrasive, and pretended to be more sophisticated and intelligent than he was. As foreman, he routinely checked on the work of others in addition to doing his own. He had just been checking on the job that M. and P. were doing on the third floor (framing doorways) and in the process spent several minutes telling obscene jokes, complaining about his wife and the employer, and then criticizing the framing job. After he had returned to the first floor where he had been working, a short conversation about L. occurred between M. and P., including some of the following comments: "Damn, does he ever say anything to make anybody feel good?" "Shit, if he don't like the way you doin' something, why don't he just say it and leave it at that? Why does he have to go on and on about it?" "Do he think we really want to hear about him and his wife?" and "I don't know why he's complaining about Y. [the employer], all that money he's getting."

Example #93
P.: "You know I actually kind of like L. I think underneath he has a good heart.
M.: "Yeah, he just tries too damn hard."
P.: "Well, you know what they say, **nothing ruins a duck but its bill**."

The proverb speech act functioned as an insult here. A component of its situational meaning is the message that, in spite of whatever favorable feelings the speaker might have toward the foreman in contemplative moments, his faults were so obvious that they were overwhelming. The particular fault that the proverb commented on was the foreman's incessant, abrasive, and inadvertently insulting talk. The grammatical meaning contains two derisive statements about the duck: one is concerned with the way he looks, the other with his voice. One suggestion is that the duck's bill makes him ugly. Another is that it gives him an unappealing voice with none of the melodic qualities associated with the singing of birds. This dual meaning at the grammatical level makes possible a dual meaning at others, or an emphasis on one aspect of meaning more than on the other. At the situational level in this speech event, the quality of voice/speaking, rather than an aspect of appearance, is emphasized and criticized. Socially, this proverb is typically applied to children and one of its connotations in this situation is that L.

is immature and either has not yet learned rules of appropriate speech or seems incapable of learning them.

The use of another proverb by P. almost led to a physical fight between him and his brother. There was an Orange Julius fast food restaurant across the street from the hotel where we were working, as well as a Chinese restaurant and several other food establishments. Most of the men from the job went to Orange Julius during break or at lunch, and it was not unusual for a number of men to give money to one person and ask him to pick up various things for them. On this occasion, several men had asked M. to get something for them, and he had taken so long in returning that a good twenty minutes of the lunch break had already gone by. When he did return, his brother was the first to accost him.

Example #9
P: [Angrily] "Man, where the hell have you been? You know that we only have a half an hour for lunch. Twenty fucking minutes is already gone."
M: "I ran into somebody I knew over there."
P: "Ran into somebody you knew?! Why can't you run into somebody you know when people ain't waiting for their food? You knew we were waiting. **If the dog hadn't stopped to shit he would've caught the rabbit.**"
M: "Wait a minute now. If you don't like the way I get the food you get your own damn food. I didn't ask to get y'all food for you anyway. And anyway, I didn't stop to shit and I ain't no damn dog. And I don't know why you trying to get all in my face about it anyway."
[At this point the two were almost rubbing chests as if they were about to fight, but some of the other men pulled them apart and cooled them down.]

The two brothers did argue from time to time but seldom had altercations as serious as this one. I suspected that the intensity of P.'s reaction had less to do with the particular situation than with other stresses, perhaps even with some tension between them related to something that had happened before they came to work that day. P. did not usually react this strongly to problems or inconveniences. M.'s reaction was accentuated because of the attack in the presence of the other men. While he was comfortable with the general roles into which the two of them customarily fit—one more impulsive and talkative, the other more pragmatic and wise—an interaction such as this one strained those roles by adding dimensions to them to which he objected. For example, the way in which P. spoke to him implied that he was an irresponsible, "baby" brother who needed reprimanding, and diminished his stature as a man in front of the other men. From his point of view, the proverb speech act and P.'s responses in general seemed extreme and harsh.

The proverb does, as we have noted, criticize by comparing the addressee to an animal—in this case a dog. At the social level, it suggests that the dog is unreliable, selfish, lazy, and easily distracted, and that the person to whom the proverb is said shares these characteristics. It also carries an implied frustration on the part of the hunter (adult) in having to acknowledge the dog's superior ability to do the task and, thus, the need to rely on him. At the same time it conveys an awareness that the animal may get distracted along the way and not do it properly. There is the further implication that it is "just like a dog" to fail to take care of primary tasks before beginning the hunt (endeavor) and that he does not have the ability to distinguish between the mundane and the important—they are both relative to him. At the situational level the proverb was an insult and a put-down. It suggested that the components of the social meaning applied to M., but, more importantly, it separated M. from the group of men by implication. This implication was an attack on M.'s manhood and sense of belonging to the group. The proverb suggested further that M. has missed out on something that he could have had if only he was more reliable or more "with it."

A final example used by P. belongs perhaps with a category of proverbs that is sometimes mentioned (Barnes-Harden 1980: 72) but seldom discussed by proverb scholars; it is triggered as much by recurrent linguistic markers that precede it as it is by a social situation. The proverb "If a dog had a square asshole, he'd shit bricks," is similar to expressions such as "Wait? Weight broke the wagon down" (Dance 1978: 307), "If a frog had wings he'd fly," "Hey! Hay is for horses," and "If frogs had wings, they wouldn't bump their ass all the time" in this way. "Wait? . . ." is customarily said in response to someone telling the speaker to wait for something. The proverbial response is usually a lighthearted way of expressing irritation at having to do so. Both of the other expressions, said in response to a conditional statement containing the word "if," are ways of saying that it is silly to suppose rather than to simply deal with what is, in fact, the case. P. used the expression in a conversation about getting a raise. He, M. and several other men were sitting around talking during a morning break. For several months we had been optimistic about getting a raise and the foreman had continually indicated that the employer was going to agree to it. The conversation was instigated almost as a mechanism for boosting morale at moments when it was low. On this occasion, Q., a nineteen-year-old Euro-American man who was hired basically to clean up debris, was expressing enthusiasm about the raise. In general, Q. was an enthusiastic person and was considered naive by the other men on the job. Much of his conversation centered on automobiles, and his main hobby was adding one thing or another to his car, a newly painted, older model with a new engine in it. A final factor in the relationship between Q. and some of the other men was that his long-range ambition was to become a policeman, which was a strike against him in the eyes of the African-American men and the foreman, who was something of a hippie.

> Example #95
> Q.: "If we get that raise I'm going to buy me some new hubs and maybe get a new stereo."
> P.: **"If a dog had a square asshole he'd shit bricks."**
> Q.: "Oh, now what's that supposed to mean? You don't think we're gonna get a raise or something?"

The speech act evoked laughter from all of the men who were present, except Q., who was noticeably embarrassed. The laughter went on for several minutes, the speech event serving as the morning's entertainment. A part of the humor lay in the grammatical image of the proverb and the ridiculous nature of the utterance. Another part of the humor evolved out of an appreciation for the verbal wit and fast comeback to Q.'s statement. There was a way in which the proverb speech act fit perfectly in the speech event. Another element of the humor lay in the situational meanings conveyed by the proverb. P. was implying that Q. was very naive; not only was he entertaining the idea that we were going to get a raise, but he was already planning how he would spend the money. The way in which he planned to spend it was also being ridiculed. While most of us were concerned with basic living expenses, Q. had nothing better to do with his money than to buy hubcaps to replace the ones that he had bought not long ago. The proverb speech act conveyed a message—"You're such an idiot. Get real"—that went beyond the immediate context and extended to how P. felt about Q. in general. Although Q. did not seem to be familiar with the proverb, he understood that he was being put down and made fun of, and that the sentiments of the speaker extended beyond this one situation. He did not seem to be sure though, whether or not the image in the proverb (the dog) was being applied to him, and so he was uncertain of how upset to be in response to it. His confusion about the proverb application emphasized the men's opinion that he was naive and added further to the humor that they obtained from the situation.

In Public

In one instance, I observed a proverb performance that functioned as part of a "rap" as well as a joke; in another, the same proverb speech act could be considered a part of a "marking" performance, also containing humor. The humor derived from the implicit sexual innuendo of the proverb metaphor, as well as from particular dynamics of the contexts in which it occurs.

In the first speech event the proverb was used by a man around forty years of age on a street corner in Richmond, Virginia. The man was standing with a group of three other men who, though not destitute or homeless, looked as if they spent a lot of their time on the street. Humorous piggy-backing on each other's comments seemed to be the general tone of their interactions, including jive and frequent hand-slapping. As a woman passed she was assailed by comments of "Hey baby!" and "Ooohh momma, you sure lookin' good!" She was a professionally dressed, African-American woman, around thirty years old, who calmly ignored the comments.

> Example #96
> A. [loudly] "Let me be your little engine 'till your big engine come." [The group cheered and slapped hands]
> B. [picking up on this line] "Yea, like they say, I might be small, but that ain't all, ain't no need to worry cause I'm never in a hurry." [This rhyme, spoken in a rhythmic voice, brought even more cheers from the group.]
> C. [responding] "Don't worry 'bout them baby, let *me* tell you, **it ain't the size of the ship, but the motion of the ocean!**"

The function of the proverb speech act is complex. Certainly, the purpose is to elicit laughter. It also functions as does a dynamic line in a sermon in a traditional Baptist church on Sunday, or as the "clincher" line at the end of a B. B. King blues verse in a packed club. That is, it becomes a climactic point in the speech event and elicits extended verbal responses from the audience. This is evidenced here by the men's laughter, whoops, "oooohhh's," and hand-slapping. In this regard, the speech act also functions in the ritual of bonding, to unify the group and create an emphatic moment of closeness.

Intertwined with the dramatic, performative aspect of the speech act is the close connection with the verbal boasting that has been going on between the men and of which their comments to the woman are a part. To the extent that they are competing to see who can come up with the most effective rap or traditional lines, in calling to the woman, the proverb speech act becomes also a cap in the boasting context. At this level, the men are not as concerned with the woman as they are with the interaction among themselves. At the same time that they are addressing her, they are performing for each other. Finally, the proverb speech act functions as a nonserious rap to the passing woman, a mechanism for making the most sexually overt suggestion possible in the most poetical, indirect manner. In effect, all of the men's comments functioned in this way. The first is a commonly known blues double entendre. The second is a combination of "jive" expressions, suggesting that the speaker takes his time in lovemaking. The proverb metaphor suggests that a man's penis size (the ship) is unimportant in comparison to his rhythm and energy, or his style, in lovemaking. The style of correlation here is similar to what Seitel refers to as "self-deprecatory for the purposes of courtesy and humor" (1969: 153).

Different dimensions of meaning evolve out of each of these distinct functions of the proverb speech act. At the social level, it means, as stated above, that a man's rhythm is more important than his penis size. But it means more than that. It also includes the attitudes that men are/should be the sexual aggressors (even conquerors), that an important element of manhood is one's sexual prowess, and that a man's pride and self-esteem are intricately linked to sexual abilities. While the social meaning of the proverb dismantles a traditional standard by which men have evaluated their status (size), it maintains the base from which that standard emerged—sexual hegemony.

At the situational levels, numerous meanings can be found. One concerns the successful one-upmanship gained by the speaker in the context of the competitive raps offered to the woman. In coming up with the most impressive rap, the speaker has defeated the other two men. A meaning in the framework of this game can be interpreted "I'm a better rapper than you," directed, of course, to the men. Ironically, another meaning in the context of the game involves the delineation of groupness that sets the men apart from the woman and other passersby. As has been noted about jokes and other conversational genres (Abrahams 1968a; Basso 1979: 73–76) they not only facilitate definitions of "in" and "out" groups, but can reflect the intimacy that exists between those involved in the speech events. The speech event here is no less than a celebration of commonly shared attitudes about manhood, and the social meaning of the proverb speech act is consistent with those attitudes. These attitudes are not only being celebrated by the men, but are announced to the woman and communicate a number of implicit messages, for example, "I would like to 'do it' to you," and "I know I'm a great lover and I know that you'd like it."

In a speech event between two women the same proverb occurs, spoken by an African-American woman, approximately thirty years old, to a coworker in the university grill. I was not able to hear the conversation that led up to the use of the proverb, but noticed that as the proverb was spoken both women were smiling as if sharing a private joke.

Example #97

"It's not the size of the ship . . . ," the first speaker declared. "Yea, that's what they say," the second speaker responded, almost laughing, but not looking up from the food cooking on the grill.

The proverb speech act functioned as a joke here, to elicit laughter and in the process to bond the two women together. I conjectured from paralinguistic features such as vocal tone, pitch, and facial expressions, that a part of the joke involved the "mocking" of the male persona, or other speakers who might be characterized to some extent by speaking this particular proverb. I assumed that the women had been talking about men either in general or in particular, and conjectured further that the proverb for these speakers contained a symbolic meaning that evolved out of experiences such as the one in example #96, in which they overheard the proverb directed to them or to other women. According to this conjecture, the proverb characterized certain male behaviors and attitudes, and this is what the women were mocking. Their mocking, which included mimetic and derisive features, focused on a component of the proverb mentioned above: the men believed themselves to be more sensitive by de-emphasizing genital size, but they still managed to convey the same attitude. I considered that perhaps the women were sharing a positive experience about making love to a man with small genitals, but this interpretation would not account for the paralinguistic components of the speech event that I observed.

In Private

Proverbs can also occur in speech events involving self-mockery and demonstrating the active engagement of a speaker in rehearsing traditional components of speech. The following example was spoken by an African-American man, X., at a junior high school in Virginia. X. was approximately eighteen years old and was a proverb master with whom I grew up. He was an only child who had basically been raised by his mother, and who had spent a great deal of time around older people. A model student, he was regarded by peers as mature for his age and recognized for his use of wise "sayings." At the time that this speech act occurred, we were both employed as custodians at the junior high school, working in the late afternoon and early hours of the evening. While taking a lunch break, X. and I played a game of basketball in the school gymnasium. The ball became lodged between the rim and the backboard, and before thinking my coworker threw a pair of pliers to get it down. The pliers struck the fiberglass backboard and it shattered instantly, leaving us stunned. In the months that followed, money was taken out of my friend's wages to pay for the backboard, and, as word got around, he was subjected to a great deal of teasing from other friends.

Example #98
On a later occasion, I asked him if he wanted to play a game of basketball and he answered sharply, "**If the dog bite you the first time it's the dog fault; if he bite you the second time, you just a fool**, cause you ought to know better!"

The speech act functioned on the situational level as a way of answering "no" to the question. Its meaning went further to suggest that playing basketball on the first occasion had been a mistake that had cost him dearly, and that he would not make the same mistake again. The entire chain of events that led to the broken backboard and subsequent loss of pay become referents of the metaphorical "dog" biting him. The grammatical meaning of the proverb suggested a drama in which the dog may have either been hidden or believed to be docile. The speech event continued, as the speaker realized the humorous effect that his expression was having on the listener. His liberal rewording of the proverb had been for dramatic and humorous effect, and once he saw the extent to which it succeeded, he ventured to continue, becoming more of a performer. "Now do I look like a fool to you? Naw sir. I'm go' do my work and sit down and read my paper. Now be cool!"

A component of the dynamics here had to do with the mocking quality in the speaker's performance. Two factors bear on this particular characteristic: (1) the speaker was involved in an internal conflict between the world of the "good student"—one who spoke grammatically and was always well-behaved—and the world of the "cool" students, who spoke in slang and were not very interested in academic pursuits, and (2) the speaker was also involved in an internal conflict in separating from home and family and becoming more independent and in deciding what aspects of various role models to choose in that transition. A part of the humor of his performance lay in his trying out a more "cool" way of expressing himself than he would have normally done, and doing so with a sense of mockery. The proverb performance represented the rehearsal of a style of speech in the presence of a friendly audience. Had the audience been different, the speaker would not have felt comfortable enough to take liberties in his performance, but would probably have spoken the proverb in its simplest form (" . . . it's your fault") and let it go at that. For a known honors student, church-goer, and "pet" of teachers and senior members of the community to adopt the mannerisms of the rougher, more streetwise students in front of those students could have opened X. up to ridicule, and to do so in front of students like himself might have elicited criticism as well.

Summary

Contemporary proverb speech events among peers illustrate characteristics different from those between parents and children, in many cases containing elements of aggression of one kind or another and often resembling in their functions genres such as capping, rapping, marking, and signifying. They frequently occur in contexts marked by competition and play, and often address the topics of talk or appropriateness in speech behavior. Relationships between words and actions, for example, as well as breeches in trust are central concerns of many of these speech events. The ritual of defense/attack is salient, and the atmosphere in which speech is regarded approaches that observed among the Anang of Africa and cited in chapter 1 as "suspicious and competitive." It seems appropriate to suggest that the category of *sanza*, which includes speech of all kinds with veiled meanings and malicious or insulting intent, is applicable to much speech behavior in certain contexts within the African-American community and that proverbs play a significant role in this type of speech. As we noted, in some contexts there are proverbs that are traditionally connected to particular situations characterized by aggressive behavior, for example, those items that were commonly heard in the poolroom or on the playground. Although we have not discussed symbolic meaning in any depth with examples in this chapter, it stands to reason that this level of meaning for many of these speakers involves an outlook that sees the world as hostile and human interactions as aggressive, with the resulting expectation that one will need to defend oneself from attack. Conversely, this level of meaning must include competition as a mechanism for establishing, defining, and celebrating close social relationships.

The discussion of proverbs among peers indicates clearly that their rhetorical function and performance is strongly influenced by the context and the relationship between speaker and audience. Furthermore, my findings lead to the observation that attitudes towards speech that are distinctive in the African-American community have a profound impact on the way in which proverbs are applied, performed, and ultimately given meanings. Playing, as Abrahams has discussed it (1974), is a component of many of these speech events and contributes to the style of proverb usage. This factor is often a background that helps to key the decoding of the proverb message. It does not, however, inhibit the serious use of proverbs. Instead, it provides a social smokescreen that compounds the indirectness or denial of personal responsibility that is already a characteristic of proverbial utterances.

In other cases, there is no component of play. A larger trope is applicable: talk, which includes the full range of linguistic behavior in the African-American community, e.g., "talking smart," "talking shit," "woofing," "running something down," "signifying," "marking," etc. The consideration of proverbial speech in this more inclusive cultural context has implications not only in the functional sphere but also in the aesthetic. When we examine the aesthetic choices from which speakers make artistic selections, we must include a wider range of metaphorical speech than simply the genre of proverbs. Such a perspective will affect the questions that are posed about proverbs and the ways in which those questions might be answered. We would ask, for example, not simply why a speaker chose a particular version of a given proverb, but why the proverb and not some other metaphorical utterance from a related genre. Or, does the speaker make a distinction between a proverb and capping? If so, what kinds of features are the focus of the differentiation?

I must note, finally, the prevalence of male speakers in the corpus of examples. This raises the question of whether or not proverbs are used more frequently by males in situations involving peers and in which children are not involved. Of course, my own gender had an impact on my data; I was more often in situations where men were gathered than I was in contexts of women. I suspect, however, that proverbs are just as often used among women, or, to put it another way, that groups of women do include proverb masters. It would be interesting to investigate whether, in these gatherings, the same aggressive speech dynamics obtained. Speech events found in literature indicate that certain forms—e. g., the curse—do, whereas others, such as capping and rapping, do not.4 Further research would be required before any conclusions could be drawn in this area.

Appendix

Organization

Much of the organization of this appendix follows the accepted format of the most scholarly proverb collections. Proverbs are listed alphabetically according to the key word, usually the first or most important noun. The key word in "Beauty is only skin deep," for example, would be "beauty," and so the proverb would be listed ahead of "There's more than one way to skin a cat," in which the key word is "cat," and listed behind "An apple a day keeps the doctor away," in which the key word would be "apple." In some cases there is no key noun in the proverb and so the item is listed according to the key verb, for instance, "What you sow you must reap," "Seeing is believing," and "Live and let live." Exceptions to these criteria are those few examples in which the key word is neither a verb or noun. "What goes around comes around," is one of these; "around" is more central and consistent than are the verbs. "Study long, study wrong," is another, "long" being more consistent than "study" (it is sometimes changed to "Think long, think wrong").

Below the listing of each proverb is the informant from whom that version comes. Informant information includes, when available: age, occupation, where the person was living when the proverb was collected, from whom the person learned the proverb, where he/she was living at that time, the date he/she first remembers hearing it, where the person he/she learned it from first learned it, and where I, the researcher, found or collected the entry. Below the informant data is listed the "usage" of the proverb: the meaning of the proverb in the informant's words, possible contexts in which it might be used, and other comments that the informant might have regarding that item. The absence of any information under "usage" indicates that there was no such information available and that the version given by that informant is identical to the one already presented; information marked with an asterisk is commentary by this researcher. Succeeding listings of informants follow the identical format of the initial entry, and are in turn followed by a "usage" for that informant. If the informant gives a different version of the proverb, that version will appear in the "usage" data, accompanied by the same kind of information we have previously discussed. The reader is referred to the discussion of items examined in the book by "In text," followed by the page number. For such entries, I have given minimum information, for data and discussion are found in the text. A number of items found in the text have not been included in the appendix; I have been unable to locate other examples of these items from African-American sources. Following the last entry of each proverb are published annotations for the proverb; the list of bibliographical entries and abbreviations for those entries comes at the end of this discussion. The first number after each abbreviation is the page number on which the entry can be found; when a second number appears, it corresponds to the numerical entry on that page. For example, ST 2616:11 indicates that the item is number eleven on page 2616 of Stevenson. The second number has only been included, however, in cases where the author actually lists proverbs numerically.

Usefulness and Scholarly Significance

This appendix is the first collection of any size of African-American proverbs to provide contextual data, informant data, and informant's interpretation of proverb meaning. A number of other issues are indirectly addressed here. By way of informant data, for example, the appendix documents the use of certain proverbs through generations from the time of the postslavery period to the present. It also provides us with a comparative basis for looking at proverb usage and meaning in connection with other ethnic groups and documents, at least suggesting routes that proverbs have taken from areas of the southern United States to the West Coast. Finally, this appendix should facilitate the discussion of meaning, context, and application of proverbial speech not only among African-Americans but among proverb users in general. In no way is this meant to be a comprehensive or inclusive collection of proverbs from African-Americans; it is a collection of some popular, predominantly metaphorical items and a documentation of some aspects of their meaning based on ethnographic research. Only proverbs for which I have been able to find contextual uses that contribute to an understanding of meaning beyond texts are included. Many more items of proverbial speech exist in the African community, and it is my hope that this work will facilitate the rigorous collection and scholarly documentation of some of their meanings and applications.

Abbreviations Used in Appendix
(for complete information, see reference list)

AC   Izett Anderson and Frank Cundall, *Jamaica Negro Proverbs and Sayings*

AP   G. L. Apperson, *English Proverbs and Proverbial Phrases*

BA   Francis Barbour, *Proverbs and Proverbial Phrases of Illinois*

BE   Martha W. Beckwith, *Jamaica Proverbs*

BH   Alene L. Barnes-Harden, "African American Verbal Arts: Their Nature and Communicative Interpretation"

BR   Francis W. Bradley, "South Carolina Proverbs"

BRE   Paul G. Brewster, "Folk 'Sayings' from Indiana"

BRU   Harold Brunvand, *A Dictionary of English Proverbs and Proverbial Phrases from Books Published by Indiana Authors before 1890*

BT   William C. Bates, "Creole Folk-lore from Jamaica: 1. Proverbs"

CH   Selwyn G. Champion, *Racial Proverbs*

DA   Jack L. Daniel, *The Wisdom of Sixth Mount Zion from Members of Sixth Mount Zion and Those Who Begot Them*

DSDJ   Jack L. Daniel, Geneva Smitherman-Donaldson, and Milford A. Jeremiah, "Makin' A Way Outa No Way: The Proverb Tradition in the Black Experience"

FA   Arthur H. Fauset, *Folklore from Nova Scotia*

FR   Harry A. Franck, "Jamaica Proverbs"

GR   Bennett W. Green, *Word-book of Virginia Folk-Speech*

HA   Margaret Hardie, "Proverbs and Proverbial Expressions Current in the United States East of the Missouri and North of the Ohio Rivers"

HO   Walter B. Hoard, *Anthology: Quotations and Sayings of People of Color*

HY   Albert M. Hyamson, *A Dictionary of English Phrases*

MKH   Mieder, Kingsbury, and Harder, *A Dictionary of American Proverbs*

NC   B. J. Whiting, "Proverbs and Proverbial Sayings," in *The Frank C. Brown Collection of North Carolina Folklore*, v. 1

OX   F. P. Wilson, *The Oxford Dictionary of English Proverbs*

PA   Elsie C. Parsons, "Riddles and Proverbs from the Bahama Islands"

PAR   Elsie C. Parsons, *Folk-Lore of the Antilles, French and English*
SM   John A. Simpson, *The Concise Oxford Dictionary of Proverbs*
SN   Emma L. Snapp, "Proverbial Lore in Nebraska"
ST   Burton E. Stevenson, *The Macmillan Book of Proverbs, Maxims and Familiar Phrases*
T   Morris P. Tilley, *A Dictionary of the Proverbs in England in the Sixteenth and Seventeenth Centuries*
TA   Archer Taylor, *The Proverb and an Index to the Proverb*
TW   Archer Taylor and B. J. Whiting, *A Dictionary of American Proverbs and Proverbial Phrases, 1820–1880*
WH   B. J. Whiting, *Modern Proverbs and Proverbial Sayings*
WS   Llewellyn G. Watson, *Jamaican Sayings: with Notes on Folklore, Aesthetics, and Social Control*
WT   B. J. Whiting, *Early American Proverbs and Proverbial Phrases*

Discography

Arnold, Kokomo
    1935 "Sissy Man Blues" (C-9654-A) Collectors' Classics CC-25.
    1935b. "Let Your Money Talk" (C-9924) Blues Classics BC-4.
    1938 "Your Way and Actions" (67344-A) Saydisc SDR-163.
Bill, Big
    1939 "Dreamy-Eyed Baby" (WC-2731-A) Mamlish S-3800.
Bland, Bobby "Blue"
    1964 "Farther up the Road," *Original Golden Hits of the Great Blues Singers* (MGH-25002) Mercury.
Bogan, Lucille
    1934 "You Got to Die Some Day" (15477-2) Roots RK-317.
Bracey, Mississippi
    1930 "You Scolded Me and Drove Me from Your Door" (404764-B) Origin Jazz Library OJL-17.
Bunn, Teddy
    1930 "It's Sweet Like So" (59739-1) Historical HLP-5.
Carr, Leroy
    1934 "Good Woman Blues" (16427-1) Yazoo L-1019.
Chatman, Peter
    1940 "I See My Great Mistake" (053595-1) RCA 730581.

Cube, Ice
1991 "A Bird in Hand," *Death Certificate* (CDL-57155) Priority.
Doyle, Little Buddy
1939 "Hard Skufflin' Blues" (MEM-17-1) Roots RL-327.
Fuller, Blind Boy
1935 "Rag, Mama, Rag" (17863-2) Blues Classics BC-6.
1938 "Big House Bound" (SC-25-1) Blues Classics BC-11.
Gibson, Clifford
1929 "Stop Your Rambling" (486-A) Yazoo L-1027.
Gillum, Bill
1939 "You Got to Reap What You Sow" (034810) RCA INT-1177.
Harlem Hamfats
1937 "Root Hog or Die" (reissued on Ace of Hearts AH-77).
Henderson, Bertha
1928 "Lead Hearted Blues" (20560-2) Biograph BLP-12037.
James, Skip
1930 "Cypress Grove Blues" (L-747-2) Biograph BLP-12015.
1966 "Crow Jane" *Skip James Today* (VSD-79219-A) Vanguard.
James, Jesse
1936 "Lonesome Day Blues" (90762-A) Ace of Hearts AH-158.
Johnson, Lil
1929 "Never Let Your Left Hand Know What Your Right Hand Is Doing" (C-3355) Historical HLP-2.
Johnson, Robert
1937 "Milkcow's Calf Blues" ARC 7-10-65, Voc 03665.
Johnson, Tommy
1928 "Bye-Bye Blues" (41838-1) Yazoo L-1007.
Jones, Maggie
1924 "Jealous Mamma Blues" (140105-1) VJM VLP-23.
King, Albert
1972 "Don't Burn Down the Bridge," *I'll Play the Blues for You* (STS-3009) Stax.
1980 "Everybody Wants to Go to Heaven" *Lovejoy* STAX STS-2040.
Kokane
1991 "Action" *Who Am I?* (EK-47356) Ruthless.
Ledbetter, Huddie
1935 "Death Letter Blues—Part 2" (16696-1) Biograph BLP-12013.

Martin, Carl
   1935 "Joe Louis Blues" (90293-A) Yazoo L-1016.
McClennan, Tommy
   1941 "It's A Cryin' Pity" (064891) Roots RL-305.
Minnie, Memphis
   1935 "He's in the Ring" (C-1099-B) Paltram PL-101.
Nickerson, Charlie
   1930 "You May Leave But This Will Bring You Back" (64733) Roots
   RL-337.
Parker, Little Junior
   1964 "Next Time You See Me," *Original Hits of the Great Blues Singers,*
   vol. 2. (MGH-25002) Mercury.
Patton, Charlie
   1929 "Pea Vine Blues" (15221-A) Yazoo L-1001.
Peterson, James and Lucky
   1972 "The Way a Tree Falls," *The Father. The Son. The Blues.* (TLP-1011)
   Today Records.
Slim, Guitar (Eddie Jones)
   [1950] 1972. "Reap What You Sow" (SPS-2120) Speciality.
Smith, Bessie
   1927 "Send Me to the 'Lectric Chair" (143576-2) Columbia CL-858.
   1933 "Do Your Duty" (152577-2) Columbia CL-856.
Smith, Trixie
   1925 "Love Me Like You Used To" (2365-?) Collectors' Classics
   CC-29.
Stetsasonic
   1991 "Don't Let Your Mouth Write a Check That Your Ass Can't Cash,"
   Blood, Sweat, and No Tears (TBCD-1024) Tommy Boy.
Stokes, Frank
   1928 "Mistreatin' Blues" (45419-1) Roots RL-308.
Temple, Johnnie
   1937 "New Louise Louise Blues" (91248-A) RBF-16.
Terry, Sonny, and Brownie McGhee
   1969 "Night and Day," *A Long Way From Home* (BLS-6028) Bluesway.
Thomas, Ramblin'
   1928 "So Lonesome" (20334-2) Yazoo L-1026.
2Pac
   1993 "Keep Ya Head Up," *Strictly For My N.I.G.G.A.Z.* (7-92209-2)
   Interscope.

Vincson, Walter

1931 "I've Got Blood in My Eyes for You" (405023-1) Mamlish S-3804.

1932 "I'll Be Gone, Long Gone" (L-1565-1) Biograph BLP-12041.

Walker, T-Bone

1970 "T-Bone Shuffle" (ST-A-69 1797 PR) Atlantic SD-8256.

Waters, Muddy

1972 "Young Fashioned Ways," *The London Muddy Waters Sessions*. (CH-60013) Chess.

[1957] 1970 "County Jail," *They Call Me Muddy Waters* (CH-1553) Chess.

[1950] 1976. "Rolling Stone" *Muddy Waters* (2-ACMB-203) Chess Blues Master Series.

Weaver, Curley

1979 "Dirty Mistreater," *Atlanta Blues-1933* (JEMF-106).

Williamson, Sonny Boy

1938 "Miss Louisa Blues" (020114) RBF RF-14.

1957 "Fattening Frogs For Snakes," *Down and Out Blues* (CH-9257) MCA-6567.

Wilkins, Robert

1935 "Dirty Deal Blues" (JAX-104) Blues Classics BC-5.

Major Informants

CLARA ABRAMS was this researcher's great-grandmother. She was born in Hanover County, Virginia, on April 20, 1898, and lived there all of her life. She was a community pillar, storyteller, and chronicler, who used proverbs abundantly. She learned many of her proverbs from her mother, and also collected poetic, wise expressions from forms of popular media such as greeting cards and calendars. I grew up with her and collected proverbs from her most of my life.

DOROTHY BISHOP was a librarian and resource specialist at Golden Gate Elementary School in Oakland, California, at the time when proverbs were being collected from her. She was raised by her grandmother, from whom she learned many proverbs. She also collected and wrote down proverb-like expressions from calendars, greeting cards, other media, and conversations. I collected proverbs from her (overhearing her use them and in interviews) during the years when I worked as a teacher at Golden Gate. She is an extremely thoughtful person who uses proverbs on every occasion.

MATTHEW BOYD was a personal friend of this researcher in Oakland, California. After living in California for almost fifteen years, he now resides in Memphis, Tennessee, where he was born. He is forty-five years old, and has recently left the insurance business to work for Federal Express. He has two children. He is a wordsmith who delights in storytelling and joking, and frequently uses proverbs in lighthearted situations as well as in more serious contexts. I have collected proverbs from him since meeting him in 1986.

PHYLLIS CARROLL was a twenty-five-year-old student living in Oakland, California, and attending the University of California, Berkeley. While growing up, she spent summers with her grandparents in Walton County, Georgia, and learned most of her proverbs from them. She collected from herself.

CHRISTINA COX was a twenty-one-year-old student living in Berkeley, California, when the proverbs were collected. She learned her proverbs from her mother, who was born in Monroe, Louisiana. Cox's mother learned proverbs from her own mother, also born in Monroe.

LA CHURANCE BOYD DAVIS was a twenty-one-year-old receptionist in Berkeley, California, at the time of collection. The proverbs were collected by Debbie Scherrer, a student at the University of California, Berkeley, in February 1969.

JEAN FOLLY is this researcher's mother. She was born on January 15, 1934, in Hanover County, Virginia, and has lived there all of her life. She was raised by her grandmother, Mrs. Clara Abrams, and has raised six children herself. She is a nurse's aid, and is deeply involved in church-related activities. She learned proverbs from her grandmother and other older people in the community, and uses them frequently in all kinds of contexts. I have collected proverbs from her most of my life.

JEROME HOLLOWAY was a twenty-two-year-old instructional assistant at Golden Gate Elementary School in Oakland, California. He learned proverbs from his mother, and used them frequently in interactions with children and adults, coworkers and parents. I collected the proverbs over a period of four years, between 1984 and 1988.

ELZADIA JAMERSON was a forty-nine-year-old nurse living in Berkeley at the time when the proverbs were collected from her. The proverbs were collected November 3, 1974, by Marilyn Jamerson, a student at the University of California, Berkeley.

MALCOLM KING has been a friend of the researcher since childhood. He was born in rural Hanover County, Virginia, in 1954 and has lived in Virginia all of his life (except for two years of military service). He works as a substance abuse program supervisor. He learned proverbs from his mother, other older people, and from literature. I collected the proverbs over a period of twenty years, between 1965 and 1985.

FRANKIE SAUNDERS was a forty-two-year-old instructor living in El Cerrito, California, at the time when the proverbs were collected from her. She learned her proverbs from her grandmother in Summerton, South Carolina. Her proverbs were collected in November 1977 by Betty Armstrong, a student at the University of California, Berkeley.

LAURA TALLIE was a forty-five-year-old instructional assistant at Golden Gate Elementary School in Oakland, California, at the time when I collected proverbs from her. She learned proverbs from her mother. She has raised four children and uses proverbs frequently with them as well as with children and adults at school. I collected proverbs from Mrs. Tallie in interviews and from overhearing her use them. She is often reluctant to use proverbs because she feels that it is her mother's role.

CHARLENE THAYER was a forty-six-year-old housewife living in Los Angeles at the time when the proverbs were collected from her. She was born in Los Angeles in 1932, and has lived there all of her life. She learned many of her proverbs from her father, who was born in New Orleans and lived there until early adulthood. The collector was Karen Thayer, a student at the University of California, Berkeley. The proverbs were collected in November 1976.

RILLEN THOMAS was a thirty-two-year-old musician/journalist living in Berkeley, California, at the time of collection. He was born in Lexington, Kentucky, and moved to Euclid, a small town near Cleveland, Ohio, when he was eight years old. He learned the proverbs from his mother and grandmother. The proverbs were collected by Joanne Harano, a student at the University of California, Berkeley, in November 1974.

MARJORIE TWITTY was a fifty-six-year-old telephone operator living in El Sobrante at the time of collection. She is of Canadian-Black ethnicity and had lived in Detroit and Seattle, where she learned some of her proverbs from friends. She moved to California in 1975. The collector was Pamela McNab, a student at the University of California, Berkeley, and the interview was conducted in October 1981.

DON WILLIAMS (an alias) was born August 13, 1910, in Mapleton, Kansas. He had three brothers and sisters, and his mother died giving birth to her last son, who also died a little later. Mr. Williams was raised by his grandparents. His grandmother was born into slavery, and she and her brother walked from Kentucky to Kansas when the slaves were freed. He tried to come to California in 1933, but was caught riding freight trains. He finally made it in 1945, working at the naval supply and serving in the army. He was married to Gerry Williams until she died in 1984. Proverbs were collected from him by his granddaughter, Kimberly Jackson, a student at Sonoma State University in Rohnert Park, California, April 11, May 11 and May 14, 1989.

GERRY ROGERS (an alias) was born March 11, 1931, in Fort Scott, Kansas. Her parents were Don and Gerry Williams. She moved to California in 1943 with her family. She worked as a nurse's aid in 1950, and began working at the county hospital in Martinez, California, and taking classes to get her LVN license, which she received in 1962. She married in 1958 and had two daughters. Proverbs were collected from her by her daughter Kimberly Jackson in April and May 1989.

Proverb Usage

Actions speak louder than words.

Infmnt: Kokomo Arnold, blues singer. See Arnold 1938.

Usage: "Now your ways and your actions speaks almost as loud as words / Because your dreamy eyes told me something, Lord, that I never heard." See Taft 1994: 240.

Infmnt: Kokane, hip hop artist. See Kokane 1991.

Usage: "Action speaks louder than words." Used in boast about having achieved material wealth, women, street reputation, and respect of peers.

Annot: BH 68; DA 2, 11; OX 3; WT 3; SM 1; ST 2616:11; TW 3; WH 4.

An apple a day keeps the doctor away.

Infmnt: Virgie Vitero, 55, housewife, Berkeley, California, 10-1-74. Berkeley Archives.

Usage: "To make young children eat more fruits."

Infmnt: Dorothy Bishop, instructional assistant, Oakland, California. Learned from grandmother in Texas. Collected 8-6-88 by Prahlad.

Usage:

Annot: AP 13; BH 64: 1; BR 60; DSDJ 499; ST 86, "Ait a happle avore gwain to bed, An' you'll make the doctor beg his bread"; TA 124; NC 362; WH 14: A103; MKH 23; SN 93; WT 14; SM 5.

What goes around comes around.

Infmnt: Walter Robinson, 28, Richmond, Virginia, 1964. Berkeley Archives.

Usage: "All the bad things that were occurring would be the reverse in years to come, or in the near future. Those on top and had got there illegally, would be on the bottom before it was all over with. Nature was in control, and she had control over the balance of nature and she does take care of her own." In text: 182-183.

Infmnt: Allane Dixon, 50, assistant librarian, Berkeley, California, 11-12-75. Learned from sister, Tennessee hills. Berkeley Archives.

Usage: "What bad things you say about someone else will eventually be told about you."

Infmnt: Dominic Pinkney, 23, student, Berkeley, California, 11-29-77. Berkeley Archives.

Usage: "For example, if you bother someone, some result will come back to you and make you suffer just as much. It denotes a conscience within the black culture that is not often emphasized. It is similar to 'What goes up must come down' or 'Do unto others as you would have them do unto you.'"

Infmnt: Bill Banks, 30, professor, Oakland, California, 2-28-74. Learned from father, Fort Valley, Georgia. Berkeley Archives.

Usage: "You're held accountable for your actions."

Infmnt: Beverly Battes, 28, seamstress, Berkeley, California, 2-5-74. Learned from mother, Bastrop, Louisiana. Berkeley Archives.

Usage: "What you put out in life will come back to you, like karma."

Infmnt: Elzadia Jamerson. Berkeley Archives.

Usage: What comes around goes around. "If someone does something that is morally wrong, they will eventually be paid back, by something happening to them."

Infmnt: Marjorie Twitty, 56, telephone operator, El Sobrante, California, 10-17-81. Learned from friends, Detroit, Michigan. Berkeley Archives. In text: 183.

Usage: "What you do to someone, someone will do to you."

Infmnt: Female, 35, student. Collected in Los Angeles, California, 3-7-83, by Prahlad. In text: 182.

Usage: *See above.

Infmnt: Male, 26, carpenter. Collected in Berkeley, California, 8-80, by Prahlad. In text: 181.

Usage: *See above.

Infmnt: Male, 27, mortgage appraiser, Detroit, Michigan, 1987. From mother, Alabama. From DA below.

Usage: "I have heard this used mostly when playing basketball. The winning team will boast of its great ability to play, and the losing team will say this to them. Then the next game, my team, which was the winning team, will lose real bad."

Infmnt: Fictional character in Gloria Naylor's *Mama Day*.

Usage: "What goes around comes around, some say," p. 15.

Annot: BH 61; DA 12:55; DSDJ 504:1.

You don't see an empty bag stand up.

Infmnt: Rosa Howard, 26, education specialist, Berkeley, California, 11-20-77. Berkeley Archives.

Usage: "What the proverb is almost always used to mean is that when one is hungry, one doesn't have the energy to work."

Infmnt: Same.

Usage: "Empty bag can't sit down, full one can't bend." Rosa's mother used the proverb to her teacher when the teacher complained about Rosa's performance in school.

Annot: AP 181-182; NC 364, "It's hard for an empty bag to stand up-right"; OX 170-171; ST 115; TW 14; T B30; MKH 36; PAR 465: 172, "You neber see empty bag 'tan' up," Grenada, 467: 215, St. Lucia; WH 18; WS 179: 5, 183: 29; FR 107:427, "Empty bag can't sit down, full one can't ben'"; HO 122, "Empty bag can't stand up"; AC 15:18, "You nebber see empty bag 'tan up"; SM 64; WT 18.

Beauty is only skin deep.

Infmnt: Ella Richardson, 21, student, Oakland, California, 11-22-71. Berkeley Archives.

Usage: "One cannot judge a person by his outward appearance. It is what lies within that actually counts. To use one proverb to describe another . . . 'you can't judge a book by its cover.' " Was used to her during a discussion about clothes.

Infmnt: Female, 64, Oakland, California, 10-31-77. Learned from mother, Georgia, 1920. Berkeley Archives.

Usage: "Beauty is only skin deep, but ugly to the bone." "Physical is superficial, but meanness, and rudeness are ugly behaviors that come out . . . even if covered by masks of beauty. In other words, 'Beauty is as beauty does.' "

Infmnt: Big Bill, blues singer. See Bill 1939. See also Taft 1994: 240.

Usage: "Beauty is only skin-deep, yeah, but ugly is to the bone / Yeah, your old man will be with you when all your pigmeat is gone."

Infmnt: Children's rhyme. See Brewer 1968: 163.

Usage: "Beauty is only skin deep and ugly is to the bone / Beauty fades away, but ugly hangs on." In text: 82.

Annot: AP 281; DA 11:5; DSDJ 504, "Beauty is only skin deep, but love is to the bone"; ST 140; BR 60; OX 38; T B170; NC 367 (ugly's to the bone); WH 36:B129; BA 12; HA 462; SN 80; MKH 41; WS 179: 9, 8; WT 23; SM 11.

If you make your bed hard, you have to lay in it.

Infmnt: Harvey Nolan Loyd, 24, surgical trainee, Berkeley, California, 12-4-69. From mother, Des Moines, Iowa, 1957. Berkeley Archives.

Usage: "One must face the consequences of his actions."

Infmnt: Kay E. McCrary, 22, student, Berkeley, California, 3-9-69. From mother, Gary, Indiana, 1967. Berkeley Archives.

Usage: "You make your bed hard and you have to lay in it, but turn over a little more often. This proverb is said to a young woman in relation to choosing a husband or complaining about having had hard luck by her mother."

Infmnt: Desdemona H. Lewis, 30, student, Hayward, California, 11-12-79. From mother, Cleburne, Texas. Berkeley Archives.

Usage: "When you make your bed hard, you have to lay in it." Her mother said it to her when she broke a house rule, got punished, and sulked. She remembers it from age 7. In text: 147-148.

Infmnt: JoNell Barnett, 45, secretary, Berkeley, California, 2-23-68. From mother, Jackson, Mississippi. Berkeley Archives.

Usage: "If you make your bed hard, you've gotta lie in it. For instance, if a girl marries a fella and her parents don't like him, she will have to put up with the conditions that follow."

Infmnt: Clara Abrams, 75. Learned from mother in Virginia. Collected in Hanover County, Virginia, by Prahlad.

Usage:

Infmnt: Male character, approximately 40, in Hurston's *Jonah's Gourd Vine*, p. 130.

Usage: The father is encouraging his wife to accept their daughter's choice in a husband, and to attend the wedding. "She done done her pickin', now leave her be. If she make her bed hard, she de one got tuh lay on it. 'Taint you. Git yo' clothes on fuh de weddin'."

Infmnt: Bessie Smith, blues singer. See Smith 1933. See also Taft 1994: 240.

Usage: "If you make your own bed hard, that's the way it lies/If I'm tired of sleeping by myself, you too dumb to realize." In text: 117.

Infmnt: Female character, approximately 60, in Naylor's *Mama Day*, p. 255.

Usage:

Infmnt: Shirley Jones, 35, secretary, San Francisco, California, 1969. From grandmother, Oklahoma. Berkeley Archives.

Usage: "You are in control of what happens or not happens. If your marriage is on the rocks and you do nothing to patch it up what happens is your fault."

Infmnt: Jean Folly. Collected in Virginia by Prahlad.

Usage: "Well, like the old folks used to say, you make your bed hard, nobody but you has to lay in it." In text: 146.

Annot: ST 142; AP 391; BR 61; DA 11:23, "If you make your bed hard, turn more often"; OX 502; T B189; NC 368; WH 37:B136, "One has made his bed and must lie on it"(varied); HA 470; SN 93; BA 13; T B189, "He that makes his bed ill lies there"; MKH 42; WS 112: 19; SM 143.

I won't let the same bee sting me twice.

Infmnt: Ida Cox, blues singer. See Charters 1963: 102.

Usage: *I won't let the same mistake happen to me again, I won't be fooled again. In text: 107.

Infmnt: Male, 30s. Collected in Richmond, Virginia, 7-78, by Prahlad.

Usage: "I ain't go' let that same bee sting me again." *Overheard on public bus.

Annot: MKH 42, "If a bee stings you once, it's the bee's fault; if a bee stings you twice, it's your own damn fault."

The blacker the berry the sweeter the juice.

Infmnt: Marjorie Twitty, 56, El Sobrante, California, 10-17-81. From friends, Seattle, Washington, 1961. Berkeley Archives.

Usage: "You say this as a compliment or in admiration of a dark-skinned Black woman."

Infmnt: Louis Williams, 37, consultant, Oakland, California, 11-79. Berkeley Archives.

Usage: "Dark-skinned sisters are very sweet if you get by the thorns—their evil humor—you'd find someone very sweet."

Infmnt: Theresa Epperson, 36, financial assistant, Berkeley, California, 11-20-83. From mother. Berkeley Archives.

Usage: "The blacker a person is the sweeter and better they are sexually."

Infmnt: Shirley White, 30, student, Albany, California, 11-74. From cousin, Charlotte, North Carolina, 1950. Berkeley Archives.

Usage: "It was a comment made after a person had been called black. In saying this my cousin was trying to make it clear that she was proud of being black and that being black was better than being brown or yellow. It also has a sexual connotation (black women were better lovers than brown or yellow women)."

Infmnt: Gerry Rogers, 57, 5-89, Richmond, California. Collected by student at Sonoma State University, Rohnert Park, California.

Usage: "This has to do with color preference. Like a berry, the darker the sweeter it is. An example is difference between dark- and light-skinned people."

Infmnt: Female, 74, housewife, Detroit, Michigan. Born in Louisiana. From DSDJ below.

Usage: "There was a class among Black folks based on color. Lighter-skinned people were considered better, and lighter-skinned Blacks got the first and best jobs. Old folks said it to boost the self-esteem of darker Black children, especially girls. They were saying 'hold your head up.'"

Infmnt: Male, 30, student, Richmond, Virginia. Collected by Prahlad ca. 1975.

Usage: "Yea, well, you know what they say . . . the blacker the berry the sweeter the juice." In text: 177.

Infmnt: Teddy Bunn, blues singer. See Bunn 1930. See also Taft 1994: 239.

Usage: "The blacker the berry, the sweetest juice / Black hair for my prejudice."

Infmnt: Leroy Carr, blues singer. See Carr 1934. See also Taft 1994: 239.

Usage: "Blacker the berry, sweeter is the juice / I got a good black woman, and I ain't going to turn her loose." In text: 110.

Infmnt: Fictional character in Hurston's *Jonah's Gourd Vine*, p. 234.

Usage: A male who has returned from France during the war is comparing French women to African-American women in the South. The speech event is along the line of "jive." "Ah could uh married one uh dem French women but shucks, gimme uh brown skin eve'y time. Blacker de berry sweeter de juice. Come tuh mah pick, gimme uh good black gal."

Infmnt: 2Pac, hip hop artist. See 2Pac 1993.

Usage: "The darker the flesh, the deeper the roots."

Infmnt: Wallace Thurman, author, 1929.

Usage: Used as title of novel: *The Blacker the Berry, The Sweeter the Juice*, New York: Macaully.

Annot: BH 64 2,3, "The blacker the berry/meat, the sweeter the juice"; DSDJ 503:4, 505; MKH 48.

Birds of a feather flock together.

Infmnt: Jean Folly, 46, 1980. Hanover County, Virginia. From grandmother, who was born in Hanover County. Collected by Prahlad.

Usage: *People who are alike tend to group themselves together. Used in explaining the meaning of "If you fool with trash it'll get in your eyes," to suggest that people will make assumptions about a person based on who that person associates with.

Annot: AP 48; BH 62:1; BR 62; DA 5:14; DSDJ 503:10; HA 462; HY 46; NC 370:14; OX 45; T B393; WH 49:B235; BA 16; TW 28; MKH 52; SM 20; WT 31.

A bird in the hand is worth two in the bush.

Infmnt: Charlene Thayer, 46, housewife, Los Angeles, California, 11-22-76. From father, 1946. Berkeley Archives.
Usage: "It is better to appreciate what one has rather than to take chances on things which are uncertain."
Infmnt: Josephine I. Austin, 36, Berkeley, California, 5-3-65. From mother, Boston, Massachusetts. Mother born in Jamaica. Berkeley Archives.
Usage: "Usually about economic situations. If a man has a job and wants to quit to look for a better one."
Infmnt: Elma Paige 53, housewife, Oakland, California, 1-23-74. From mother, Lumberton, Mississippi. Berkeley Archives.
Usage: "A bird in the hand is better than two in the bush."
Infmnt: Ice Cube, hip hop artist. See Cube 1991.
Usage: "A bird in the hand is worth more than a Bush." *A "bird" refers to a kilogram of cocaine. Used to argue that selling cocaine is more economically productive than any of President George Bush's inner-city economic programs. A criticism of Bush and the impact of his programs on black men and black families.

Annot: AP 48; DA 3:50; DSDJ 499; SN 70:270; ST 182:6; TW 27-28; BR 62; OX 59; TA 13,22; T B363; NC 370; WH 47:B229; HA 461; BA 16; BRU 10; MKH 51; WT 3T.

But iffen a bird fly up in de sky it mus' come down sometimes.

Infmnt: Sara Ford, ex-slave. See Rawick 1972: S. 1, v. 4, Tex., pts. 1 and 2, 42. In text: 67.
Usage:
Infmnt: Henry Washington, 35, student, University of Missouri, Columbia. From family, Centralia, Missouri. Collected by student, Dove Reynolds, March 1993.

Usage: "There was never a bird that flew so high that he didn't have to swoop down to shit. Don't get above yourself. If you get a good job, don't forget the little people, cause there'll be a day you need those little people. You'll have to come back, and if they're not there, no matter how much money you have, you'll be shit out of luck."

Annot: WH 257:G82, "What goes up must come down"; MKH 52, "There never was a bird who flew so high but what he came down again," "Every high-flying bird must at some time make light"; SM 62

The early bird catches the worm.

Infmnt: Jean Folly, 46, Hanover County, Virginia. From grandmother, Hanover County. Collected by Prahlad.

Usage:

Annot: AP 173: 4; BH 67; BR 61; DA 3:49, "The early bird gets the worm"; DSDJ 502; HA 464; HY 127; OX 211; NC 371; T B368; WH 49:B236; TW 28; BA 16; MKH 52; BRU 10; SM 62.

Never bite off more than you can chew.

Infmnt: Mary Jane Simmons, ex-slave. Rawick 1972: S. S. 1, v. 4, Ga., 570. In text: 48.

Usage: *Don't take on more than you can handle.

Infmnt: Clara Abrams, 76, Hanover County, Virginia. Collected by Prahlad.

Usage: *Don't take on more than you can handle.

Annot: ST 190; TY 12; BH 61:2, "Don't bite off more than you can chew"; BR 62; BR 32; DA 7:3, "Don't bite off more than you can chew"; HY 47; NC 371, "He bites off . . ."; TA 12.

De bline am temptin' to lead de bline.

Infmnt: Malindy Smith, ex-slave, Mississippi. Rawick 1972: S. S. 1, v. 10, Miss., 1994.

Usage: "De blind leadin' de blind." In text: 71.

Infmnt: Male preacher, 1940s. (?) See J. Mason Brewer, 1968: 134.

Usage: "I wishes to further say, dat I sees in dis congregation, a big flock of black sheep without a shepherd; one in which de bline am 'temptin' to lead de bline."

Infmnt: Dorothy Bishop. Collected by Prahlad.

Usage: "Lord, the blind leading the blind."

Infmnt: Jean Folly. Collected by Prahlad.

Usage: "The blind leading the blind, and neither one of them knows where they're going."

Annot: AP 56; DA 5:4, "The blind can't lead the blind"; DSDJ 503:2; NC 372, "If the blind lead the blind both shall fall into the ditch"; OX 50; ST 199; TW 32-33; HY 51; T:B452; WH 55:B283, "The blind leading the blind"; BA 18; MKH 56; SM 21; WT 35.

Blood is thicker than water.

Infmnt: Male ex-slave, South Carolina. Rawick 1972: S. 1, v. 3, S. C., 51.

Usage: "You know blood is thick."

Infmnt: Clara Abrams, 80, Hanover County, Virginia, 7-78. From mother. Collected by Prahlad.

Usage: *In tight situations people are always going to side with their relatives rather than an outsider.

Annot: AP 56; BH 65:2; NC 372; OX 68; Vance Randolph, *The Devil's Pretty Daughter*, 143; ST 202:7; TW 33; BR 62; WH 56:B291; SN 107; BA 18; BRV 13; MKH 57; WT 36; SM 22.

Can't get blood out a turnip.

Infmnt: Male student, 20, U.C.-Berkeley, 1980. Collected by Prahlad.

Usage: In response to a demanding assignment.

Infmnt: Female student, 21, V.C.U., Richmond, Virginia, 1975. Collected by Prahlad.

Usage: In reponse to an overdue student loan payment.

Annot: AP 56; BH 69:29; BR 62; DA 6:25, "You can't get blood out of a turnip"; GR 36; HA 472; TA 12; T B466; NC 372, "As much blood as a turnip," "No more blood than a turnip," "You can't get blood out of/from a turnip," "You can't git blood out of a turnip, but you can get the turnip"; WH 57:B299, varied; SN 74; TW 34; BA 18; MKH 58; WH 36; SM 21; OX 869.

Don't judge a book by its cover.

Infmnt: Gerry Rogers, 57, retired, 5-89, Richmond, California. Collected by student for a class paper.

Usage: "Cannot tell by looking at someone what they are like. My cousin wouldn't bathe and change clothes and we would think he was stupid because of his appearance but he was actually smart."

Annot: BH 61:2, "You can't judge a book by its cover"; DSDJ 503:6; WH 65:B351, "Never judge . . ."; HA 465, " . . . by its binding"; SN 84; BA 20; MKH 62; ST 83:3; SM 23.

You know what side your bread is browned on.

Infmnt: Bill Banks, 30, professor, Oakland, California, 2-28-74. From father, Fort Valley, Georgia. Berkeley Archives.

Usage: "You know who you can depend on (financial and otherwise) to support you."

Infmnt: Black male, 30s, Oakland, California, 7-87. Collected by Prahlad.

Usage: "She knows what side her bread is buttered on."

Annot: AP 64; ST 232; HY 62; NC 375, "He know on which side his bread is buttered"; OX 81; TA 188; T B623; WH 71: B398, "To butter one's bread on both sides"; SN 95; BA 22; MKH 68, "Don't butter your bread on both sides"; WT 44.

Don't cross the bridge before you get to it.

Infmnt: Christina Cox, 21, student, Berkeley, California, 11-21-71. Berkeley Archives.

Usage: "Worrying about something before it's even happened is always a waste of time and energy." In text: 151.

Infmnt: Female, 30, Oakland, California. Berkeley Archives.

Usage: "We'll cross that bridge when we get to it." *Used as a way of avoiding answering a child's questions about doing something in the future. In text: 152.

Infmnt: Jean Folly, 50, Hanover County, Virginia. From older people. Collected by Prahlad.

Usage: "We'll have to cross that bridge when we get to it." *Used as words of consolation and to remind one not to worry about the future. In text: 150.

Annot: AP 123; BH 65:9, "We'll cross that bridge when we get to it"; DA 8:35, "Never cross a bridge before you get to it"; NC 388; OX 156; ST 244:11 2377: 12; TW 43; BR 63; WH 74:426, "One should not cross . . ."; SN 83; HA 462; BA 23; OX 156; MKH 71; WS 260:214; SM 45.

Never burn your bridges behind you.

Infmnt: Jerome Holloway, 25, instructional assistant, 6-88, Oakland, California. Collected by Prahlad.

Usage: "Well, you know what they say, never burn your bridges behind you." *Spoken about an acquaintance who had recently been fired from a job. Apparently that particular person had exploited all of his friends in an effort to move up the ladder. The proverb was applied to the situation of that person not having anyone who would sympathize with him when he was fired. In text: 176.

Infmnt: Gerry Rogers, 57, retired, 5-89, Richmond, California. Collected by student at Sonoma State University for class paper.

Usage: "Don't get mad and say nasty things to someone because you never know when you might need them."

Infmnt: Don Williams, 79, retired, 5-89, Richmond, California. Born Mapleton, Kansas, moved to California in 1945. Interviewed by student from Sonoma State University, Rohnert Park, California.

Usage: "Don't burn your bridge behind you. Don't close the door and not be able to open it again. An example is if you are living together with a person and get into an argument, don't say or do things and not be able to go back."

Infmnt: Albert King, blues singer. See King 1972.

Usage: "Don't burn down the bridge, cause you might wanna come back / And the grass ain't no greener, on the other side of the track." In text: 115.

Annot: BH 62:5, "Don't burn the bridge that carried you across"; DSDJ 503, "Don't burn down bridges you have to cross"; WH 75:B428, "To burn one's bridges"; TA 198; BA 23; MKH 71; HY 55; ST 245; WS 181:16; FR 99:79, "Don't broke down de bridge you jus' cross"; AC 21:104.

New brooms sweep clean but old broom knows where the dirt is.

Infmnt: Charlene Thayer, 46, housewife, Los Angeles, California, 11-22-76. Berkeley Archives.

Usage: "The old broom has become accustomed to its job and therefore fits into them (corners) from repeated use. A new thing or person may be attractive and new but lacks the specific practical experience of the old one."

Infmnt: Female, 40, domestic, Los Angeles, California, 1-14-68. From Dallas, Texas, 1950. Berkeley Archives.

Usage: " . . . an old broom know all the corners." Literal. "A friend said this when trying to decide which of two brooms to use."

Annot: AP 443; NC 376, " . . . but an old brush knows the corners/fine de corner/ corners of the house"; SN 93:3; ST 246-247; TW 44; BR 64; HY 250; OX 450; TA 51; T B682; WH 75:B432; BA 24; BRV 16; MKH 72; AC 21:105; FR 108:458; WT 47; SM 161.

You can't have your cake/pie and eat it too.

Infmnt: Jean Folly, Hanover County, Virginia. Collected by Prahlad.

Usage: "You want to have your cake and eat it too. You can't do both."

Infmnt: Matthew Boyd, 40, insurance salesman, Oakland, California, 1987. Collected by Prahlad.

Usage: *Said to his four-year-old year-old daughter who wanted to keep her toys so that others could not play with them, but did not want to play with them herself. "You want your cake and eat too."

Annot: BH 61; DSDJ 503, "cake"; AP 178; BR 64; HA 465; HY 70; OX 215; NC 379 "you cannot"; T C15; WH 88:C11, "One cannot have his cake . . ."; SN 94; TW 52; BA 28; MKH 79; WT 53; SM 109.

There's more than one way to skin a cat.

Infmnt: Rillen Thomas, Berkeley, California. 11-8-74. From Kentucky. Berkeley Archives.

Usage:

Infmnt: Jean Folly, Hanover County, Virginia. Collected by Prahlad.

Usage: *There's more than one way of doing whatever is in question.

Infmnt: Don Williams, Richmond, California. Collected by student from Sonoma State University for class paper.

Usage: "There is more than one way to skin a cat. If you are trying to beat someone and cannot. An example is a horse trader trying to sell a horse and it was wind-broke, they put a lemon up the horse's nose so you couldn't hear it wheeze."

Infmnt: Gerry Rogers. Collected by student from Sonoma State University.

Usage: "There is more than one way to do something."

Infmnt: Female character in Naylor's *Mama Day*, p. 67.

Usage:

Annot: NC 382, "There are more ways of killing a cat than by choking her with butter" (butter/ cream; pig/dog; skin); BR 64; AP 88; BH 70:58; WH 670:W74; OX 872; TW 396-397; BRU 151; MKH 87; T W156, "There are more ways to kill a dog than hanging"; 242.

Don't let the cat out the bag.

Infmnt: Jean Folly. Collected by Prahlad.

Usage: *Be discreet. Don't give away too much, especially specific secrets.

Infmnt: Laura Tallie, instructional assistant, Oakland, California. Collected by Prahlad.

Usage: Same as above.

Annot: AP 89; OX 362; ST 295:6; TW 61; WH 100:C104, "To let the cat . . ."; BRE 266; SN 65; BA 31; BRU 21-22.

Charity begins at home.

Infmnt: Charity Jones, 84, Friars Point, Mississippi, 11-17-38. See Rawick 1972: S. S. 1, v. 8, Miss., 1193.

Usage: In text: 71.

Imfmnt: Clara Abrams, Hanover County, Virginia, 12-78. From mother. Collected by Prahlad.

Usage: *Be loving with people in your home first and with outsiders second. Said to great-grandchildren.

Annot: AP 91-92; BH 71:13; NC 382; OX 115; ST 322-323:7; TW 65; WH 105:C141; BR 65; HA 462; SN 87; BA 32; MKH 92; T C251; WT 66; SM 34.

Chickens comin' on the roost.

Infmnt: Dave Barnett, 20, student, Berkeley, California, 2-15-68. From mother, Pine Bluff, Arkansas. Berkeley Archives.

Usage: "Chickens goin' come on the roost. Whatever you do to other people, someone might do it to you."

Infmnt: Female character in Naylor's *Mama Day*, p. 56.

Usage: "All chickens come home to roost."

Annot: NC 388; SN 70:246; ST 332:7; TW 67. See also Bambara 1980: 69. In news footage of Malcolm X, used as "America's chickens coming home to roost," referring to the violence that America was founded on coming back to haunt the country. Spoken in specific response to the news of John F. Kennedy's assassination. BR 65; GR 21; HA 462; AP 130; OX 162; TA 10; WH 108:C164, "Chickens (curses) come home to roost"; BA 33; TW 67; MKH 95; ST 332:17; WS 262:10; SM 47.

Don't count your chickens before they hatch.

Infmnt: Elma Paige, 53, housewife, Oakland, California, 2-23-74. From Lumberton, Mississippi. Berkeley Archives.

Usage: "Don't plan your life based on what's promised to you, but on what you already have."

Infmnt: Jean Folly. Collected by Prahlad.

Usage: *Don't base your plans on things that haven't actually materialized.

Infmnt: Gerry Rogers. Richmond, California.

Usage: "Never count your chickens before they are hatched. Don't plan on doing something until you have the money because something might happen."

Infmnt: Don Williams. Richmond, California.

Usage: "Never count your chickens before they hatch. An example is two brothers who were farmers named Frank and George. Frank paid someone to help with the work. George didn't have anyone to help him because he figured he could save money and would have more money than his brother. George died because he worked himself to death."

Annot: AP 95; BH 64; DA 8:36; DSDJ 503; OX 42; NC 383; ST 332:8; 334:6; TW 67; WH 109:C166, "To count . . ."; TA 28; BR 65; HA 465; SN 70; BA 33; BRU 24; T C292; MKH 95; WT 69; SM 43.

The bigger they come, the harder they fall.

Infmnt: Carl Martin, blues singer. See Martin 1935.

Usage: "Now he's a natural born fighter who likes to fight them all / The bigger they come, he says, the harder they fall." See Taft 1994: 239.

Infmnt: Memphis Minnie, blues singer. See Minnie 1935.

Usage: "Joe Louis is a two-fist fighter, and he stands six feet tall / And the bigger they come, he say, the harder they fall." See Taft 1994: 239.

Annot: MKH 610, "The bigger the tree, the harder she falls"; OX 373; ST 748:13.

You're known by the company you keep.

Infmnt: Jean Folly. Collected by Prahlad.

Usage: *A person is judged by the kind of people that he spends his time with.

Infmnt: Male, 12, student, Oakland, California, 2-12-86. From mother. Collected by Prahlad.

Usage: "Don't hang around with people that do bad things 'cause then people will think you're bad too."

Annot: AP 394; BH 62; OX 138; SN 107:101, 107:119; ST 386-387; TW 78, FY; BA 115, "A man is known . . ."; MKH 108; WS 138: 133; WT 81; SM 40.

Just let your conscience be your safety guide.

Infmnt: Maggie Jones, blues singer. See Jones 1924.

Usage: "Just let your conscience be your safety guide / Anything wrong with me is a mitten to a side." See Taft 1994: 240. In text: 117.

Infmnt: Matthew Boyd, 40, insurance salesman. Collected by Prahlad in Oakland, California, 1988.

Usage: "Well, let your conscience be your guide."

Annot: BH 71; MKH 113.

Too many cooks spoil the pot.

Infmnt: Elzadia Jamerson, 11-3-74. Berkeley Archives.

Usage: "If you have too many people thinking that they know everything, the project won't turn out well."

Infmnt: Clara Abrams. Collected by Prahlad.

Usage: *Too many people's input on a given project can ruin the results.

Annot: AP 640; BH 69; NC 386, (broth); OX 831; SN 93:41; ST 419:5; TW 79; WH 130:C323, (broth); TA 142, (broth); T C642; HA 465; PAR 467:224, pt. 3 (soup) St. Lucia; ST 419:5; MKH 116; WS 244:15; FR 106:353, "Too much cook spoil the soup"; WT 83; SM 228.

Why buy a cow when you can get the milk for nothing?

Infmnt: Bill Hastie, 22, Berkeley, California, 2-10-69. From Chicago, 1960. Berkeley Archives.

Usage: "Why should you marry a girl when you can enjoy the benefits of marriage (sex, in particular) without the responsibility of it?" Used by a mother to give her daughter advice: don't be free with sex, or no one will marry you.

Infmnt: Charlene Thayer. Berkeley Archives.

Usage: *Told to her and her two sisters by father, to "school" them on proper conduct with men before marriage He also used in reference to other people who were living together but not married. There is no use in buying something or making a restricting commitment if it is already being given without the red tape (marriage). "Why buy the cow when you can get the milk free."

Infmnt: Robert Boyd, 28, statistician, Berkeley, California, 10-30-74. Berkeley Archives. From Euro-American male, Washington, D.C., 1966.

Usage: "Why buy a cow when milk is so cheap? Why get married before you're financially and mentally ready if you just want companionship and sex; there are plenty of girls around to let you have both."

Annot: DA 5:17, "Why buy the cow when you can get the milk free?"; ST 446; OX 151; Partridge 450; WH 135:C372, "Why keep a cow when milk is so cheap?"—varied (bull/beef); BA 41; MKH 123; T C767, "Who would keep a cow when he may have a quart of milk for a penny?"; SM 44.

The woman rocks the cradle, I declare she rules the home.

Infmnt: Blind Lemon Jefferson, blues singer. See "That Growling Baby Blues" in Oliver 1960b: 329.

Usage: *The person in charge of the childcare and domestic chores is undeniably the person who controls the home or domestic domain. In text: 101.

Infmnt: Herman Johnson, blues singer. See "Crawlin' Baby Blues" in Oster 1969: 385.

Usage: See above.

Annot: ST 1061, "The hand who rocks the cradle rules the home"; WH 282:H44; OX 347; MKH 276; ST 1060:2; TW 169.

You've got to crawl before you can walk.

Infmnt: Mrs. Laura Tallie, Oakland, California. Collected by Prahlad.

Usage: *Don't expect to achieve everything at once. It takes time to reach one's goals, so be patient and go one step at a time.

Annot: BH 63; DA 12:72; BA 42; AP 214, "First creep, then go"; OX 120; ST 722; MKH 125; WH 138; T:C820; WS 256:167; BT 42:74, "Pickney mus' creep before him walk" ; AC 93:1048; WS 114:23; SM 240; WT 70.

Every crow thinks her crow is the blackest.

Infmnt: Barbara Lashley, 45, student/singer, Berkeley, California, 10-10-79. From mother, South Carolina. Berkeley Archives.

Usage: "When they (mother and neighbors) discussed a particular person who bragged about their children's appearances or achievement, someone would say, 'every crow thinks her crow is the blackest.' "

Infmnt: Clara Abrams, 80, Hanover County, Virginia. Collected by Prahlad.

Usage: *Every mother thinks that her child is the best, smartest, most outstanding, etc.

Annot: AP 124; OX 156; ST 462: 4; TW 85, "Every crow thinks its own young one's the whitest"; SN 70; BA 43; T C851, "fairest, whitest"; MKH 128; WS 90:286; BT 40:28, "John Crow tink him pickny white"; FR 100:118; AC 73:779; HO 134; WT 88.

What's done in dark will come to light.

Infmnt: LaChurance Boyd Davis, 21, Berkeley, California, 11-25-68. Berkeley Archives.

Usage: "Things done in the dark soon come to the light. If you do things sneaky, something will happen to make it known, like when girls in high school get pregnant." Common in Church of Living God, Oakland, California. Used often by her mother as well, who used to say, "As sure as La Churance is your name, as sure as you are you, things done in the dark soon come to light."

Infmnt: Elzadia Jamerson, 49, Berkeley, California, 11-3-74. Berkeley Archives.

Usage: "What is done in darkness shall soon come to light. Anything which is covered up in dishonesty will eventually be exposed." Heard as a child. Applied to the Watergate scandal, 1973-74.

Infmnt: Female character in Naylor's *Mama Day*, p. 121.

Usage: "The truth had to come to light."

Annot: BH 65:5, "What you do in the dark will come to the light"; DA 12:51, "What is done in the dark will come to light"; DSDJ 504:3, "What happens in the dark must come to light"; ST 537:9.

You have to eat a peck of dirt before you die.

Infmnt: Kay E. McCrary, 22, Berkeley, California, 3-2-69. From Lee County, Georgia, 1956. Berkeley Archives.

Usage: "Told to young mother who was hypersensitive about germ contact for her child. Usually said by an older person to a germ-conscious person who is always telling the children not to touch or put things in their mouths. A way of rationalizing the unsanitary living conditions of many Negro homes."

Infmnt: Clara Abrams. Collected by Prahlad.

Usage: *Told to children who might be upset by small amounts of dirt on food that they have dropped on the floor. A way of saying, "It's not such a big deal and, in fact, if you live a long life, there's no telling how many times you may have to eat (or to accept) something that falls a little bit below your standards."

Annot: WH 479:P83, "To eat . . ."; Taylor 1962:2, "You must eat"; MKH 151; ST 581:5; OX 214; SM 63.

You can't teach an old dog new tricks.

Infmnt: Jean Folly. Collected by Prahlad.
Usage:

Infmnt: Matthew Boyd, insurance salesman, Oakland, California. From family in Tennessee. Collected by Prahlad.

Usage:

Annot: BH 66; DSDJ 503; AP 158; BR 71; HA 465; NC 399; OX 805; T D500; TW 105; BA 52; WH 179:D251; MKH 162; ST 615:6; SM 221; WT 118.

The dog that brings a bone carries a bone.

Infmnt: Fictional character in Hurston's *Jonah's Gourd Vine*, p. 195.

Usage: "Ah ain't tole yuh nothin', and you be keerful uh dese folks dat totes yuh news. Uh dog dat'll bring uh bone will keep one. You know dat's de truth."

Infmnt: Laura Tallie, Oakland, California. Collected by Prahlad.

Usage: "If a dog'll bring a bone he'll carry one." *Said about a person who gossips a lot.

Annot: BH 69:7; DA 5:18, "A dog that will bring a bone will carry a bone"; WH 175: D221, " . . . brings a bone will pick a bone"; OX 196, "Dog that fetches . . ."; MKH 158; ST 1012:12; WS 183:30; FR 100:83, "De dog that fetch a bone will carry 'way another"; SM 58.

Don't let the dog bite you twice.

Infmnt: Gerald Green, dentist, San Francisco, California, 11-74. Berkeley Archives.

Usage: "If you had a bad experience don't repeat it."

Infmnt: Malcolm King, Hanover County, Virginia. Collected by Prahlad.

Usage: "I ain't gonna let the same dog bite me twice. If the dog bites you the first time it's the dog's fault, but if he bites you the second time it's your fault." *Anyone can make a mistake once, but only a stupid person would make the same mistake repeatedly, especially if it led to a painful experience. In text: 191.

Annot: An analog of "Don't let the same bee sting you twice." MKH 160.

If you lie down with dogs, you'll get up with fleas.

Infmnt: Charlene Thayer. Berkeley Archives.

Usage: "If a person associates with or indulges in something it will be reflected on his character . . . it will become a part of him." Used by mother to say "associate with decent people and not 'riffraff.' " Like "Birds of a feather flock together."

Infmnt: JoNell Barnett, 45, secretary, Berkeley, California, 2-25-68. From mother, Jackson, Mississippi, 1928. Remembers hearing it at 5 years old. Berkeley Archives.

Usage: "If you waller with the dog, you'll get up with fleas. If you associate with bad people, you'll get bad habits. It is used by a parent in warning a child not to associate with certain people whom the parent considers undesirable."

Infmnt: Mrs. Clara Abrams. Collected by Prahlad.

Usage: Said about an apparently decent minister who had been be-friended by a group of women in the church, known for their gossip and less-than-Christian behavior.

Annot: NC 398; BR 61; DA 10; DSDJ 504; T D537; WH 176: D225; MKH 160; ST 610:7; AC 39:327 (sleep/ketch); OX 460; SM 132; WT 116.

Let sleeping dogs lie.

Infmnt: Lillie Knox, ex-slave. See Rawick 1972: S. S. 1, v. 11, N. C. and S. C., 234.

Usage: *Leave potentially explosive situations alone. In text: 67.

Infmnt: Clara Abrams. Collected by Prahlad.

Usage: See above.

Annot: AP 578; BR 70; DA 7:23, "Let a sleeping dog lie"; HA 463; OX 456; T W7; NC 398; WH 176:D228; BA 52; SN 64; ST 6164; MKH 160; HO 131; SM 205.

If you play with a dog they'll lick you.

Infmnt: Beverly Swayza, 22, cashier, Richmond, California, 10-74. From grandmother. Berkeley Archives.

Usage: "If you deal with someone who is nasty, sooner or later, they will say something nasty to you." *Used to her after a fight with a coworker she had never trusted.

Infmnt: Mrs. Laura Singleton, 63, housewife, Richmond, California, 10-74. From grandmother, De Ridder, Louisiana. Berkeley Archives.

Usage: "Used to warn parents that if you played with a child too much, or gave it too much attention the child will get out of hand, spoiled, and will sass you and give you trouble, like a dog that is poorly trained that jumps on you and licks you."

Infmnt: Martha White, 31, student, Albany, California, 11-74. From mother, New York City, 1950s. Berkeley Archives.

Usage: Play with a dog he will lick your mouth. "She (informant's mother) usually said it after telling us to go away that she didn't play with children. The analogy between this saying and her belief could be that when you play with a dog he tries to do what he is not supposed to do—lick your mouth, and if you were to play with a child it would mean that child may behave in some disrespectful way towards the parent."

Infmnt: Rosie Lee Luckett, 65, retired domestic. From Chicago, Illinois, and before that Mississippi, 1958. Berkeley Archives.

Usage: "Play wid uh dog, he'll lick yo mouf. One must be aware of starting something that they won't like." *Beware of starting something that you would not really like to continue.

Infmnt: Clara Abrams, Hanover County, Virginia. Collected by Prahlad.

Usage: "Play with a puppy he'll lick your mouth."

Infmnt: Dorothy Bishop, 57, instructional assistant, Oakland, California, 3-87. Collected by Prahlad.

Usage: *If you play with children, or are too informal with them, they'll embarrass you or get you into trouble by either acting too familiar with you in public, or by somehow betraying the trust that you place in them.

Infmnt: Jerome Holloway, Oakland, California. Collected by Prahlad.

Usage: "Play with a puppy they will lick you." *Spoken to a classroom of fourth graders who had been creating havoc in the halls while waiting for the speaker to come and take them outside for P.E. In text: 175.

Annot: DA 11:25, "If you play with a puppy, he will lick you in the mouth"; DSDJ 504 (lick your face); WS 96:310; AC 29:326; HO 121, "If you play with dog, dog bites you"; FR 105:305, "Play wid puppy dem lick you mout."

Nothing ruins a duck but its bill.

Infmnt: Desdemona H. Lewis, 30, student, Hayward, California, 11-12-79. From mother, Texas. Berkeley Archives.

Usage: "During my childhood I had a tendency to talk too much and become argumentative in family activities. She usually said this after one of my rambunctious episodes. I always took it to mean you are a lovely child if you keep your mouth shut."

Infmnt: Laurie Tallie, outreach consultant, Oakland, California. Collected by Prahlad.

Usage: "Talking too much. Getting the wrong thing, carrying the wrong message. They talk but they really don't know if it's true or not. Said about people who gossip."

Infmnt: Male, carpenter, 20. Collected in Berkeley, California, 1977, by Prahlad.

Usage: *Said to a fellow carpenter about an overbearing foreman. In text: 184.

Annot: None found to date.

Don't put all your eggs in one basket.

Infmnt: Irene P. Harmon, 52, San Rafael, California, 9-9-80. Berkeley Archives.

Usage: "Always look out for him/herself."

Infmnt: Charlene Thayer, 46. Berkeley Archives.

Usage: "Don't risk all your assets on one venture. Have more than one resource to depend on."

Infmnt: Jean Folly. Collected in Virginia by Prahlad.

Usage: *Always save some of your resources for yourself, especially as concerns relationships. In text: 149.

Infmnt: Clara Abrams. Collected in Virginia by Prahlad.

Usage:

Annot: AP 180-181; NC 403 (too many eggs; "the man who puts his eggs all in one basket, should watch that basket"); OX 218; SN 93:14; ST 672; TW 118; WH 198:E52; BR 72; HA 462; BA 57; T E89; MKH 177; SM 64.

Your eyes are bigger than your stomach.

Infmnt: Viola Winters, 68, Oakland, California, 11-3-71. Berkeley Archives.

Usage: "I tell my children this saying whenever they ask for more of anything than I feel that they are able to eat."

Infmnt: Jean Folly. Collected in Virginia by Prahlad.

Usage: *Same as above.

Annot: AP 195; BH 61; BR 74; HA 472; OX 235; TA 130; T E261; GR 36; NC 404 (belly); WH 209:E129, varied, "To have . . ."; BA 60; ST 733; MKH 191; WS 116:33.

Every shut eye ain't sleep, and every grinning mouth ain't happy.

Infmnt: Frankie Saunders, 42, instructor, El Cerrito, California, 11-4-77. From South Carolina. Berkeley Archives.

Usage: "Just because someone is not looking in your direction it doesn't mean they don't see what you are doing."

Infmnt: James and Lucky Peterson, blues singers. See Peterson 1972: "Every Goodbye Ain't Gone."

Usage: *Everyone pretending to be oblivious to what is happening may not be so. "Every goodbye ain't gone, every shut eye sure ain't sleep." In text: 104.

Annot: NC 404, "don't mean sleep"; DA 11:4, " . . . and every goodbye ain't gone"; WH 42.

Don't fatten frogs for snakes.

Infmnt: Frankie Saunders, 42, from grandmother, South Carolina. Berkeley Archives.

Usage: "It means that you are not supposed to teach people a lot of things within one specific area because in the end they will turn on you and leave you without gratitude. They will also begin thinking that they are too good for you and often leave you for someone or something else. Also used when speaking of relationship. Mostly told among females. It means that a woman should not put too much in a relationship for a man, especially when there are no strings attached, because when he reaches a stage when he is confident and comfortable he will leave her for someone else."

Infmnt: Sonny Boy Williamson (Rice Miller), blues singer. See Williamson 1957.

Usage: "Took me a long time to find out my mistake / But I'll betcha my bottom dollar / I ain't go fatten no more frogs for snakes."

Infmnt: Peter Chatman, blues singer. See Chatman 1940.

Usage: "Because I'm tired of fattening frogs for snakes / After these long many years, believe I just see my great mistake." See Taft 1994: 233.

Annot: None found to date.

What God got lot out for a man, he'll get it.

Infmnt: Ex-slave. See Rawick 1972: S. 1, v. 3, S. C., 63.
Usage: In text: 74.
Infmnt: Minister, 1940s (?). See Brewer 1968: 119.
Usage: "And whatever fer you all this morning, just hold yer cups, and whatever fer yer all yer git it. Kinda like a mail-carrier or post office; give yer whatever fer you."
Infmnt: Clara Abrams. Collected in Virginia by Prahlad.
Usage: "If it's for you, you'll get it." *Don't worry about goals that you want to achieve, because if it's meant for you to achieve them, you will.
Infmnt: Jean Folly. Collected in Virginia by Prahlad.
Usage: *Same as above.

Annot: None found to date.

What's good for the goose is good for the gander.

Infmnt: Female, 40s, librarian, Oakland Public Library, Oakland, California, 3-87. Collected by Prahlad.
Usage: *If something is appropriate for one person in a particular situation, then it should be appropriate just as well for someone else.
Infmnt: Elzadia Jamerson, 49, nurse, 11-3-74, Berkeley, California. Berkeley Archives.
Usage: "What's good for the gander is good for the goose. What one has, whether it is good or bad, is good for another."
Infmnt: Female, 16, student. Collected in Oakland, California, 7-81 by Prahlad.
Usage: *Same as above.
Infmnt: Male, 17, student, Berkeley, California, 7-81. Collected by Prahlad.
Usage: "What's right for the gander may not be good for the goose. What's good for one person might be bad for someone else, because everybody's different."
Annot: ST 1011; WH 548:S54, "Sauce for the goose is sauce for the gander"; BRU 51, 123; MKH 262; WS 84:259; OX 699; WT 379; SM 197.

The grass is always greener on the other side.

Infmnt: Albert King, blues singer. See King 1972.

Usage: "The grass always looks greener on the other side of the tracks."
In text: 115.

Infmnt: Matthew Boyd. Collected in Oakland, California, 2-88, by
Prahlad.

Usage: *Said in reference to a person who was thinking about "cheating
on his wife."

Annot: BH 62:7; DA 11:8; WH 268:G173, "The grass is (looks) greener
on the other side"; AP 302, "Hills are green afar off"; HA 463;
SN 73; ST 591; BA 79; T N115; MKH 265; SM 100.

All that glitters is not gold.

Infmnt: Little Junior Parker, blues singer. See Parker 1964.

Usage: "It's a true true saying / all that shines' not gold."

Infmnt: An anonymous male on a bus, approximately 30, San Francisco,
California. Collected by Prahlad, 1980.

Usage: *Spoken to another man about an attractive woman who had just
gotten on the bus. While one man seemed enthralled with the
woman's appearance, the speaker remained aloof and uninter-
ested, seeming somewhat cynical.

Annot: BH 66; DA 11:18, "All that glitters ain't gold"; DSDJ 504; AP
6; BR 77; HA 461; OX 316; TA 36; T A146; NC 416; BA 77,
"All is not gold that glitters"; TW 154; PAR 484:592, pt. 3, "Not
everything that glitters is gold," St. Thomas; MKH 256; WT
181; SM 92.

Don't bite the hand that feeds you.

Infmnt: Male, about 45, minister, Hanover County, Virginia, 7-80. Collected by Prahlad.

Usage: *Don't alienate or betray those who have supported you, or who
are continuing to support you.

Infmnt: Dr. Clayton, 1940s, blues singer.

Usage: "He bites the hand that feeds him, soon as he gets enough for to
eat." Spoken about the Japanese in reference to the bombing of
Pearl Harbor. See Oliver 1968: 278. In text: 108.

Annot: DA 7:15, "Never bite the hands that feed you"; DSDJ 503; NC
419; HY 47; TA 37; WH 284:H51, "To bite . . ."; ST 1242:9; BA
83; MKH 275; OX 64; WT 195.

Don't let your left hand know what your right hand is doing.

Infmnt: Lil Johnson, blues singer. See Johnson 1929.

Usage: "Listen people to what I'm telling you / Don't let your left hand know what your right hand do." See Taft 1994: 240.

Infmnt: Matthew Boyd, 40, insurance salesman. Collected by Prahlad in Oakland, California, 1988.

Usage: Said in discussion about the issue of divulging information from friends.

Annot: DA 7; MKH 276; WT 194; WH 283; ST 54:1.

To bury the hatchet.

Infmnt: Ex-slave. See Rawick 1972: S. 1, v. 4, Tex., pts. 1 and 2, 11.

Usage: "Bury de hatchet." In text: 45.

Infmnt: Malcolm King, 27, Ashland, Virginia. Collected by Prahlad.

Usage: "They may as well get over it and bury the hatchet." Said about two friends who had been quarrelling and had stopped speaking to each other.

Annot: AP 289; OX 92; SN 110; ST 1087; TA 191; TW 173; T H209, to "hang up . . ."; BA 85; WH 291:H103; BRU 66; MKH 285, "Nobody ever forgets where he buried a hatchet"; WT 201.

Two heads are better than one.

Infmnt: Female, about 35, maid, Los Angeles, California, 11-81. Berkeley Archives.

Usage: "Two heads are better than one, even if one is a wooden head. Always talk out what you are doing."

Infmnt: Clara Abrams. Collected in Virginia by Prahlad.

Usage: *Two people can often come up with ideas or solutions more efficiently than one person.

Annot: AP 655; OX 690; ST 1096:1, TW 177; WH 297:H144, "Two (three) heads . . ."; BR 78; HA 465; TA 61; BA 86; MKH 288; T H281; SM 233; WT 206.

A hard head makes a soft back.

Infmnt: Phyllis Carroll, 25, student, Oakland, California, 11-74. Berkeley Archives.

Usage: "To me it always threatened a whipping to a child who wouldn't behave."

Infmnt: Phyllis Carroll. From grandmother, Walton County, Georgia. Berkeley Archives.

Usage: "A hard head makes a hard bed. It always meant that stubborn or misbehaving children would learn the hard way; that is we would be hurt."

Infmnt: Claudine Hammonds, 21, student, Richmond, California, 11-24-78. From grandmother. Berkeley Archives.

Usage: "Hard head makes a sore butt. My mother would always say, 'Alright, a hard head makes a sore butt,' whenever we wouldn't pick up toys or go to sleep. It meant that if we didn't start doing what we were told to do, we would get a spanking."

Infmnt: Male, 37, administrator, Kensington, California, 11-12-77. From father, Danville, Illinois, 1940. Berkeley Archives.

Usage: "A hard head makes a soft behind."

Infmnt: Marilyn Boyd, student, Kensington, California, 11-71. Berkeley Archives.

Usage: "A hard head makes a soft behind."

Infmnt: Charlene Thayer. From father. Berkeley Archives.

Usage: "A hard head makes a soft back."

Infmnt: Darryl Parker, 26, lawyer, Berkeley, California, 7-21-81. From father, East Harlem, New York, 1969.

Usage: Was more of a rebuttal than a disguised threat of punishment. His father would only repeat the proverb to him whenever he was stubborn or wouldn't listen.

Infmnt: Clara Abrams. Collected by Prahlad in Virginia.

Usage: *If you don't do what you're supposed to be doing or you ignore the directions of adults, you could get into trouble or be hurt.

Infmnt: Vertis Crawford, 20, student, Oakland, California, 1-5-66. From father, 1959. Berkeley Archives.

Usage: "A hard head makes a sore butt."

Infmnt: Dorothy Bishop, instructional assistant, Oakland, California, 1-88. Collected by Prahlad.

Usage: "A hard head makes a sore ass. If you don't mind, you'll get a whipping."

Infmnt: Don Williams. Collected by student from Sonoma State University, Rohnert Park, California.

Usage: "A hard head makes a soft behind."

Infmnt: Gerry Rogers. Collected by student from Sonoma State University.

Usage: "A hard head makes a soft behind. If they tell you not to go outside and walk on the street because it has glass and you walk on the street and cut your feet, it is your own problem."

Annot: BH 65, "A hard head makes/carries a soft ass"; DSDJ 503, "A hard head makes a soft behind"; WH 293:H123, "soft behind," "soft ass"; also "soft heart"; NC 421, "A hard head and soft mind."

Last hired, first fired.

Infmnt: Ex-slave. See Rawick 1972: S. S. 1, v. 4, Ga., pt. 2, 405.

Usage: "Last hired." In text: 75.

Infmnt: Male, 30, graduate student, U. C. L. A., 1984. Collected by Prahlad.

Usage: In conversation about the difficulty even highly educated African-Americans have finding jobs.

Annot: WH 361:L48, "Last in, first out."

You can catch more bees with honey than vinegar.

Infmnt: Gerry Rogers. Collected by student from Sonoma State University, Rohnert Park, California.

Usage: "You can get a person to do things for you when you are nice rather than being mean. An example is with a boyfriend, instead of being demanding with him, it is better if you are nice to him instead of always arguing."

Infmnt: Don Williams. Collected by student from Sonoma State University.

Usage: "Being nice you can make more friends than being nasty."

Annot: DA 2:22, "You can draw more flies with honey than you can with vinegar"; AP 220; HA 462; NC 410, "flies with a spoonful honey than a gallon of vinegar"; TA 10; T F403; MKH 306; SM 113; WT 159.

You can take a horse to water, but you can't make him drink. You can send a fool to college and you cannot make him think.

Infmnt: Mary Richardson, 52, teacher, Berkeley 10-28-71. From mother, Monroe, Louisiana, 1930. Berkeley Archives.

Usage: "When describing anyone in a position of opportunity and doesn't make good use of that opportunity." In text: 140.

Infmnt: Eva Phillip, 52, housekeeper, San Francisco, California, 2-24-68. From grandmother, Jackson, Louisiana, 1926. Berkeley Archives.

Usage: "You can lead a horse to water but you can't make it drink. You can't make anyone do something they don't want to."

Infmnt: Dorothy Bishop, instructional assistant, Oakland, California, 10-86. Collected by Prahlad.

Usage: "You can lead a horse to water, but you can't make him drink." *You can send children to school, but you can't force them to learn. You can present people with opportunities, but you can't make them take advantage of them. In text: 138.

Annot: AP 314; BH 66 (lead/horse; take/mule); DA 6:21; DSDJ 503:9; NC 428; OX 449; SN 65:77; ST 1179-1180:9; TW 191; WH 322:H316, "One may lead . . ."; BA 95; BR 80; HA 465; T H682; TA 10, 151; MKH 312-313; WS 235:71; HO 125; WT 223; SM 115.

Don't change horses in the middle of the stream.

Infmnt: Male principal, Liberty Junior High School, Hanover County, Virginia, 1980. Collected by Prahlad.

Usage: *In response to my expressing doubts about continuing in graduate school.

Infmnt: Matthew Boyd, 40. Collected by Prahlad in Oakland, California, 1989.

Usage: *In a conversation about the possibility of changing careers. "Well, they say not to change horses in the middle of a stream."

Infmnt: Male, 25. Collected by Prahlad on basketball court, Berkeley, California, 1988.

Usage: "Don't change dicks in the middle of a screw." Said to an opposing team member who wished to switch teams.

Annot: BH 64; DA 7:24; BR 80; HT 80, 334; NC 427, "Don't swap horses while crossing a river"; OX 791; TA 37; TW 191; BA 94; MKH 311; SM 34.

Don't look a gift horse in the mouth.

Infmnt: Female student, U. C.-Berkeley, 1979. Collected by Prahlad.

Usage: "Don't kick a gift horse in the mouth." *Said in response to her own complaints about how difficult her assignments were, to suggest that she should be glad for the opportunity to attend a university as prestigious as Berkeley.

Infmnt: Malcolm King, Ashland, Virginia. Collected in Ashland, 1991, by Prahlad.

Usage: *In a conversation about his job, with which he was not completely satisfied. The proverb was used to express the fact that, although the job was not perfect, he still considered himself lucky to have it.

Annot: BH 69; DA 7:24; AP 245-246; BR 80; HA 464; HY 159; NC 427, "Never"; OX 301; TA 158:65; T H678; WH 324:H329, "To look a gift horse . . ."; SN 65; ST 1182; TW 191; BA 75; BRU 72; MKH 311; SM 91.

People who live in glass houses shouldn't throw stones.

Infmnt: Don Williams. Collected by student from Sonoma State University in Rohnert Park, California.

Usage: "If you are doing the same thing as someone else you can't gossip about them. An example is a preacher can't tell you not to have an affair with a woman when he is doing it himself."

Infmnt: Matthew Boyd. Collected by Prahlad in Oakland, California, 1988.

Usage: "If you live in a glass house you can't throw stones." *Said about someone who had been unfaithful to his wife when the topic of her having an affair came up. The general message was that the man had no right to complain about his wife's activities.

Annot: BH 66; DA 11:37, "If you live in a glass house, don't throw stones"; BR 80; HA 464; SN 84; TW 194; TA 74, 84, 141; MKH 252-253; WT 225; SM 92.

It's better to climb on top of the house and sit than to live inside with a nagging woman.

Infmnt: Ex-slave woman. See Rawick 1972: S. 1, v. 6, Ala. and Ind., 45.

Usage: "It's better to climb on top of the house and sit den to live inside wid a naggin' 'oman." In text: 73.

Infmnt: Male minister, about 50, Providence Baptist Church, Hanover County, Virginia, 1976. Collected by Prahlad.

Usage: "It's better to sit on top of the house than to live inside in confusion."

Annot: ST 2581:2.

A leopard don't change his spots.

Infmnt: Ex-slave. See Rawick 1972: S. S., v. 1, Okla., 118.

Usage: "You got to go slow and not try to change the leopard spots quick." In text: 68.

Infmnt: Female character in Naylor's *Mama Day*, p. 121.

Usage: "A leopard don't hide his spots but for so long."

Annot: WH 368:L109; OX 456; TW 121-122; MKH 369; T L206; WT 132; SM 131.

Live and let live.

Infmnt: See Bumble Bee Slim, "You Got to live and let live" in Oliver 1960a: 109.

Usage: *See above. In text: 117.

Infmnt: Howard Roundtree, 50, New York, born Virginia.

Usage: "We believe in live and let live. I don't go out here looking for no trouble. I pay my debts. I go to work. And I do my level best to help anybody . . ." (Gwaltney 1980: 63).

Annot: AP 375; BH 67; NC 438; OX 473; SN 88:43; ST 1408:7; TW 226; BR 82; BA 111; T L380; MKH 381; WH 380: L196; WT 265; SM 136.

Study long, study wrong.

Infmnt: Betty A. Robinson, 21, student, Richmond, California. Berkeley Archives.

Usage: It is a mechanism used to hurry a slow player. Used while playing dominoes, checkers, or cards.

Infmnt: Sandra Alsbrook, 22, Berkeley, California, 11-4-65. From St. Paul, Minnesota, 1961. Berkeley Archives.

Usage: "If you think long, you think wrong. It urges a person to just be natural and go ahead and act . . . a Negro cultural value." *This proverb is often used with games such as dominoes and cards to encourage players not to take so long in making their moves.

Infmnt: Male student, 30, in game room of student union, Virginia Commonwealth University, Richmond, Virginia, 1976. Collected by Prahlad.

Usage: *Said when another person with whom he was playing took a long time to make a move (chess, checkers, cards, pool, etc.).

Annot: MKH 569.

Look before you leap.

Infmnt: Gerry Rogers. Collected by student from Sonoma State University, Rohnert Park, California.

Usage: "Don't do anything unless you know it is okay. Don't make a decision unless you are absolutely sure."

Infmnt: Don Williams. Collected by student from Sonoma State University.

Usage: "Don't leap until you know where you are going to land. An example is if you have a good marriage, don't break it off to go with someone else."

Annot: BH 64; DA 7:31; NC; 438; AP 380; BR 83; HA 464; HY 226; OX 482; TA 45; TW 228; BA 112; T 6429; MKH 384; WH 383:L216; ST 1452:2; WT 267; SM 138.

Once a man, twice a child.

Infmnt: Herman Harris, 25, student, 3-27-64. Berkeley Archives.

Usage: Used by people when they are referring to the very silly behavior of an old person who supposedly should know better.

Infmnt: Laura Tallie, outreach consultant, Oakland, California. Collected by Prahlad.

Usage: "An example is like my mother, once a woman, twice a child. You're a baby, then you're grown, then when you get in you late years, you can't do for yourself. Your children have to bathe you and do for you because you're sick."

Annot: AP 464-465; BH 68:1; OX T M570; NC 441; MKH 403; WT 70.

An idle mind is a devil's workshop.

Infmnt: Juanita Barnes, 40, Oakland, California, 7-17-71. From Galveston, Texas. Berkeley Archives. In text: 27.

Usage:

Infmnt: Jim Ashe, 21, Sacramento, California, 10-17-74. Berkeley Archives.

Usage:

Infmnt: Lynell Brazier, 20, Berkeley, California, 11-13-74. From Kilgore, Texas. Berkeley Archives.

Usage:

Infmnt: Wyatt Frieson, 51, accountant, Norco, California, 11-22-84. From Gallaway, West Virginia, 1940. Berkeley Archives.

Usage: "Idle time is the Devil's workshop."

Infmnt: Jean Folly, Hanover County, Virginia. Collected by Prahlad.

Usage: "Idle mind is the devil's workshop. Idle hands are the devil's workshop." *If you're not busy you might get into trouble.

Infmnt: Female character in Naylor's *Mama Day*, p. 216.

Usage: "Idle hands are the devil's workshop."

Annot: DA 4:83; MKH 411; WS 133:107, "Idle head"; FR 102:192, "Idle man head a debil workshop"; OX 395; SM 118.

Money talks.

Infmnt: Male, about 25, Oakland, California, 12-84. Overheard on public bus, collected by Prahlad.

Usage: *The amount of money that you have is what counts. If you don't have enough money, be quiet.

Infmnt: Male, graduate student, Oakland, California, 7-10-82. From Denver, Colorado, 1974. Berkeley Archives.

Usage: "Money talks and bullshit walks. The proverb makes a distinction between what is real and important (money) and what is trivial (bullshit)." *Used to indicate to someone that mouthing off amounts to nothing, whereas money has real power in the world.

Infmnt: Kokomo Arnold, blues singer. See Arnold 1935. See also Taft 1994: 240-241.

Usage: "Let your money talk, let your money talk, so we can / hear, so we can hear / If you ain't coming back, tell me right now; leave a dime for beer." In text: 117.

Annot: AP 423:38; Patridge, 528; BH 68, "Money talks, niggers walk," "Money talks and bullshit walks"; WH 418:M209, "Money talks," varied; BR 86; SN 90; ST 1617:2; TA 9; MKH 417; SM 154.

Money is the root of all evil.

Infmnt: Henre Necaise, ex-slave, Mississippi. See Rawick 1972: S. S. 1, v. 9, Miss., 1633. In text: 48.

Usage:

Infmnt: Deacon, 64, Hanover County, Virginia, 7-80. Collected by Prahlad.

Usage: *Used to mean that money was the cause of disharmony and bad feelings between people within the church.

Infmnt: Lazy Slim Jim, blues singer.

Usage: "Money is the root of all evil, look what it has done for me / Cause me to leave my baby, now I'm living in misery," See Oliver 1960: 129.

Annot: BH 63 (love of money; money); BR 85; DA 2:29, (the love of money); HY 297; TA 49; NC 446; I Timothy 6:10; WH 387:L248, "The love of money . . ."; BRU 89; TW 230; MKH 416; ST 1608:1; OX 150; WT 270.

One monkey don't stop no show.

Infmnt: Marjorie Twitty, 56, telephone operator, El Sobrante, California, 10-17-81. From Detroit, Michigan, 1964. Berkeley Archives.

Usage: "It would be used, for instance, in a situation where a woman has invited a man over for dinner and he doesn't show up. You would say this to yourself or to your friends. It would also be used when you break up with a guy and you're really hurt inside but you don't want to show it. You would say this to your friends or to yourself as a comfort."

Infmnt: Marilyn Boyd, 36, Kensington, California, 11-14-77. From Danville, Illinois, 1950. Berkeley Archives.

Usage: "If someone gets mad and says that he is going to quit playing, someone will pipe in and say, 'Go on and quit, one monkey don't stop no show.' They are telling him to go on and quit, they don't care, and that they will keep playing without him. Plus they add insult by comparing him to a monkey." In text: 174-175.

Infmnt: Phyllis Carroll, 25, Oakland, California, 11-74. Berkeley Archives.

Usage: *Used as above about people who were rowdy and were put out of dances. "One monkey don't spoil the show." In text: 175.

Infmnt: Jerome Holloway, 25, instructional assistant, Oakland, California, 3-86. Collected by Prahlad.

Usage: *Used as above to boys who quit a kickball game. In text: 172.

Annot: BH 66 (above version plus a second—"but he can sho mess up one"); DA 6:22; DSDJ 503.

Hard times will make a monkey eat cayenne pepper.

Infmnt: Mary Ann Pollar, 41, concert promoter, Oakland, California, 10-26-69. From Texas. Berkeley Archives.

Usage: "If a monkey had gone a long time without eating, he would eat whatever became available to him." *If a person was poor enough, or in severe enough a situation, he would eat whatever was available in order to survive. In text: 157.

Infmnt: Lois Page, 67, housewife, East Orange, New Jersey, 3-74. Berkeley Archives.

Usage: "Never say what you will or will not do. You never know when circumstances will change your fortunes and then just like the monkey, who hated them, ate red peppers and cried his eyes out. A monkey will eat red peppers and cry his eyes out." In text: 158.

Infmnt: Sammy Davis, Sr., 72, retired, Los Angeles, California, 2-3-74. Berkeley Archives. From grandmother, North Carolina, 1909.

Usage: "Hard times make a monkey eat red pepper when he don't care for Black. In those days they fixed your plate and you ate everything on it or what you didn't eat then you ate the next morning for breakfast." The informant had objected to some food on his plate when his grandmother told him this proverb. The proverb means that when times get bad and there is a shortage, that one has to eat or make do with whatever there is around. In text: 156.

Annot: PAR 460:73, part 3, "Hunger make monkey blow fire," Grenada; MKH 419, "Monkeys in hard times eat red peppers"; WH 630.

Don't let your mouth write a check that your behind can't cash.

Infmnt: Maxine Hudnall, 35, clerk, Oakland, California, 11-27-71. From Oakland Army Base, 1970.

Usage: "My informant told me that someone in her office told this to another worker that had a tendency to overdo everything."

Infmnt: Bill Banks, 30, professor, Oakland, California, 2-28-74. From father, Fort Valley, Georgia. Berkeley Archives.

Usage: "Don't let your mouth write a ticket your ass can't cash. Don't take a position that you can't defend."

Infmnt: Emma Gordan, 69, Berkeley, California, 10-71. Berkeley Archives.

Usage: "Your mouth is going to cause you a check, your ass is going to have to chase." *Used often by adults to children, as a way of saying "If you talk too much you may not be able to talk your way out of the situation." Used by peers on the verge of going from a verbal fight to a physical one. Means: Don't make statements that you cannot physically back up. In text: 169.

Infmnt: Female student, 11, Oakland, California, 1986. Collected by Prahlad.

Usage: Used in confrontation with another student. In text: 169.

Infmnt: Stetsasonic, hip hop artist. See Stetsasonic 1991.

Usage: "Don't let your mouth write a check that your ass can't cash." *Don't "talk trash" about people unless you can back it up with lyrical or musical skills, wealth, or physical combat.

Annot: BH 64 (plus two additional versions: "Don't write a check your behind can't cash," and "Don't let your head start something your ass can't handle").

Don't take any wooden nickels.

Infmnt: Louis Williams, 37, 11-79. Oakland, California. Berkeley Archives.

Usage: "Be careful when you accept things from people. Don't accept empty promises."

Infmnt: Laura Tallie. Collected in Oakland by Prahlad.

Usage: *Same as above. Especially as regards deals that may look or sound good but that are really designed to trick you out of your money.

Annot: DA 7; TY 12; WH 446:N68; BA 128; MKH 430.

Don't jump from the frying pan into the fire.

Infmnt: Elzadia Jamerson, nurse, Berkeley, California, 11-3-74. From Louisiana. Berkeley Archives.

Usage: "Be satisfied where you are, because the situation could get worse."

Infmnt: Clara Abrams. Collected in Virginia by Prahlad.

Usage: "Out of the frying pan and into the fire." *Used to refer to someone who is getting out of one undesirable situation and getting into an even less desirable one.

Infmnt: Albert King, blues singer. See King 1972.

Usage: "Now it seems like you gonna jump / From the frying pan into the fire." In text: 115-116.

Annot: AP 240; BH 69:23, "He/she jumped out of the pan/skillet into the fire"; NC 413; OX 292; ST 814:1; TW 147; TA 158, 186; WH 244:F282, " . . . out of the frying pan into the fire"; BA 72; BR 75; HA 470; SN 95; BRU 5405; MKH 448-449; WT 170.

A thin pan gwine to git hot quicker than a thick one.

Infmnt: James Johnson, ex-slave, 79. See Rawick 1972: S. 1, v. 3, S. C., 43. In text: 69.

Usage:

Annot: MKH 448, " . . . , an' cold the same way."

Don't cast your pearls before swine.

Infmnt: Jean Folly. Collected in Virginia by Prahlad.

Usage: *Don't waste your time giving your best to people or to situations that are not up to your standards or that will devalue your true worth.

Infmnt: Male Preacher, 1940s (?). See J. Mason Brewer 1968: 135.

Usage: "Cast not your pearls before a hawg, nor feed holy things to er dawg." *The second half added humorously because a dog had entered the church. This was the minister's metaphorical response to the situation. In text: 38.

Annot: AP 488; BR 87; DA 7:10; DSDJ 503; HY 267; OX 617; TA 30, 186; T P165; NC 455-456; WH 478:P76, "To cast pearls before swine"; SN 62; ST 1768:13; TW 278; BA 136; BRV 107; MKH 456; WS 217:198; WT 330; SM 176.

A picture is worth a thousand words.

Infmnt: Male, 35. Collected in San Francisco, California, 8-87, by Prahlad.

Usage: *Used in response to another man's question: "What does she look like?" "A picture is worth a thousand words." Means that seeing something for one's self is more meaningful than hearing someone else's description.

Infmnt: Female, 21. Collected in Richmond, Virginia, 3-80, by Prahlad.
Usage: *Overheard in a restaurant, conversation between two university
         students. Did not hear enough of the conversation to interpret
         the meaning.
Annot: ST 2611:3; MKH 463; SM 177.

The Lord don't like little pitchers with big ears.

Infmnt: Female, 40s.
Usage: *Used to a child to say that the child should not be listening to
         the adult's conversation. See Angelou 1970: 127.
Infmnt: Clara Abrams. Collected by Prahlad.
Usage: "Little pitchers with big ears." *Used to refer to children who are
         trying to overhear conversation between adults.
Annot: AP 372; BR 72; GR 31; HA 464; OX 471; T P363; WH 497:P230,
         "Little pitchers (pigs, jugs) have long ears," varied; SN 93; ST
         1806; BA 141; MKH 466; SM 135.

Don't buy a pig in a bag.

Infmnt: Clara Abrams. Collected in Virginia by Prahlad.
Usage: *Don't be deceived by outward appearances. Especially in regards
         to choosing a marital partner. Take time to thoroughly know the
         person before marrying them and bringing them home. See Folly
         1982: 235-236.
Infmnt: Laura Tallie. Collected in Oakland, California, by Prahlad.
Usage: "Buying a pig in a bag."
Infmnt: Roosevelt Sykes, blues singer.
Usage: "But women are so tricky / they'll try to tell you white is black
         / To get a woman nowadays / is just like buying a pig in a sack"
         See Oliver 1960a: 99.
Annot: Buying a pig in a sack ("poke"). AP 494; NC 458; OX 95; ST 1791-
         1792:10; TW 284; WH 489:P157; T P304; BRU 109; MKH 463-
         464; WS 97: 313 (puss in a bag); AC 98:1109, "Nebber buy puss
         in a bag"; WT 335.

Root, pig, or die.

Infmnt: Ex-slave. See Rawick 1972: S. 1, v. 6, Ala. and Ind., 41.
Usage: In text: 70.

Infmnt: Rube Witt, 87, ex-slave. See Rawick 1972: S. 1, v. 5, Tex., pts. 3 and 4, 209.

Usage: "Root hawg or die." In text: 70.

Infmnt: Miss Jane Pittman, an elderly, fictional character in Ernest Gaines's *The Autobiography of Miss Jane Pittman.*

Usage: "Root hog or die." "Yankee money came in to help the South back on her feet—yes, but no Yankee troops. We was left there to 'root hog or die.'" See Gaines 1971: 70.

Infmnt: Harlem Hamfats (vocalist Herb Morand). See Harlem Hamfats 1937.

Usage: "Root hog or die" (refrain of song).

Annot: MKH 516; ST 1147:9; TA 90; BA 91; SN 66; TW 184; BRU 70.

From pillar to post.

Infmnt: Clara Abrams. Collected in Virginia by Prahlad.

Usage: Said about the demands of modern society and the constant effort that it takes to keep up. "Look like they keep you going from pillar to post."

Infmnt: Ex-slave. See Rawick 1972: S. S. 1, v. 1, Ala., 411.

Usage: "From piller ter post." In text: 75.

Annot: AP 496; TA 193; WH 491:P182; BRU 109, 112; TW 285; T P328.

The pot calling the kettle black.

Infmnt: Doris Daniels, 30, student, 2-23-74, Berkeley, California. From mother, Texas. Berkeley Archives.

Usage: "That's like the pot calling the kettle black. If you accused another student of cheating on the test when you yourself had also cheated on the exam, it would be like the 'pot calling the kettle black.'"

Infmnt: Rillen Thomas, 32. Berkeley Archives.

Usage: "Pot calling the kettle black."

Infmnt: Katherine Hack, 22, student, Oakland, California, 2-13-69. From mother, Compton, California, 1960. Berkeley Archives.

Usage: "The skillet called the pot black. This is a proverb which means that a person who is talking about another is like the person he is talking about."

Infmnt: Clara Abrams. Collected in Virginia by Prahlad.

Usage: "The kettle calling the pot black and the frying pan standing up for witness." See Folly 1986: 238. In text: 143-144.

Infmnt: Dorothy Bishop, Oakland, California. Collected by Prahlad.

Usage: "Yea, the pot calling the kettle black." In text: 141.

Infmnt: Female character in Hurston's *Jonah's Gourd Vine*. See Hurston [1934] 1987:230.

Usage: "Dey chunkin stones at yo' character and sayin' you ain't fit. Pot calling de kittle black."

Annot: AP 507, BH 69:30, "The pot can't call the kettle black"; NC 461; OX 421; ST 1840:14; TW 293; WH 506:P297, varied; HA 471; SN 93; TA 158, 170; BA 144; PAR 467:223, pt. 3, St. Lucia; MKH 476; WS 211:170, 212:176; WT 344.

A watched pot never boils.

Infmnt: Elzadia Jamerson, 11-3-74. Berkeley Archives.

Usage: "Refers to raising children. If something is carefully guided, it will never get out of control, and always be a success."

Infmnt: Laura Tallie. Collected in Oakland by Prahlad.

Usage: "A watched pot never boils."

Annot: AP 669; BR 88; DA 11:20; GR 18; HA 462 (kettle); OX 869; WH 507:P303, varied; SN 93; ST 1839:6; BA 144; MKH 475; SM 242.

An ounce of prevention is worth a thousand pounds of cure.

Infmnt: Charlene Thayer, Los Angeles, California, 11-22-76. Berkeley Archives.

Usage: "Just a small amount of time taken to prevent something bad from happening is well worth one's while."

Infmnt: Dorothy Bishop. Collected in Oakland by Prahlad.

Usage: "An ounce of prevention is worth a pound of cure."

Annot: AP 511; BH 64:3; DA 3: 44 (a pound of cure); DSDJ 502; NC 454; OX 646; ST 1877:4; TW 272; WH 510:P324, "Prevention is better than cure"; BR 89; HA 461; SN 87; BA 132; MKH 482-483; WT 347; SM 183.

Spare the rod.

Infmnt: Blind Boy Fuller, blues singer. See Fuller 1938.

Usage: "Then I sent for my friend; please spare the rod / Then my friend sent me word; Lord, the job was too doggone hard." See Taft 1994: 241.

Infmnt: Muddy Waters, blues singer. See Waters 1970.

Usage: "I call my friends, I said 'please spare the rod' / You know what my friends said, 'Muddy the times is too doggone hard.'" *In blues, the traditional proverb "spare the rod and spoil the child" seems to have been transformed. It is shortened and used to mean "lend me a hand" or "help me out."

Annot: BH 70; DSDJ 503; OX 759; WT 366; SM 209; ST 344:8; TW 309; WH 534.

When in Rome do as the Romans do.

Infmnt: Jean Folly. Collected in Virginia by Prahlad.

Usage: In response to procedural requirements on her job that conflicted with her idea of how things should be done. "Well, I guess sometimes you have to do as the Romans do."

Infmnt: Male ex-slave. See Rawick 1972: S. S. 2, v. 7, Tex., 2593.

Usage: "When in Rome do as Rome do." In text: 59.

Annot: T R165; AP 537; TA 40; BR 90; HA 465; SN 109; TW 310; WH 536:R126; BA 154; MKH 515; ST 2005:1; SM 193; OX 683; WT 368.

Hoe your row.

Infmnt: Ex-slave. See Rawick 1972: S. S. 1, v. 12, Okla., 111, 118.

Usage: In text: 75.

Infmnt: Clara Abrams. Collected by Prahlad.

Usage: "He's really had a tough row to hoe."

Annot: BA 155; ST 2397; TW 313; WH 539:R15, varied; BRU 120; MKH 517.

Seeing is believing.

Infmnt: Manda Boggan, 80s, Mississippi, 1930s. See Rawick 1972: S. S. 1, v. 10, Miss., 4.

Usage: *One can believe in what one sees with one's own eyes. In text: 63.

Infmnt: Male, 80s, ex-slave, Mississippi.

Usage: Same as above. See Rawick 1972: S. S. 1, v. 10, Miss., 5. In text: 64.

Infmnt: Sonny Terry, blues singer, approximately 65. See Terry and McGhee 1969.

Usage: "Seeing is believin' / That's what the old folks always told me. / But you know I can't see love but I can feel it, / And that's good enough for me." In text: 103.

Annot: AP 556; BH 65; NC 471; ST 2105:12; TW 321-322; WH 551: S92; MKH 530; SM 199.

Two clean sheets don't smut.

Infmnt: Clara Abrams. Collected by Prahlad.

Usage: *Used to mean that if two people, married or not, engage in sex, their actions will be "clean" as long as they are not otherwise sinners. Reportedly used as a rationalization by persons engaged in adultery.

Infmnt: Male, 80s, ex-slave. See Rawick 1972: S. S. 1, v. 3, Ga., 74.

Usage: Same as above. In text: 72.

Annot: See Cohn 1935: 184. "Like rubbing two clean sheets together; dey can't soil each other." See also Rawick 1972: S. S. 1, v. 7, Okla. and Miss., 23, "She didn't want no Negro man smutting her sheets up." Perhaps the expression "smutting up" was commonly used to refer to sexual relations; MKH 534, "One clean sheet will not soil another."

It's not the size of the ship, but the motion of the ocean.

Infmnt: Venetia L. Terrell, 26, student, Albany, California, 12-5-70. From other black students, Atlanta, Georgia, 1963. Berkeley Archives.

Usage: "One has to look for definitive meanings in life, one has to understand nuances of each event in question in order to understand the event."

Infmnt: Carol Clark, 24, student, Berkeley, California, 10-18-70. From girl friend, Berkeley, 1970. Berkeley Archives.

Usage: "It's not the size of the ship that makes you sea sick, but the motion of the ocean. It's not the size of a man's genitals that make you have an orgasm but the way he uses it."

Infmnt: Portia Stewart, 36, counselor, Oakland, California, 11-19-83. From other students. Berkeley Archives.

Usage: "Is really related to sexual beliefs. That a man who has a small penis cannot perform well sexually, but according to this proverb, it may not be the case. You can't base all your ideas by the size of a person but what a person can do."

Infmnt: Gloria Frank, student, Berkeley, California. Berkeley Archives.

Usage: "It's not the size of the ship but the motion of the waves."

Infmnt: Anonymous male, 40s, Richmond, Virginia, 3-80. Collected by Prahlad.

Usage: "It's not the size of the ship but the motion of the ocean." In text: 188.

Infmnt: Anonymous female, 20s, Richmond, Virginia, 7-82. Collected by Prahlad.

Usage: "It's not the size of the ship but the motion of the ocean." In text: 190.

Annot: None found to date.

If the shoe fits, wear it.

Infmnt: Felix Leatherwood, 21, Berkeley, California, 3-10-74. From Chicago. Berkeley Archives.

Usage:

Infmnt: Betty Armstrong, student, Oakland, California, 10-13-77. Berkeley Archives.

Usage: "If the shoe fits wear it. If it don't then squeak! If you think the phrase fits you then accept it, but if you don't think so, accept it anyways because it surely does fit you." *If you feel that a certain statement or accusation applies to you, accept that it does.

Annot: TW 328; BR 91; AP 81; DA 11:29; TA 18; NC 473; NC 379 (cap); WH 560:S155; HA 463; SN 105; BA 162; ST 2097:1; TW 328; MKH 536; WT 390.

Nothing comes to a sleeper but a dream.

Infmnt: Anonymous male, 30s, Greyhound bus crossing the country, 1978. Collected by Prahlad.

Usage: *You may as well wake up because nothing of importance will happen to you while you are asleep.

Infmnt: Thelma Folly, 29, from Richmond, Virginia. Collected by Prahlad.

Usage:

Annot: None found to date.

What you sow you must reap.

Infmnt: Shirley Jones, 35, secretary, San Francisco, California, 5-9-69. From mother, Oklahoma. Berkeley Archives.

Usage: "If someone do someone wrong you will get the worse done to you."

Infmnt: Ex-slave. See Rawick 1972: S. 1, v. 3, S. C., pt. 4, 157. Mack Taylor, 97, 1930s.

Usage: "What you sow you sure to reap." *Black people helped to make America a prosperous country and they have a right to the benefits. "Us fell de forests for corn, wheat, oats, and cotten; drained de swamp for rice; built de dirt roads and de railroads; and us old ones is got a fair right to our part of de pension." In text: 53.

Infmnt: Mr. Calhoun, 98, ex-slave, Texas, 1930s. See Rawick 1972: S. S. 2, v. 3, Tex. 606.

Usage: "You shall reap when you laborth." *A slave is not stealing if he takes crops from the garden of the master because he put all of the work into raising the crop; therefore he has a right to benefit from the food. In text: 51.

Infmnt: Jane Johnson, 90, ex-slave, South Carolina, 1930s. See Rawick 1972: S. 1, v. 3, pt. 3, 51.

Usage: "You knows dat if you sows evil you is sho' gwine to gather evil in time." *The white people who have fought against the freedom of black people will one day suffer for their deeds. In text: 50.

Infmnt: Henry Gibbs, 85, ex-slave, Mississippi. See Rawick 1972: S. S. 1, v. 8, Miss., 828.

Usage: "I gwine reap what I sow." *If one lives a good life one will go home to God after death. In text: 56.

Infmnt: Ophelia Jemison, ex-slave, South Carolina. See Rawick 1972: S. S. 1, v. 11, N. C. and S. C., 223.

Usage: "What you sow in wicked doings you sure reap down dere." *People who live a wicked life will go to hell. In text: 56.

Infmnt: Hager Brown, about 90, ex-slave, Murrels Inlet, South Carolina. See Rawick 1972: S. S. 1, v. 11, S. C., 77.

Usage: "Man shill, 'Reap what he sow.' Bible say, Honor you Father and Mother. You reap or chillun reap." *Used to say that if the parents don't live to suffer for their moral transgressions, then their children will. In text: 57.

Infmnt: Peetie Wheatstraw, blues singer, 1930s. For transcription of song "Ice and Snow Blues," see Garon 1971: 30.

Usage: "Baby, now, you know you got to reap, baby, Just what, what you sow." *Used as refrain to mean that the woman who has mistreated him will receive mistreatment in the future. In text: 92.

Infmnt: Guitar Slim (Eddie Jones), blues singer, 1950s. See Slim [1950] 1972.

Usage: "They say you got to reap baby / You got to reap—just what you sow." *Used in same way as previous example. In text: 92-93.

Infmnt: Bobby "Blue" Bland, blues singer, 1950s. See Bland 1964.

Usage: "You got to reap just what you sow / That old saying is true, Like you mistreat someone / Someone's gonna mistreat you." *Used as in above examples. In text: 93.

Infmnt: Bill Gaither, blues singer, 1930s. For transcription, see "Sing Sing Blues" in Oliver 1960b: 248.

Usage: "My mother told me, 'Son, you've got to reap just what you sow' / Now I'm behind these hard stone walls, may never see the streets no more." *Used to mean that crime leads to punishment. In text: 99.

Infmnt: Jesse James, prisoner making blues recording, 1936, Oklahoma. See Oliver 1960b: 257-258.

Usage: "I been to the Nation, 'round the Territo'. / You heah me talkin' to ya, gotta reap what ya sow." *Used as above. A possible indication that the U.S. government will reap misfortune for its treatment of the Native American and black people. In text: 99.

Infmnt: Skip James, blues singer, 1930s. See "Cypress Grove Blues" in Sackheim 1969: 177.

Usage: "Well the old people told me / baby, but I never did know / The Good Book declares you've got to / reap just what you sow."

Infmnt: Curley Weaver, blues singer. See Weaver 1979.

Usage: "And you mistreat me baby / you drove me from your door. / And the Good Book tell you baby / Ummm, you bound to reap what just what you sow." In text: 95.

Infmnt: Lucille Bogan, blues singer. See Bogan 1934.

Usage: "You may be beautiful but, baby, you got to die some day / And you going to reap what you sow for treating me this a-way." See Taft 1994: 235.

Infmnt: Mississippi Bracey, blues singer. See Bracey 1930.

Usage: "You scold me, faro, now; drove all from your door / Well the Good Book say you got to reap just what you sow." See Taft 1994: 235.

Infmnt: Blind Boy Fuller, blues singer. See Fuller 1935.

Usage: "Mind, mama, what you sow/You got to reap just what you sow." See Taft 1994: 235.

Infmnt: Clifford Gibson, blues singer. See Gibson 1929.

Usage: "Oh it seems so different; you don't care for me no more / But some day, baby, you're going to reap just what you sow." See Taft 1994: 235.

Infmnt: Bill Gillum, blues singer. See Gillum 1939.

Usage: "That's why I'm leaving; I ain't got no place to go / Because the Good Book says you going to reap just what you sow." See Taft 1994: 235.

Infmnt: Bertha Henderson, blues singer. See Henderson 1928.

Usage: "Lord, Lord, can't rest no place I go / Blues is driving me crazy; must be reaping what I sow." See Taft 1994: 235.

Infmnt: Tommy Johnson, blues singer. See Johnson 1928.

Usage: "Says Good Book tell you, reap just what you sow / Going to reap it now or, baby, reap it by-and-by." See Taft 1994: 235.

Infmnt: Tommy McClennan, blues singer. See McClennan 1941.

Usage: "But that's al right, babe, got to reap just what you sow / But don't forget that night I knocked upon you door." See Taft 1994: 235.

Infmnt: Charlie Patton, blues singer. See Patton 1929.

Usage: "Yes I cried last night, and I ain't going to cry no more / But the Good Book tell us, you got to reap just what you sow." See Taft 1994: 235.

Infmnt: Bessie Smith, blues singer. See Smith 1927.

Usage: "I want to take a journey to the devil down below / I done killed my man; I want to reap just what I sow." See Taft 1994: 160.

Infmnt: Trixie Smith, blues singer. See Smith 1925.

Usage: "Please come back and love me like you used to; I think about you every day / You reap just what you sow in the sweet by-and-by, and be sorry that you went away." See Taft 1994: 236.

Infmnt: Frank Stokes, blues singer. See Stokes 1928.

Usage: "Now you mistreat me; oh baby, drove me from you door / Now the Good Book say, mama, you got to reap just what you sow." See Taft 1994: 236.

Infmnt: Ramblin' Thomas, blues singer. See Thomas 1928.

Usage: "Oh my mama told me when I first left her door / Said be careful in your traveling son; you got to reap just what you sow." See Taft 1994: 236.

Infmnt: Robert Wilkins, blues singer. See Wilkins 1935.

Usage: "Oh baby, I'm so glad that this whole round world do know / That every living creature, mmm, reap just what they sow." See Taft 1994: 236.

Infmnt: Sonny Boy Williamson, blues singer. See Williamson 1938.

Usage: "Now Miss Louisa, she mistreated me, and she drove me from her door / Now that will be all right; Louisa, you will have to reap just what you sow." See Taft 1994: 236.

Infmnt: Gracie, fictional character in Toni Cade Bambara's *The Salt Eaters*. See Bambara 1980: 69.

Usage: "A matter of reap what you sow, I guess." *Used to mean that medical epidemics are a result of the white scientific community's playing around and experimenting with viruses.

Infmnt: Black slaves, slavery and postbellum period, spirituals.

Usage: "You shall reap jes' what you sow, Brother / You shall reap jes' what you sow, / On the mountain, in the valley / You shall reap jes / what you sow." *Referent unclear. See Lovell 1972: 117, 126.

Annot: AP 591; BH 61; BR 92; DA 10; DSDJ 499; OX 757; NC 479; T S687; Galations 6:7; WH 585:S364, "As one sows . . ."; SN 61; BA 117; ST 2179:4; BRU 117; MKH 554-555; WT 408; SM 208.

A stitch in time saves nine.

Infmnt: Hawkins Ingram, 30, student, Oakland, California, 10-29-74. From mother, Texas. Berkeley Archives.

Usage: *Do what is supposed to be done when it is due so that the task will not multiply itself by virtue of the delay.

Infmnt: Dorothy Bishop. Collected in Oakland, 8-88, by Prahlad. From grandmother, Texas.

Usage: Same as above.

Infmnt: Malindy Smith, ex-slave. See Rawick 1972: S. S. 1, v. 10, Miss.,
          1.
Usage: In text: 71.
Annot: AP 603; BH 69:1; DA 3:43; NC 481; OX 775; TW 354; WH
          595:S460; BR 93; HA 462; SN 93; ST 2216:6; BA 173; TA 14;
          MKH 564; SM 213; WT 415.

Rolling stones gather no moss.

Infmnt: La Churance Boyd Davis, 21, Berkeley, California, 2-6-69.
          Berkeley Archives.
Usage: "Don't stay in one place too long, keep pushing."
Infmnt: Marvin Barbour, 40. Berkeley Archives.
Usage: "Used to a depressed person to get them going."
Infmnt: Sheri Grant, 22. Berkeley Archives.
Usage: "If you don't keep working, your mind will stagnate."
Infmnt   Dorothy Bishop. Collected by Prahlad in Oakland, California.
Usage:
Infmnt: Ex-slave. See Rawick 1972: S. S. 2, v. 7, Tex., 2593.
Usage: "They say a rollin' stone gathers no moss." In text: 59.
Infmnt: Charlie Nickerson, blues singer. See Nickerson 1930.
Usage: "You quit me, pretty mama, because you couldn't be my boss /
          But a rolling stone don't gather no moss." See Taft 1994: 239. In
          text: 110.
Infmnt: Johnnie Temple, blues singer. See Temple 1937.
Usage: "Louise got ways like a rolling stone / When she leave a man, he
          have to grieve and moan." See Taft 1994: 239. In text: 110.
Annot: AP 537; DA 3:48; NC 481; OX 682; ST 2218-2219:6; TW 355.
          Blues singer Muddy Waters based one of his better-known songs
          on this proverb. The song "Rolling Stone" inspired the famous
          rock group to name themselves the Rolling Stones (Waters 1950);
          BA 173; BR 93; HA 461; SN 73; TA 44; T S885; MKH 565; WH
          597:S484; BRU 134; PAR 462:121, pt. 3, Grenada, "Rolling stone
          ketch no moss but him gader polish all de same"; R & B song,
          "Papa Was a Rollin' Stone"; SM 193; WT 416.

The straw that broke the camel's back.
Infmnt: Clara Abrams. Collected by Prahlad.

Usage: *The last thing, after a large number of previous factors, which sends a situation over the edge.

Infmnt: Ophelia Jemison, 80s, ex-slave. See Rawick 1972: S. S. 1, vol. 11, 212.

Usage: "It was de straw dat broke de camel's back." In text: 65.

Annot: TW 54, "That order jest broke the camel's back"; AP 351; HY 330; OX 443; NC 482; T F158, "feather/horse"; WH 600:S503, "The last straw that broke the camel's back"; ST 2226; BA 174; BRU 20; MKH 567.

Different strokes for different folks.

Infmnt: Dorothy Bishop. Collected by Prahlad.

Usage: *One way of being or of doing things will not work for everybody. In text: 129.

Infmnt: Norma Geraldine Jett, 58, Richmond, California, 5-18-89.

Usage: "All people don't like the same thing."

Infmnt: Male student, 30, student union game room, Richmond, Virginia. Collected by Prahlad.

Usage: Said in defense of another student who is in an interracial relationship and being criticized for it. In text: 179.

Annot: BH 63; also the name of a recent television sitcom, "Different Strokes"; MKH 569.

Talk is cheap.

Infmnt: Kokane, hip hop artist. See Kokane 1991.

Usage: "Talk is cheap."

Infmnt: Jerome Holloway, instructional assistant, Oakland, California. Collected by Prahlad.

Usage: *Used in reponse to the rumor that school employees would be getting a raise.

Annot: BH 68; MKH 581; TW 365; WH 612.

As de tree fall dar mus it lay.

Infmnt: Male, preacher. See Hatcher 1908: 175.
Usage:

Infmnt: James and Lucky Peterson, blues singers. See Peterson 1972.

Usage: "The way a tree falls, that's the way it lie. / The way a man live, that's the way he die." In text: 113.

Annot: AP 644-645; NC 489, "As the tree falls, so shall it lie"; T T503; MKH 610; ST 2368: 6; WH 452; WS 261:1; AC 114:1302, "Where de exe fall de tree, dere shall it lay"; OX 505; WT 452; ST 2368:6; SM 229.

If you fool with trash, it'll get in your eyes.

Infmnt: Clara Abrams. Collected by Prahlad.

Usage: *If a person associates with people of bad character, they'll become like those people, and they'll get into bad situations. In text: 145.

Infmnt: Male, deacon, 60s. Collected by Prahlad in Hanover, Virginia, 1976.

Usage: "Fool with trash, it'll sure get in your eyes, ain't that what they say?"

Annot: NC 489, "If you associate with trash, you'll flounder with trash"; DA 11:27, "If you play . . ."; MKH 608, "blow in our eyes."

Don't trouble trouble until trouble troubles you.

Infmnt: David Roth, 28, psychiatrist, Albany, California, 7-17-71. Berkeley Archives.

Usage: "Don't rock the boat, let sleeping dogs lie, would be in the same vein."

Infmnt: Jean Folly. Collected in Virginia by Prahlad.

Usage: "Don't trouble trouble and trouble won't trouble you." *Don't look for problems, don't stir up problems and you'll be less likely to be bothered by them.

Annot: AP 646; BR 73; DA 7:12; DSDJ 503 (Never trouble trouble . . .); NC 489; WH 645:T280; SN 83; BA 187; ST 2377: 7; HO 132; AC 115:1312, "Nebber trouble trouble till trouble trouble you"; MKH 612; SM 230.

Let every tub sit on its own bottom.

Infmnt: Elzadia Jamerson, 49, nurse, Berkeley, California, 11-3-74. From mother. Berkeley Archives.

Usage:

Infmnt: Charlene Thayer, 46. Berkeley Archives.

Usage: "Every tub stands on its own bottom. Everyone should be able to stand on his own two feet, be self-reliant. If someone who is lazy were to stand on Telegraph Avenue and ask for handouts simply because he did not want to work, people passing would have every right to refuse him money and to say, 'Every tub stands on his own bottom.' "

Infmnt: Mildred Glover, Richmond, California, 3-1-74, Oakland. House-wife. Learned in Oakland, California in family. Berkeley Archives.

Usage: "Every tub stands on its own bottom. Each person carries his own weight . . . responsible for seeing that your own needs are met."

Annot: AP 193; BH 67, "Every feet must stand on its own bottom"; NC 490; OX 845; ST 2397:4; TW 384; BR 96; GR 22; HA 463; TA 65; T T596; WH 649:T306, (tub, barrel); SN 93; BA 188; MKH 618; FR 101:126, "Ebery tub sit down pon him own bottom"; WT 456; SM 232; ST 2397:4.

Every man should live under his own vine and fig tree.

Infmnt: Jim Allen, male, ex-slave. See Rawick 1972: S. S. 1, v. 6, Miss., 13. In text: 61.

Usage:

Infmnt: Ex-slave. See Rawick 1972: S. 1, v. 4, Tex., pts. 1 and 2, 189-190.

Usage: "Every man has to serve God under his own vine and fig tree." In text: 61.

Annot: None to date.

An empty wagon rattles.

Infmnt: Roy Smith, 51, vulcanizer, Berkeley, California, 6-20-71. Berkeley Archives.

Usage: *Used to refer to people who talk a lot. "A talkative person is like an empty wagon that rattles because that person has nothing important to say but keeps on prattling endlessly about nothing."

Infmnt: Female, 40, teacher, Ashland, Virginia, 1972. Collected by Prahlad.

Usage: *Used as "Empty wagons make the most noise," to a student who talked too much in class. Implied that the student didn't have very much in his head—"empty wagon."

Annot: AP 182; BE 47; BR 72; DA 28, "An empty wagon/pitcher makes a lot of noise"; DSDJ 503, "An empty wagon makes a lot of noise"; HA 464; OX 20; NC 491, "rattles most"; "empty vessels make the most sound"; "rumbles loud"; "a leary/light cart maketh the most noise"; WH 661:W3, "Empty wagons make the most noise"; BR 101 (barrel); TW 391 (vessel); BA 10; T V36; MKH 637; ST 676:17; FR 101:168, "Holla goadie mek de mos' noise"; HO 128 (empty barrel); WS 186:44 (barrel); SM 64.

It'll all come out in the wash.

Infmnt: Clara Abrams. Collected by Prahlad.
Usage: *Used to mean that eventually the truth will come out. Used especially to refer to situations where there is a question of a coverup.

Infmnt: Allane Dixon, 50, assistant supervisor, U. C. B. Library, Berkeley, California, 11-12-75. From mother, Louisiana. Berkeley Archives.
Usage: "What does not come out in the wash, comes out in the rinse. Whatever you are trying to keep secret will eventually become known to all, i.e., Watergate."

Annot: WH 664:W25, "To come out in the wash"; SN 93; BA 192; ST 2455:13; OX 135; MKH 640.

Still waters run deep.

Infmnt: Lulu B. Perovich, 72, retired teacher's aid, Berkeley 11-21-79. From Alto, Texas. Berkeley Archives.
Usage: "Silent person is a deep thinker. Therefore, don't play that person for a fool."

Infmnt: Dorothy Bishop. Collected by Prahlad.
Usage: *Don't underestimate people who are quiet. They may be very profound and intense people.

Infmnt: Female character in Naylor's *Mama Day*. See Naylor 1988:245.
Usage: "Still waters run deep."

Annot: AP 602-603; BH 70:33; BR 96; DA 11 (water/runs,); HA 464; OX 775; TA 67; T W123; NC 493; WH 666:W42; SN 74; TW 394; BA 193; MKH 642; ST 1894:3; AC 101:1145, "Sof'ly riber run deep"; BT 42:67; FR 105:318; HO 120; WT 471; SM 213.

You never miss your water 'til your well runs dry.

Infmnt: Laura Tallie. Collected in Oakland, California, by Prahlad.

Usage: In text: 153.

Infmnt: Harvey Nolen Loyd, 24, Berkeley, California, 12-4-69. From Des Moines, Iowa, 1955. Berkeley Archives.

Usage: "After living at home and having your folks take care of you, one day you'll have to get out in the world and take care of yourself. Then you realize how good it was at home."

Infmnt: Mary Golden, 27, student, Oakland, California, 2-23-74. From mother, Mississippi, when she was 12. Berkeley Archives.

Usage: "You don't miss your water 'til the well runs dry. You don't miss or appreciate a good person until you lose him." Her mother used it upon hearing the news that her aunt had divorced her husband.

Infmnt: LaChurance Boyd Davis, 21, 11-27-68. From older relatives, Lake Water, Texas, 1951. Berkeley Archives.

Usage: "You never miss your water 'til the well runs dry. You don't know what you've achieved in life until it's gone in one sweep."

Infmnt: Earkie Lee Moss, 51, government employee, San Francisco, California, 1968. From mother, Texas, 1925. Berkeley Archives.

Usage: "You never miss your water 'til your well goes dry. You don't pay much attention to something until you don't have it anymore. You could use it in a case where someone's husband's left her and now she all of a sudden starts talkin' about him, when you never heard her mention his name before."

Infmnt: Dorothy Bishop. Collected by Prahlad.

Usage: Same as above.

Infmnt: L. C. Williams, blues singer.

Usage: "Yes you never miss your water, water, water / baby till your well's gone dry / Yes you never miss your loved one/ son, until she says goodbye" See Sackheim 1969: 126. In text: 86.

Infmnt: Skip James, blues singer. See James 1966.

Usage: "You never miss your water / till your well runs dry / I never miss crow Jane / till the day she died."

Infmnt: Kokomo Arnold, blues singer. See Arnold 1935.

Usage: "Says I never missed my water, not until my well run dry / Says I never missed sweet Annie, not until she said goobye." See Taft 1994: 238.

Infmnt: Huddie Ledbetter, blues singer. See Ledbetter 1935.

Usage: "You don't miss your water 'til your well go dry / You don't miss pretty mama 'til you shake your hand goodbye." See Taft 1994: 238.

Infmnt: Walter Vincson, blues singer. See Vincson 1932.

Usage: "There's no use to grieve, no use to cry / You sure miss your water honey, when your well go dry." See Taft 1994: 238.

Infmnt: Male blues singer. See Evans 1982: 54.

Usage: In text: 88.

Annot: AP 670; BH 63 (You don't miss . . .); BR 97; HA 465; NC 493; WH 666:W41, " . . . not to miss the water 'till the well runs dry"; OX 344; ST 2459:2; MKH 642; WS 131:98; AC 116:1342, "Man nebber know de use a water till de tank dry"; SM 152.

Only a squeaking wheel gets the grease.

Infmnt: Carrie Williams, 27, nurse. Berkeley, California, 4-27-64. Berkeley Archives.

Usage: "If you have something to complain about do it loudly enough and long enough and something will be done about it."

Infmnt: Charlene Thayer. Berkeley Archives.

Usage: "The squeaky hinge gets the oil. If one needs or wants attention, he's got to ask for it. Go after the things you need or want."

Annot: WH 678:W128, "The squeaky wheel (axle, gate) gets the grease," varied; ST 2483:6; MKH 650.

A whistling woman and a crowing hen will not come to good.

Infmnt: Evelyn Allan, 37, Berkeley, California, 11-6-74. From Kansas. Berkeley Archives.

Usage: "Just as a chicken is going in the pot to fry, so will a woman if she don't act like a lady."

Infmnt: Student, Berkeley, California, 11-20-79. From father, Iuka, Mississippi, 1934. Berkeley Archives.

Usage: "A crowing hen and a whistling woman come to no good."

Infmnt: Female, 64, housewife, Oakland, California, 10-31-71. From mother, Chicago, Illinois, and Montgomery, Georgia. Berkeley Archives.

Usage: "Whistling girls and cackling hens, come to no good ends. When girls whistled they weren't acting ladylike and it might interfere with them getting a young man interested in them."

Infmnt: Phyllis Carroll, 25, student, Oakland, 11-74. From aunt, Ellenboro, North Carolina, 1963. Berkeley Archives.

Usage: "Whistling women and crowin' hens never come to no good en'."

Infmnt: Leann Johnson, 27, nurse, San Francisco, California, 11-1-77. From grandfather. Berkeley Archives.

Usage: "Whistling kids and cackling hens all come to no good end."

Infmnt: Lettie Frieson, 55, nurse, Norce, California, 11-21-84. From mother, Jasper, Alabama, 1940. Berkeley Archives.

Usage: "A whistling woman or a crowing hen, would never come to a good end."

Annot: AP 680; BH 71:67; BR 97; ASDJ 503; GR 18; OX 155; TA 35, 61, 72 (girl); NC 495-496; ST 2505:5; BA 75; MKH 651, (girl); WH 305; SM 245.

White folks got the money and niggers got all the signs.

Infmnt: Juliaette Robinson, 46, machinist, Richmond, California, 7-74. Berkeley Archives.

Usage: "This told of the economic situation, it was said at that point in time Black folks had little or no money, but superstitions were always being told about something or other."

Infmnt: Lou Posey, 37, Berkeley, California, 11-28-70. Berkeley Archives.

Usage: "The niggers got all the signs and the white man got all the money." "The informant claims that this is a common saying in all black communities, throughout the U.S. This saying reflects the common belief among blacks that white people do not have superstitions, but teach superstitions to blacks to keep them in an inferior social and economic position."

Infmnt: Fictional character in Zora Neale Hurston's *Jonah's Gourd Vine*. See Hurston [1934] 1987: 289.

Usage: Mrs. Lovelace is reflecting on her own superstition after inviting John, the main character, to sit down on her step. "Naw, it 'taint. If you set on de steps you'll git all de pains in de house. Ha, ha! Ah reckon you say niggers got all de signs and white folks got all de money."

Annot: None found to date.

Where's there's a will there's a way.

Infmnt: Little Buddy Doyle, blues singer. See Doyle 1939.

Usage: "Good Book trying to tell us, where's there's a will, there's a way / But it seem like the many ways draining out of me more and more every day." See Taft 1994: 241. In text: 117.

Infmnt: Matthew Boyd, 45, insurance salesman, Columbia, Misouri. Collected by Prahlad, 3-94.

Usage: Used to encourage himself to remain positive when discouraged about living in Tennessee. (He had relocated from Oakland to Tennessee and found it difficult to acclimate to the new environment.)

Annot: DA 4, 12; MKH 655; OX 891; TW 402; SM 245; ST 2510:12; WH 683.

Notes

CHAPTER ONE

1. Yankah (1989a: 78–79) notes that proverbs among the Akan are often used to reject the rhetoric or meaning of the proverbial wisdom, a usage that is also found among African-American speakers. Such instances indicate clearly that one cannot draw conclusions about the values of speakers simply from the texts of proverbs.

2. See Hain 1951. Unfortunately, my competence in German is not sufficient to allow me to read this work critically.

CHAPTER TWO

1. See Rawick 1972. This work is composed of published texts of interviews with ex-slaves conducted by the Federal Writers' Project in 1936–1938. Rawick's original compilation consisted of volumes 1–19, Series 1 and Series 2. Subsequent volumes are entitled Supplemental Series 1 and Supplemental Series 2. Between the original and subsequent volumes, these extensive sets include material from every region of the United States. I have surveyed all of the original volumes and all but a few of the supplemental ones. In the passages cited the emphasis is mine.

2. Rawick writes, "The narratives were tapping an oral tradition about slavery among black people, as well as the 'memories' of those who had been born as slaves. They provide a link between personal recollection on the one hand and 'common knowledge,' lore and folksay, on the other, as historical source material" (S. S. 1, v. 3, Ga., pt. 1, p. xix).

3. William Bascom has discussed this tale in depth, documenting it as an example of a tale of African origin. See "African Folktales in America: 1. The Talking Skull Refuses to Talk," in *Research in African Literatures* 8, no. 2 (1977): 266–291. Reprinted in William R. Bascom, *Contributions to Folkloristics* (Meerut: Folklore Institute, 1981), pp. 185–211.

4. This strategy is similar to that found among the Akan of West Africa. See Yankah 1989: 171.

5. Rawick 1972: S. S. 1, v. 3, Ga., pt. 1, 49, and S. S. 1, v. 4, Ga. pt. 2, 488.

6. For a complete volume of conversion narratives see Clifton H. Johnson, ed., *God Struck Me Dead* (Philadelphia: Pilgrim Press, 1969).

7. See Kirshenblatt-Gimblett (1973) for a discussion of this proverb.

8. Mieder (1989: 195–221) discusses this proverbial expression, giving an example of it in a mid-nineteenth-century song entitled "Root, Hog, or Die." Originally published as "Proverbs in American Popular Songs," *Proverbium* 5 (1988): 85–86.

CHAPTER THREE

1. Smith's discussion of fictive and natural discourse is especially helpful in establishing a distinction between the two types of discourse. She writes, "By 'natural discourse' I mean here all utterances—trivial or sublime, ill-wrought or eloquent, true or false, scientific or passionate—that can be taken as someone's saying something, somewhere, sometime, that is, as the verbal acts of real persons or particular occasions in response to particular sets of circumstances" (1978: 15–16).

2. Other scholars have discussed structural similarities between proverbs and other conversational genres. See, for example, Roger D. Abrahams, "A Rhetoric of Everyday Life: Traditional Conversational Genres," *Southern Folklore Quarterly* 32 (1968): 48–59; and Alan Dundes, "On the Structure of the Proverb," *Proverbium* 25 (1975): 961–973. See also Alan Dundes, *Analytic Structures in Folklore* (The Hague: Mouton, 1975), pp. 103–118; and Wolfgang Mieder and Alan Dundes, eds., *The Wisdom of Many: Essays on the Proverb* (New York: Garland Publishing, 1981), pp. 43–64.

3. Taft (1994:237) refers to such lines as "proverb-formulas."

4. Many scholars have described this propensity of Africana speakers. See Hurston ([1934] 1969: 39–46); Abrahams (1976); Smitherman (1986); and Kochman (1970: 145–162).

5. Ferris is one scholar who has drawn this comparison. He writes that "[g]riots are traveling African musicians whose songs preserve tribal stories and legal codes," and that "African griots, slave singers, and country and urban bluesmen share a common musical tradition as their lyrics speak of movement across land and water and the singer's separation from loved ones" (1978: 25, 182). See also Paul Oliver, *Savannah Syncopators* (London: Studio Vista, 1970), pp. 43–55.

6. The spiritual verse "You shall reap jes' what you sow, Brother (Sister, Sinner) / You shall reap jes' what you sow / On the mountain, in the valley / You shall reap jes' what you sow" may have been sung to warn a fellow member of the enslaved community to be careful of his/her actions, or may have been directed toward whites. Without emic information we can only speculate. This,

however, represents the only stanza of a spiritual that contains a traditional proverb. See Lovell 1972: 117, 126.

7. For printed texts of sermons, see Zora Neale Hurston, *Mules and Men* (Philadelphia: J. P. Lippincott, 1935); William Harrison Pipes, *Say Amen Brother!* (New York: William Frederick Press, 1951); Courlander (1976); Brewer (1968); Hughes and Bontemps (1958); and Bradford (1935: 16–17).

8. I am assuming that the references to "the Nation" and "the Territo'" here signify the pre-1912 Indian territory of Oklahoma; thus, the verse is a depiction of obvious American social injustices.

9. It may be significant that the proverb is changed from "rules the world," to "rules the home." See appendix.

10. Examples of proverbs in soul and rhythm and blues include Tyrone Davis's "What Goes Up Must Come Down" (see Ferris [1978:73]); Aretha Franklin's "For every chain there's a weak link" and "A slip of the lip will sink a ship" from her popular song "Chain, Chain, Chain," and "Still waters runs deep" from the song by the same title; Clarence Carter's "Lovin' eyes can never see" from "When a Man Loves a Woman," and numerous others, mainly from the height of Motown's popularity in the 1970s.

CHAPTER FOUR

1. Although the heaviest period of concentration on my collection occurred while I was working on my dissertation, I actually began collecting in my adolescence. I was always interested in proverbs and collected them from my great-grandmother and from magazines and calendars. The formal period of collection began after I took a folklore class from Dr. Daryl Dance in 1975 at Virginia Commonwealth University in Richmond, Virginia. Thus, some of the examples referred to in this study predate my declaring of proverbs as the focus of my dissertation research and the beginning of rigorous collection efforts. Some of the speech events that occurred in those years in Virginia are approximations, which I have recalled with as much accuracy as possible. Most of those recorded in California were written down immediately after I heard them.

2. Abrahams (1974: 240–262) discusses the distinctions between African-American speech behavior as it occurs in the home and on the street, suggesting that the former is characterized by decorum and the latter by loud talking and play. I am not in complete agreement with Abrahams on the degree to which this distinction holds true.

3. See Smitherman 1986. Cultural continuities proposed by early scholars such as Janhetz Jan and Herskovits have been amplified by more recent works such as Levine (1977) and Vlach (1991).

4. The interview was conducted at Mrs. Bishop's home in Oakland, California, on August 6, 1988.

5. Mieder (1989: 317–333) devotes a chapter to the proverb "Different strokes for different folks." He argues the African-American origin of the proverb, saying that its meaning is "that people are entitled to or insist on living their lives the way they see fit."

6. Peter Seitel has compared proverb usage to shamanistic rituals, focusing on the rhetorical, diversionary strategy of the two. See "Proverbs and the Structure of Metaphor among the Haya of Tanzania," Ph. D. diss. (University of Pennsylvania, 1972), 251.

7. Levine (1977: 3–80) discusses this component of early African-American religion, arguing that the worldview of slaves encompassed the mythological and real figures and events from the past and that these were considered a part of the present. According to him, this expansive and sacred view of time gave way to a more secular and limited view beginning around the antebellum period. I suggest that closer scrutiny of particular rituals in certain contexts reveals that this perception has not entirely disappeared.

8. This function is similar to what Bronner (1985: 126–144) observed pertaining to elderly chain carvers. Carving often reminded them of experiences in their youth and helped them to cope with the anxiety of aging and isolation.

9. Another item, "Lauros catch meddlers," was also used in this way. See Folly (1982:240).

Chapter Five

1. Mitchell-Kernan and Kernan (1977: 189–208) have written about children's insults and directives in children's speech. Their research touches on the proliferation of aggressive speech acts and the associations of power inherent in these that may influence their frequency.

2. This phrase was taken from a television commercial advertising a fast-food hamburger restaurant. The question referred to competitors' hamburgers and implied that they were less substantial and contained a lower percentage of beef. Ironically, this commercial was an innovation on the expression "What's your beef?", a metaphorical reference to an issue or problem. Around the school, children used it in any situation in which there was some insufficiency involved, usually to tease or insult one another. For example, a boy might say it about a girl to indicate that she was not attractive. Or members of one team might say it to the other team to imply that they weren't very good players. Very young children, such as those in first through third grades, often applied the expression incorrectly, but nevertheless enjoyed saying it. See Barrick (1986: 43–46).

3. "Insults" are another related children's genre. For a discussion of insults and their relationship to values, see Mitchell-Kernan and Kernan (1975: 307–315).

4. I base this statement on works by such authors as Toni Morrison, Alice Walker, Zora Neale Hurston, Toni Cade Bambara, and Paule Marshall. There are in these works few occasions of aggressive, competitive interactions between women of the sort that characterize many male encounters.

References

Abrahams, Roger D. 1963. *Deep Down In the Jungle*. Chicago: Aldine Publishing Co.

———. 1968a. "A Rhetoric of Everyday Life: Traditional Conversational Genres." *Southern Folklore Quarterly* 32: 48–59.

———. 1968b. "Introductory Remarks to a Rhetorical Theory of Folklore." *Journal of American Folklore* 81: 143–158.

———. 1970. "Patterns of Performance in the British West Indies." In *Afro-American Anthropology*, ed. Norman E. Whitten, Jr., and John F. Szwed, pp. 163–180. New York: The Free Press.

———. 1972a. "Proverbs and Proverbial Expressions." In *Folklore and Folklife: An Introduction*, ed. Richard M. Dorson, pp. 117–127. Chicago: University of Chicago.

———. 1972b. "Joking: The Training of the Man of Words in Talking Broad." In *Rappin' and Stylin' Out*, ed. Thomas Kochman, pp. 215–240. Urbana: University of Illinois Press.

———. 1974. "Black Talking on the Streets." In *Explorations in the Ethnography of Communication*, ed. Richard Bauman and Joel Sherzer, pp. 240–262. London: Cambridge University Press.

———. 1976. *Talking Black*. Rowley: Newbury House Publishers.

———. 1983. *The Man-of-Words in the West Indies*. Baltimore: The Johns Hopkins University Press.

Achebe, Chinua. 1959. *Things Fall Apart*. Greenwich: Fawcett Crest.

———. 1967. *A Man of the People*. New York: Doubleday.

———. 1969. *Arrow of God*. New York: Anchor Books.

Albertson, Chris. 1975. *Bessie Smith, Empress of the Blues*. New York: Schirmer Books.

Albig, William. 1931. "Proverbs and Social Control." *Sociology and Social Research* 15: 527–535.

Alexander, Tamar, and Galit Hasan-Rokem. 1988. "Games of Identity in Proverb Usage: Proverbs of a Sephardic-Jewish Woman." *Proverbium* 5: 1–14.

Allen, William Francis, Charles Pickard Ware, and Lucy McKim Garrison.

[1867] 1965. *Slave Songs of the United States*. Reprint, New York: Oak Publications.

Anderson, Izett, and Frank Cundall. 1927. *Jamaica Negro Proverbs and Sayings*. Jamaica: The Institute of Jamaica.

Angelou, Maya. 1970. *I Know Why the Caged Bird Sings*. New York: Random House.

Apperson, G. L. 1929. *English Proverbs and Proverbial Phrases*. London: J.M. Dent and Sons.

Arewa, E. Ojo. 1970. "Proverb Usage in a 'Natural' Context and Oral Literary Criticism." *Journal of American Folklore* 83: 430–437.

Arewa, E. Ojo, and Alan Dundes. 1964. "Proverbs and the Ethnography of Speaking Folklore." *American Anthropologist* 66, part 2, no. 6: 70–85. Reprinted in *Essays in Folkloristics*, ed. Alan Dundes, pp. 50–70. Meerut: Folklore Institute, 1978.

Armstrong, R. Plant. 1971. *The Affecting Presence: An Essay in Humanistic Anthropology*. Urbana: University of Illinois Press.

———. 1993. *The Powers of Presence*. Philadelphia: University of Pennsylvania Press.

Arora, Shirley L. 1982. "Proverbs in Mexican American Tradition." *Aztlan* 13: 43–69.

———. 1984. "The Perception of Proverbiality." *Proverbium: Yearbook of International Proverb Research* 1: 1–38. Reprinted in *Wise Words: Essays on the Proverb*, ed. Wolfgang Mieder, pp. 3–29. New York: Garland Publishing, Inc., 1994.

———. 1994. "Proverbs and Prejudice: El Indio in Hispanic Proverbial Speech." *Proverbium* 11: 27–46.

Bambara, Toni Cade. 1980. *The Salt Eaters*. New York: Random House.

Barbour, Francis. 1965. *Proverbs and Proverbial Phrases of Illinois*. Carbondale: Southern Illinois Press.

Bard, Marjorie. 1992. "Relating Intrapersonal Storying (Idionarrating) and Interpersonal Communicating." *Southern Folklore* 49: 61–72.

Barley, Nigel. 1972. "A Structural Approach to the Proverb and Maxim with Special Reference to the Anglo-Saxon Corpus." *Proverbium* 20: 737–750.

———. 1974. "The Proverb and Related Problems of Genre-Definition." *Proverbium* 23: 880–884.

Barlow, William. 1989. *Looking Up and Down: The Emergence of Blues Culture*. Philadelphia: Temple University Press.

Barnes, Daniel R. 1979. "Telling It Slant: Emily Dickinson and the Proverb." *Genre* 12: 219–241. Reprinted in *Wise Words: Essays on the Proverb*, ed. Wolfgang Mieder, pp. 439–465. New York: Garland Publishing, Inc., 1994.

Barnes-Harden, Alene Leett. 1980. "African American Verbal Arts: Their

Nature and Communicative Interpretation (A Thematic Analysis)." Ph.D. diss., State University of New York at Buffalo.

Barrick, Mac E. 1986. "'Where's the Beef'?" *Midwestern Journal of Language and Folklore* 12: 43–46.

Barton, William E. 1899. *Old Plantation Hymns*. Boston: Lamson, Wolffe and Company.

Bascom, William R. 1954. "Four Functions of Folklore." *Journal of American Folklore* 67: 333–349.

———. 1965. "Stylistic Features of Proverbs, a Comment." *Journal of American Folklore* 78: 69.

———. 1972. "Shango in the New World." In *Occasional Publication of the African and Afro-American Research Institute* No. 4, p. 14. Austin: University of Texas.

———. 1977. "Oba's Ear: A Yoruba Myth in Cuba and Brazil." In *African Folklore in the New World*, ed. Daniel J. Crowley, pp. 3–19. Austin: University of Texas Press.

Basgoz, Ilhan. 1993. "Proverb Image, Proverb Message, and Social Change." *Journal of Folklore Research* 30: 127–142.

Basso, Keith H. 1976. "Wise Words of the Western Apache: Metaphor and Semantic Theory." In *Meaning in Anthropology*, ed. K.H. Basso and Henry A. Selby, pp. 93–121. Albuquerque: University of New Mexico Press.

———. 1979. *Portraits of the "Whiteman": Linguistic Play and Cultural Symbols Among the Western Apache*. New York: Cambridge University Press.

Bates, William C. 1896. "Creole Folklore from Jamaica." *Journal of American Folklore* 9: 38–42.

Bauman, Richard. 1977. *Verbal Art As Performance*. Reprint, Prospect Heights, Ill.: Waveland Press, 1984.

———. 1983. "The Field Study of Folklore in Context." In *Handbook of American Folklore*, ed. Richard Dorson. Bloomington: Indiana University Press.

———. 1986. *Story, Performance, and Event: Contextual Studies of Oral Narrative*. Cambridge: Cambridge University Press.

Bauman, Richard, and Neil McCabe. 1970. "Proverbs in an LSD Cult." *Journal of American Folklore* 83: 318–324.

Baumgarten, Franziska. 1952. "A Proverb Test for Attitude Measurement." *Personal Psychology* 5: 249–261.

Beckwith, Martha W. 1925. *Jamaica Proverbs*. New York: Vassar College.

———. 1928. *Jamaica Folklore*. New York: Memoirs of the American Folklore Society.

Ben-Amos, Dan. 1972. "Toward a Definition of Folklore in Context." In *Toward New Perspectives in Folklore*, ed. Americo Paredes and Richard Bauman, pp. 3–19. Austin: University of Texas Press.

———. 1977. "The Context of Folklore: Implications and Prospects." In

Frontiers of Folklore, ed. William Bascom, pp. 36–53. Boulder: Westview Press for the AAAS.

Ben-Amos, Dan, and Kenneth S. Goldstein, eds. 1975. *Folklore: Performance and Communication*. The Hague: Mouton.

Bergmann, Karl. 1936. "Deutsche Heimatliebe und Wandersehnsucht in Sprache und Sprichwort." *Zeitschrift für Deutschkunde* 50: 337–343.

Blassingame, John W. 1972. *The Slave Community*. New York: Oxford University Press.

Bornstein, Valerie. 1991. "A Case Study and Analysis of Family Proverb Use." *Proverbium* 8: 19–28.

Bradford, Roark. 1935. "Swing Low Sweet Chariot." *Colliers* 21 (Sept.): 16–17.

Bradley, Francis W. 1937. "South Carolina Proverbs." *Southern Folklore Quarterly* 1: 57–101.

Brandes, Stanley H. 1974. "The Selection Process in Proverb Use: A Spanish Example." *Southern Folklore Quarterly* 38: 167–186.

Brewer, J. Mason. 1933. "Old Time Negro Proverbs." In *Spur-of-the-Cock*, ed. J. Frank Dobie, pp. 101–105. Austin: Texas Folklore Society. Reprinted in *Mother Wit From the Laughing Barrel*, ed. Alan Dundes, pp. 246–250. Englewood Cliffs, N.J.: Prentice Hall, 1973.

———. 1965. *Worser Days and Better Times*. Chicago: Quadrangle Books.

———. 1968. *American Negro Folklore*. New York: New York Times Book Co.

Brewer, Patricia J. 1973. "Age, Language, Culture, Previous Knowledge and the Proverb as Social Metaphor: A Study in Relationships." Ph.D. diss., University of Pennsylvania.

Brewster, Paul G. 1939. "Folk 'Sayings' from Indiana." *American Speech* 14: 261–268.

Briggs, Charles L. 1980. *The Wood Carvers of Córdova New Mexico: Social Dimensions of an Artistic "Rivival."* Knoxville: University of Tennessee Press.

———. 1985. "The Pragmatics of Proverb Performances in New Mexican Spanish." *American Anthropologist* 87: 793–810. Reprinted in *Wise Words: Essays on the Proverb*, ed. Wolfgang Mieder, pp. 317–349. New York: Garland Publishing, Inc., 1994.

———. 1988. "Proverbs." In *Competence in Performance: The Creativity of Tradition in Mexicano Verbal Art*, pp. 101–135, 380 (notes). Philadelphia: University of Pennsylvania Press.

———. 1993. "Metadiscursive Practices and Scholarly Authority in Folkloristics." *Journal of American Folklore* 106: 387–434.

Bronner, Simon J. 1985. *Chain Carvers: Old Men Crafting Meaning*. Lexington: The University Press of Kentucky.

Brookes, Stella Brewer. [1950] 1970. *Joel Chandler Harris-Folklorist*. Athens: The University of Georgia Press.

Brown, Frank C. 1964. *North Carolina Folklore*. Vol. 7, ed. Wayland D. Hand. Durham: Duke University Press.

Brown, H. Rap. 1972. "Street Talk." In *Rappin' and Stylin' Out*, ed. Thomas Kochman, pp. 205–208. Urbana: University of Chicago Press.

Brown, Sterling A. 1930. "The Blues as Folk Poetry." *Folk-Say* 2: 324–339.

Brunvand, Harold. 1961. *A Dictionary of English Proverbs and Proverbial Phrases from Books Published by Indiana Authors before 1890*. Bloomington: Indiana University Press.

Bryant, Margaret M. 1951. "Proverbial Lore in American Life and Speech." *Western Folklore* 10: 134–142.

Callahan, John F. 1988. *In the African-American Grain: The Pursuit of Voice in Twentieth-Century Black Fiction*. Chicago: University of Illinois Press.

Campbell, Theophine Maria. 1975. "African and Afro-American Proverb Parallels." Master's thesis, University of California at Berkeley.

Carlisle, Natalie Taylor. 1926. "Old Time Darky Plantation Melodies." *Publication of the Texas Folk-Lore Society* No. 5: 137–144.

Carnes, Pack, ed. 1988. *Proverbia in Fabula: Essays on the Relationship of the Fable and the Proverb*. Bern: Peter Lang.

———. 1991. "The Fable and the Proverb: Intertexts and Reception." *Proverbium* 8: 55–76. Reprinted in *Wise Words: Essays on the Proverb*, ed. Wolfgang Mieder, pp. 467–493. New York: Garland Publishing, Inc., 1994.

Carter, Harold A. 1976. *The Prayer Tradition of Black People*. Valley Forge: Judson Press.

Chambers, John W., Jr. 1977. "Proverb Comprehension in Children." Ph.D. diss., University of Cincinnati.

Champion, Selwyn G. 1938. *Racial Proverbs*. London: George Routledge.

Chapman, Abraham, ed. 1972. *New Black Voices*. New York: Mentor Books.

Charters, Samuel B. 1963. *The Poetry of the Blues*. New York: Oak Publications.

———. 1975a. *The Legacy of the Blues*. London: Calder and Boyars.

———. [1959] 1975b. *The Country Blues*. New York: Da Capo Press.

Christensen, James Boyd. 1958. "The Role of Proverbs in Fante Culture." *Africa* 28: 232–243.

Cohn, David D. 1935. *Where I Was Born and Raised*. London: University of Notre Dame Press.

Cone, James H. 1972. *The Spirituals and the Blues*. New York: The Seabury Press.

Courlander, Harold. 1963. *Negro Folk Music, U.S.A.* New York: Columbia University Press.

———. 1976a. *A Treasury of Afro-American Folklore*. New York: Crown Publishers.

———. 1976b. *Afro-American Folklore*. New York: Crown Publishers, Inc.

Craddock, John R. 1954. "Sin-Killer's Sermon." *Publication of the Texas Folklore Society* 26: 175–182.

Crepeau, Pierre. 1978. "The Invading Guest: Some Aspects of Oral Transmission." *Yearbook of Symbolic Anthropology* 1: 11–29. Reprinted in *The Wisdom of Many: Essays on the Proverb*, ed. Wolfgang Mieder and Alan Dundes, pp.86–110. New York: Garland Publishing, 1981.

Crystal, David. 1971. "Prosodic and Paralinguistic Correlates of Social Categories." In *Social Anthropology and Language*, ed. Edwin Ardener, pp. 185–206. London: Tavistock.

Cubelic, Turtko. 1974. "The Characteristics and Limits of Folk Proverbs within the System and Structure of Oral Folk Literature." *Proverbium* (Helsinki) 23: 821–827.

Dance, Daryl C. 1978. *Shuckin' and Jivin': Folklore from Contemporary Black Americans*. Bloomington: Indiana University Press.

Daniel, Jack. 1973. "Towards an Ethnography of Afro-American Proverbial Usage." *Black Lines* 4: 3–12.

———. 1979. *The Wisdom of Sixth Mount Zion from Members of Sixth Mount Zion and Those Who Begot Them*. Pittsburgh: self published.

Daniel, Jack, Geneva Smitherman-Donaldson, and Milford A. Jeremiah. 1987. "Makin' A Way Outa No Way: the Proverb Tradition in the Black Experience." *Journal of Black Studies* 17: 482–508.

Davis, Arthur P., and Saunders Redding, eds. 1971. *Cavalcade: Negro American Writing from 1760 to the Present*. Boston: Houghton Mifflin Co.

Davis, Natalie Zemon. 1975. "Proverbial Wisdom and Popular Errors." In *Society and Culture in Early Modern France*, pp. 227–346. Stanford: Stanford University Press.

Deetz, James. 1977. *In Small Things Forgotten: The Archaeology of Early American Life*. New York: Anchor Press.

Delano, Isaac. 1966. *Yoruba Proverbs: Their Meaning and Usage*. Oxford: Oxford University Press.

de Weever, Jacqueline. 1991. *Mythmaking and Metaphor in Black Women's Fiction*. New York: St. Martin's Press.

Doar, David. 1932. "Negro Proverbs." *The Charleston Museum Quarterly* 2: 1, 23–24.

Dolby-Stahl, Sandra. 1988. "Sour Grapes. Fable, Proverb, Unripe Fruit." In *Proverbia in Fabula: Essays on the Relationship of the Fable and Proverb*, ed. Pack Carnes, pp. 295–309. Bern: Peter Lang.

Donker, Marjorie. 1992. *Shakespeare's Proverbial Themes: A Rhetorical Context for the 'Sententia' as 'Res'*. Westport, Conn.: Greenwood Press.

Dorson, Richard. 1977. "The African Connection: Comments on *African Folklore in the New World*," ed. Daniel J. Crowley, pp. 87–91. Austin: University of Texas Press.

Douglass, Frederick. [1855] 1969. *My Bondage and My Freedom*. New York: Dover Publications, Inc.

Dundes, Alan. 1964. "Text, Texture, and Context," *Southern Folklore Quarterly* 28: 257–265.

———, ed. 1973. *Mother Wit From the Laughing Barrel*. Englewood Cliffs, N.J.: Prentice-Hall Inc.

———. 1975. "On the Structure of the Proverb." *Analytic Essays in Folklore*. The Hague: 103–118. Reprinted in *The Wisdom of Many: Essays on the Proverb*, ed. Wolfgang Mieder and Alan Dundes, pp. 43–64. New York: Garland Publishing, 1981.

———. 1977. "African and Afro-American Tales." In *African Folklore in the New World*, ed. Daniel J. Crowley, pp. 35–53. Austin: University of Texas Press.

Eckert, Rainer. 1982. "Zum Problem der Identität phraseologischer Wendungen." *Linguistische Studien*, Series A, Arbeitsberichte, no. 95: 1–33.

Elchinova, Magdalena. 1988. "Poslovitsite i pogovorkite v plana na ezika i v plana na rechta." *Bulgarski folklor* 14:3, 8–16.

Endstrasser, Vilko. 1991. "Poslovice u kontekstu." *Narodna umjetnost* 28: 159–190.

Epstein, Dena J. 1977. *Sinful Tunes and Spirituals*. Urbana: University of Illinois Press.

Evans, David. 1982. *Big Road Blues: Tradition and Creativity in the Folk Blues*. Berkeley: University of California Press.

Evans-Pritchard, E. E. 1963a. "Meaning in Zande Proverbs." *Man*: 4–7.

———. 1963b. "Sixty-One Zande Proverbs." *Man*: 136–137.

———. 1964. "Zande Proverbs: Final Selection and Comments." *Man*: 1–5.

Fanon, Frantz. [1952] 1967. *Black Skin, White Masks*. New York: Grove Press, Inc. First published in Paris as *Peau Noire, Masques Blancs*.

Fauset, Arthur H. 1931. *Folklore from Nova Scotia*. New York: Memoirs of the American Folk-Lore Society: 24.

Felman, Shoshana. 1983. *The Literary Speech Act*. Ithaca, N.Y.: Cornell University Press.

Ferris, William. 1978. *Blues from the Delta*. London: November Books.

Finnegan, Ruth. 1970. *Oral Literature in Africa*. Oxford: Clarendon Press. One chapter, "Proverbs. The significance and Concept of the Proverb. Form and Style. Content. Occasions and Functions. Specific Examples: Jabo, Zulu; Azande. Conclusion," reprinted in *The Wisdom of Many: Essays on the Proverb*, ed. Wolfgang Mieder and Alan Dundes, pp. 10–42. New York: Garland Publishing, 1981.

Firth, Raymond. 1926. "Proverbs in Native Life, with Special Reference to Those of the Maori." *Folk-lore* 37: 134–153, 245–270.

Fisher, Judith Tougas. 1981. "Adolescent Proverb Comprehension: Racial Similarities and Differences." Ph.D. diss., Florida State University.

Fisher, Miles Mark. 1953. *Negro Slave Songs in the United States*. New York: Cornell University Press.

Fisher, William Arms. 1926. *Seventy Negro Spirituals*. New York: Chas. H. Ditson and Co.

Fleischer, Wolfgang. 1987. "Sur funktionalen Differenzierung von Phraseologismen in der deutschen Gegenwartssprache." In *Beiträge sur allegemeinen und germanistischen Phraseologieforschung*, ed. Jarmo Korhonen, pp. 51–63. Oulu: Oulun Yliopisto.

Folly, Dennis W. 1982. "Getting the Butter From the Duck: Proverbs and Proverbial Expressions in an Afro-American Family." In *A Celebration of American Family Folklore*, ed. Steven J. Zeitlin, Amy J. Kotkin, and Holly Cutting Baker, pp. 232–241. New York: Pantheon Books.

———. 1991. "The Poetry of African-American Proverb Usage: A Speech Act Analysis." Ph.D. diss., University of California at Los Angeles.

Folsom, Steven. 1993a. "A Discography of American Country Music Hits Employing Proverbs: Covering the Years 1986–1992." In *Proceedings for the 1993 Annual Conference of the Southwest/Texas Popular Association*, ed. Sue Poor, pp. 31–42. Stillwater, Okla.: The Association.

———. 1993b. "Form and Function of Proverbs in Four Country Music Hits from 1992." In *Proceedings for the 1993 Annual Conference of the Southwest/Texas Popular Culture Association*, ed. Sue Poor, pp. 27–31. Stillwater, Okla.: The Association.

———. 1993c. "Proverbs in Recent American Country Music: Form and Function in the Hits of 1986–87." *Proverbium* 10:65–88.

Franck, Harry A. 1921. "Jamaica Proverbs." *Dialect Notes* 5, pt. 4: 98–108.

Freud, Sigmund. [1905] 1960. *Jokes and Their Relationship to the Unconscious*. London: The Hogarth Press.

Fry, Gladys Marie. 1975. *Nightriders in Black Folk History*. Knoxville: University of Tennessee Press.

Gaines, Ernest. 1971. *The Autobiography of Miss Jane Pittman*. New York: Dial Press.

Garon, Paul. 1971. *The Devil's Son-in-Law*. London: November Books.

———. 1975. *Blues and the Poetic Spirit*. New York: Da Capo Press.

Gates, Charlene. 1991. "'The Work Is Afraid of Its Master': Proverb As Metaphor for a Basketmaker's Art." *Western Folklore* 50: 255–276.

Gates, Henry Louis. 1988. *The Signifying Monkey: A Theory of Afro-American Literary Criticism*. New York: Oxford University Press.

Georges, Robert A. 1981. "Proverbial Speech in the Air." *Midwestern Journal of Language and Folklore* 7: 39–48.

Giovannini, Maureen J. 1978. "A Structural Analysis of Proverbs in a Sicilian Village." *American Ethnologist* 5: 322–333.

Glassie, Henry. 1975. *Folk Housing in Middle Virginia*. Knoxville: University of Tennessee Press.

Goodwin, Paul D., and Joseph W. Wenzel. 1979. "Proverbs and Practical Reasoning: A Study in Socio-Logic." *Quarterly Journal of Speech* 65: 289–302. Reprinted in *The Wisdom of Many: Essays on the Proverb*, ed. Wolfgang Mieder and Alan Dundes, pp. 140–160. New York: Garland Publishing, 1981.

Gordon, Edward. 1959. *Summarian Proverbs: Glimpses of Everyday Life in Ancient Mesopotamia*. Philadelphia: University Museum, University of Pennsylvania.

Gossen, Gary H. 1973. "Chamula Tzotzil Proverbs: Neither Fish Nor Fowl." In *Meaning in Mayan Languages*, ed. Munro S. Edmonson, pp. 205–233. The Hague. Reprinted in *Wise Words: Essays on the Proverb*, ed. Wolfgang Mieder, pp. 351–391. New York: Garland Publishing Inc., 1994.

Green, Barbara L. 1984. "Solace, Self-Esteem, and Solidarity: The Role of Afro-American Folklore in the Education and Acculturation of Black Americans." *Texas Journal of Education* 11:91–98.

Green, Bennett W. 1899. *Word-book of Virginia Folk-Speech*. Richmond: W. E. Jones.

Green, Thomas, and William Pepicello. 1986. "The Proverb and Riddle as Folk Enthymemes." *Proverbium* 3:33–45.

Grice, H. Paul. 1975. "Logic and Conversations." In *Syntax and Semantics 3: Speech Acts*, ed. P. Cole and J.L. Morgan, pp. 41–58. New York: Academic Press.

Grobler, Gerhardus M. 1994. "The Right to Be Understood: Interpreting the Proverb in an African Society." *Proverbium* 11: 93–102.

Gumperz, John J., and Dell Hymes, eds., 1964. *The Ethnography of Communication. American Anthropologist Special Publication* 66 (6) pt. 2: 2ff.

Gwaltney, John Langston. 1980. *Drylongso*. New York: Random House.

Hain, Mathilda. 1951. *Sprichwort und Volksprache*. Giessen: Wilhelm Schmitz Verlag.

Halliday, M. A. K. 1977. "Text as semantic choice in Social Contexts." In *Grammars and Descriptions*, ed. T.A. van Dijk and J.S. Petöfi, pp. 176–225. Berlin: de Gruter.

Haralambos, Michael. 1970. "Soul Music and Blues: Their Meaning and Relevance in Northern United States Black Ghettos." In *Afro-American Anthropology*, ed. Norman E. Whitten, Jr., and John F. Szwed, pp. 367–383. New York: The Free Press.

Hardie, Margaret. 1925–29. "Proverbs and Proverbial Expressions Current in the United States East of the Missouri and North of the Ohio Rivers." *American Speech* 4: 461–472.

Harmon, Marion F. 1914. *Negro Wit and Humor*. Louisville, Ky.: Harmon Publishing Co.

Harris, Joel Chandler. [1881] 1921. *Uncle Remus, His Songs and Sayings*. New York: Grosset and Dunlap.

Harrison, R. C. 1926. "The Negro as Interpreter of his own Folk-Songs." *Publication of the Texas Folk-Lore Society* 5: 143–144.

Hasan-Rokem, Galit. 1982. "The Pragmatics of Proverbs: How the Proverb Gets Its Meaning." In *Exceptional Language and Linguistics*, ed. Loraine K. Obler and Lise Menn, pp. 169–173. New York: Academic Press.

———. 1990. "The Aesthetics of the Proverb: Dialogue of Discourses from Genesis to Glassnost." *Proverbium* 7: 105–116.

Hatcher, William E. 1908. *John Jasper*. New York: Negro Universities Press.

Herskovits, Melville. 1930. "Kru Proverbs." *Journal of American Folklore* 43: 225–293.

———. 1941. *The Myth of the Negro Past*. New York: Harper. Reprint Boston: Beacon Press, 1958.

———. 1943. "Some Next Steps in the Study of Negro Folklore." *Journal of American Folklore* 56: 1–7.

———. 1945. "Problem, Method and Theory in Afro-American Studies." *Afroamerica* 1: 5–24. Reprinted in *Phylon* 7 (1945): 337–354.

Herzog, George, and C. G. Blooah. 1936. *Jabo Proverbs from Liberia*. London: Oxford University Press.

Hoard, Walter B. 1973. *Anthology: Quotations and Sayings of People of Color*. San Francisco: Robert D. Reed.

Holdcroft, David. 1978. *Words and Deeds: Problems in the Theory of Speech Acts*. Oxford: Clarendon Press.

Holt, Grace Sims. 1972. "Stylin' Outta the Black Pulpit." In *Rappin' and Stylin' Out*, ed. Thomas Kochman, pp. 189–204. Urbana: University of Illinois Press.

Honeck, Richard P., Katherine Voegtle, Mark A. Dorfmueller, and Robert R. Hoffman. 1980. "Proverbs, Meaning, and Group Structure." In *Cognition and Figurative Language*, ed. Richard P. Honeck and Robert R. Hoffman, pp. 127–161. Hillsdale, N.J.: Lawrence Erlbaum Associates.

Hudson, Catherine. 1972. "Traditional Proverbs as Perceived by Children From an Urban Environment." *Journal of the Folklore Society of Greater Washington* 3: 17–24.

Huggins, Nathan Irvin, ed. 1976. *Voices from the Harlem Renaissance*. New York: Oxford University Press.

Hughes, Langston, and Arna Bontemps. 1958. *Book of American Negro Folklore*. New York: Dodd, Mead and Co.

Hulme, Edward. [1902] 1968. *Proverb Lore*. Detroit: Gale Research.

Hurston, Zora Neale. 1942. "Story in Harlem Slang." *The American Mercury* 45:

84–96. Reprinted in *Mother Wit From the Laughing Barrel*, ed. Alan Dundes, pp. 222–237. Englewood Cliffs, N.J.: Prentice-Hall, Inc., 1973.

———. [1934] 1969. "Characteristics of Negro Expression." In *Negro Anthology*, ed. Nancy Cunard, pp. 39–46. New York: Negro University Press.

———. [1937] 1979. *Their Eyes Were Watching God*. Urbana: University of Illinois Press.

———. [1934] 1987. *Jonah's Gourd Vine*. London: Virago Press.

Hyamson, Albert M. 1922. *A Dictionary of English Phrases*. London: Routledge.

Hymes, Dell. 1964. "Toward Ethnographies of Communication." In *The Ethnography of Communication*, ed. John Gumperz and Dell Hymes, pp. 1–34. *American Anthropologist Special Publication* 66 (6) pt.2.

———. 1972. "Models of Interaction of Language and Social Life." In *Directions in Sociolinguistics*, ed. John Gumperz and Dell Hymes, pp. 35–71. New York: Holt, Rinehart and Winston.

———. 1974. "Ways of Speaking." In *Explorations in the Ethnography of Speaking*, ed. Richard Bauman and Joel Sherzer, pp. 443–451. Cambridge: Cambridge University Press.

Jason, Heda. 1971. "Proverbs in Society: The Problem of Meaning and Function." *Proverbium* (Helsinki) 17: 617–623.

Johnson, Guy B. 1930. *Folk Culture on St. Helena Island*. Chapel Hill: University of North Carolina Press.

Johnson, James Weldon, ed. 1937. *The Books of American Negro Spirituals*. 2 vols. New York: Viking Press.

Johnston, Thomas F. 1973. "Tsonga Proverbs in Cultural Context." *Tennessee Folklore Society Bulletin* 39: 3, 69–76.

Jones, LeRoi. 1963. *Blues People*. New York: William Morrow and Co.

———, and Larry Neal, eds. 1968. *Black Fire*. New York: William Morrow and Co.

Jordan, Rosan A. 1982. "Five Proverbs in Context." *Midwest Journal of Language and Folklore* 8: 109–115.

Katz, Bernard, ed. 1969. *The Social Implications of Early Negro Music in the United States*. New York: Arno Press.

Keil, Charles. 1966. *Urban Blues*. Chicago: The University of Chicago Press.

Kemper, Susan. 1981. "Comprehension and the Interpretation of Proverbs." *Journal of Psycholinguistic Research* 10: 2, 179–198.

Kerdilès, Yann. 1984. "Les acteurs langagiers dans les proverbes." In *Richesse du proverbe*, ed. Francois Suard and Claude Buridant, pp. 95–105. Lille: Université de Lille.

Kirshenblatt-Gimblett, Barbara. 1973. "Toward a Theory of Proverb Meaning." *Proverbium* (Helsinki) 22: 821–827. Reprinted in *The Wisdom of Many:*

Essays on the Proverb, ed. Wolfgang Mieder and Alan Dundes, pp. 111–121. New York: Garland Publishing, 1981.

Kochman, Thomas. 1970. "Toward an Ethnography of Black American Speech Behavior." In *Afro-American Anthropology*, ed. Norman E. Whitten, Jr., and John F. Szwed, pp. 145–162. New York: The Free Press.

Krikmann, Arvo. [1974] 1984. "On Denotative Indefiniteness of Proverbs." *Proverbium* 1: 47–91.

———. [1974] 1985. "Some Additional Aspects of Semantic Indefiniteness." *Proverbium* 2: 58–85.

———. 1994. "The Great Chain Metaphor: An Open Sesame for Proverb Semantics?" *Proverbium* 11: 117–124.

Kuhel, Pat. 1991. "Lebanese-American Proverbs and Proverbial Lore." *Mid-American Folklore* 19: 110–117.

Labov, William. 1972. "Rules for Ritual Insults." In *Rappin' and Stylin' Out*, ed. Thomas Kochman, pp. 265–314. Urbana: University of Illinois Press.

Leiber, Michael D. 1984. "Analogic Ambiguity: A Paradox of Proverb Usage." *Journal of American Folklore* 97: 423–441. Reprinted in *Wise Words: Essays on the Proverb*, ed. Wolfgang Mieder, pp. 99–127. New York: Garland Publishing, Inc., 1994.

Levin, Iu. I. 1984. "Proverbial'noe prostranstvo." In *Paremiologicheskie issledovaniia*, ed. Griogorii L'vovich Permiakov, pp. 108–126. Moskva: Nauka. Also appeared as "Zu einigen Besonderheiten des semiotischen Status von Sprichwörtern" in *Semiotische Studien sum Sprichwort. Simple Forms Reconsidered I*, ed. Peter Grzybek and Wolfgang Eismann. Tübingen: Gunter Narr, 1984, 379–385; and as "L'espace proverbial," in *Tel grain tel pain. Poetique de la sagesse populaire.* ed. G.L. Permiakov. Moscou: Éditions du Progrés, 1988, 139–167.

Levine, Lawrence. 1977. *Black Culture and Black Consciousness*. Oxford: Oxford University Press.

Levy, Isaac Jack, and Rosemary Levy Zumwalt. 1990. "A Conversation in Proverbs: Judeo-Spanish Refranes in Context." *Proverbium* 7: 117–132.

Lopes, Ana Cristina M. 1991. "Texte proverbial et construction du sens." *Degrés: Revue de synthèse à orientation sémiologique* 66: c1–c12.

Lovell, John, Jr. 1972. *Black Song: The Forge and the Flame*. New York: The Macmillan Company.

Lutzer, Victoria D. 1988. "Comprehension of Proverbs by Average Children and Children with Learning Disorders." *Journal of Learning Disabilities* 21: 104–8.

MacDonald, Donald. 1966. "Proverbs, Sententiae, and Exempla in Chaucer's Comic Tales: The Function of Comic Misapplication." *Speculum* 41:453–465.

Malone, Kemp. 1929. "Negro Proverbs from Maryland." *American Speech* 4: 285.

Maryland, James. 1972. "Shoeshine on 63rd." In *Rappin' and Stylin' Out*, ed. Thomas Kochman, pp. 209–214. Urbana: University of Illinois Press.

Maw, Wallace H., Ethel W. Maw, and Jane B. Laskaris. 1976. "Contrasting Proverbs as a Measure of Attitudes Toward Curiosity-Related Behavior of Black and White College Students." *Psychological Reports* 39: 1229–1230.

McAdoo, Harriette, and Margaret Rukuni. 1993. "A Preliminary Study of Family Values of the Women of Zimbabwe." *Journal of Black Psychology* 19: 1, 48–62.

McIlhenny, E. A. 1933. *Befo' de War Spirituals*. Boston: The Christopher Publishing House.

Messenger, John. 1959. "The Role of Proverbs in a Nigerian Judicial System." *Southwestern Journal of Anthropology* 15: 64–73.

Mieder, Wolfgang. 1974a. "The Proverb and Anglo-American Literature." *Southern Folklore Quarterly* 38: 49–62.

———. 1974b. "The Essence of Literary Proverb Studies." *Proverbium* (Helsinki) 23: 888–894. Reprinted in *New York Folklore Quarterly* 30 (1974): 66–76.

———. 1975. *Das Sprichwort in unserer Zeit*. Frauenfeld.

———. 1978. "The Use of Proverbs in Psychological Testing." *Journal of the Folklore Institute* 15: 45–55.

———. 1987. *Tradition and Innovation in Folk Literature*. Hanover, N.H.: University Press of New England.

———. 1988. "Proverbs in American Popular Songs." *Proverbium* 5: 85–101.

———. 1989. *American Proverbs: A Study of Texts and Contexts*. New York: Peter Lang.

———, and Barbara Mieder. 1977. "Tradition and Innovation: Proverbs in Advertising." *Journal of Popular Culture* 11: 308–319.

———, and Alan Dundes. 1981. *The Wisdom of Many: Essays on the Proverb*. New York: Garland Publishing, Inc.

———, Stewart A. Kingsbury, and Kelsie B. Harder, eds. 1992. *A Dictionary of American Proverbs*. New York: Oxford University Press.

Milner, G. B. 1969a. "What is a Proverb?" *New Society* 332: 199–202.

———. 1969b. "Quadripartite Structures." *Proverbium* (Helsinki) 14: 379–383.

Mitchell-Kernan, Claudia. 1972a. "Signifying and Marking: Two Afro-American Speech Acts." In *Directions in Sociolinguistics: The Ethnography of Communication*, ed. John J. Gumperz and Dell Hymes, pp. 161–178. New York: Holt, Rinehart and Winston.

———. 1972b. "Signifying, Loud Talking, and Marking." In *Rappin' and Stylin' Out*, ed. Thomas Kochman, pp. 315–335. Urbana: University of Illinois Press.

Mitchell-Kernan, Claudia, and Keith T. Kernan. 1975. "Children's Insults: America and Somoa." In *Sociocultural Dimensions of Language Use*, ed. Mary Sanches and Ben G. Blount, pp. 307–315. New York: Academic Press.

———. 1977. "Pragmatics of Directive Choice Among Children." In *Children's Discourse*, ed. Susan Ervin-Tripp and Claudia Mitchell-Kernan, pp. 189–208. New York: Academic Press.

Monye, Ambrose A. 1988. "Proverbial Lore in Aniocha Oral Literature." Ph.D. diss., University of Nigeria at Nsukka.

Morgan, Kathryn. 1980. *Children of Strangers: The Stories of a Black Family*. Philadelphia: Temple University Press.

Morrison, Toni. 1987. *Beloved*. New York: Alfred A. Knopf.

Murray, Albert. 1976. *Stomping the Blues*. New York: McGraw Hill Book Company.

Naylor, Gloria. 1988. *Mama Day*. New York: Random House.

Nippold, Marilyn A., Stephanie A. Martin, and Barbara J. Erskin. 1988. "Proverb Comprehension in Context: A Developmental Study with Children and Adolescents." *Journal of Speech and Hearing Research* 31: 19–28.

Norrick, Neal. 1982. "Proverbial Perlocutions: How to Do Things With Proverbs." *Grazer Linguistisch Studien* 17–18: 169–183. Reprinted in *Wise Words: Essays on the Proverb*, ed. Wolfgang Mieder, pp. 143–157. New York: Garland Publishing Inc., 1994.

———. 1985. *How Proverbs Mean*. New York: Mouton.

———. 1994. "Proverbial Emotions: How Proverbs Encode and Evaluate Emotion." *Proverbium* 11: 207–215.

Nuemann, Siegfried. 1987. " 'Dat seggt man, wenn . . .' Sagwörter im Munde eines alten mecklenburgischen Maurers." *Kikut. Plattdütsch gistern un hüt*, no. 12: 55–61.

Nwachukwu-Agbada, J. O. J. 1991. "Aliases Among the Anambra-Igbo: The Proverbial Dimension." *Names* 39: 2, 81–94.

Oakley, Giles. 1976. *The Devil's Music*. New York: Taplinger Publishing Company.

Ogede, Ode S. 1993. "Proverb Usage in the Praise Songs of the Igede: *Adiyah* Poet Micah Ichegbeth." *Proverbium* 10: 237–256.

Ojoade, J. Olowo. 1980. "African Proverbial Names: 101 Ilje Examples." *Names* 28: 195–214.

Okumu, Charles. 1992. "The Form of Okot p'Bitek's Poetry: Literary Borrowing from Acoli Oral Traditions." *Research in African Literature* 23: 3, 53–66.

Oledzki, Jacek. 1979. "On Some Maxims on African Cars." *Africana Bulletin* 28: 29–35

Oliver, Paul. 1960a. *Blues Fell This Morning*. New York: Horizon Press.

———. 1960b. *The Meaning of the Blues*. New York: Collier Books.

————. 1984. *Blues Off the Record*. New York: Hippocrene Books Inc.

Omijeh, Matthew. 1973. "Bini Proverb-Names: An Aspect of African Oral Literature." *The Nigerian Field* 38: 90–96.

Osofsky, Gilbert, ed. 1969. *Puttin' On Ole Massa: Slave Narratives of Henry Bibb, William Wells Brown, and Solomon Northup*. New York: Harper and Row.

Oster, Harry. 1969. *Living Country Blues*. Detroit: Folklore Associates.

Page, Mary H., and Nancy D. Washington. 1987. "Family Proverbs and Value Transmission of Single Black Mothers." *The Journal of Social Psychology* 127: 49–58.

Papp, György. 1988. "A proverbiumok jelentéstani, kommunikacio-elméleti vizsgalata." *Tanulmanyok. A Magyar Nyelv, Irodalom és Hungarologiai Kutatasok Intézetének Kiadvanya* 21: 103–129.

Parker, Carol. 1975. " 'White is the Color.' " *Western Folklore* 34: 153–154.

Parsons, Elsie C. 1919. "Riddles and Proverbs from the Bahama Islands." *Journal of American Folklore* 32: 439–441.

————. 1943. *Folk-Lore of the Antilles, French and English*. New York: Memoirs of the American Folk-Lore Society: 26, pt. 3: 457–487.

Pasamanick, Judith R. 1982. "The Proverb Moves the Mind: Abstraction and Metaphor in Children Six-Nine." Ph.D. diss., Yeshiva University.

————. 1983. "Talk 'Does' Cook Rice: Proverb Abstraction through Social Interaction." *International Journal of the Sociology of Language* 44: 5–25.

————. 1985. "Watched Pots Do Boil: Proverb Interpretation through Contextual Illustration." *Proverbium* 2: 145–183.

Peck, Richard. 1966. " 'Out of Sight' is Back in View." *American Speech* 41: 78–79.

Penavin, Olga. 1979. "A proverbiumokrol. A jugoszlaviai magyarok szolas- és közmondaskinese alapjan." *Hungarologiai Közlemények* 11:39–40, 155–180.

Penfield, Joyce. 1983. *Communicating with Quotes: The Igbo Case*. Westport, Conn.: Greenwood Press.

Penn, Nolan E., Teresa C. Jacob, and Malrie Brown. 1988a. "Comparison Between Gorham's Proverbs Test and the Revised Shipley Institute of Living Scale for a Black Population." *Perceptual and Motor Skills* 66: 839–845.

————. 1988b. "Familiarity with Proverbs and Performance of a Black Population on Gorham's Proverbs Test." *Perceptual and Motor Skills* 66: 847–854.

Permyakov, G. L. 1979. *From Proverb to Folk-Tale: Notes on the General Theory of Cliché*, trans. Y. N. Filippov. Moscow: Nauka Publishing House.

Petry, Sandy. 1990. *Speech Acts and Literary Theory*. New York: Routledge.

Pitts, Arthur William. 1966. *John Donne's Use of Proverbs in His Poetry*. Ph.D. diss., Louisiana State University.

Porter, Kenneth. 1965. "Racism in Children's Rhymes and Sayings, Central Kansas, 1910–1918." *Western Folklore* 24: 191–196.

Prahlad, Sw. Anand (Dennis Folly). 1994. "No Guts, No Glory": Proverbs, Values and Image among Anglo-American University Students." *Southern Folklore* 51:3, 285–298.

———. 1995. "Persona and Proverb Meaning in Roots Reggae: Proverbs of the Itals Reggae Group." *Proverbium* 12: 275–293.

Priebe, Richard. 1971. "The Horses of Speech: A Structural Analysis of the Proverb." *Folklore Annual* 3: 26–32.

Raboteau, Albert J. 1978. *Slave Religion.* New York: Oxford University Press.

Randolph, Vance. 1955. *The Devil's Pretty Daughter and Other Ozark Folk Tales.* New York: Columbia University Press.

Rawick, George P., ed. 1972. *The American Slave: A Composite Autobiography.* 30 vols. Westport, Conn.: Greenwood Publishing Company.

Roberts, John W. 1978. "Slave Proverbs: A Perspective." *Callaloo* 1: 129–140.

———. 1989. *From Trickster to Badman: The Black Folk Hero in Slavery and Freedom.* Philadelphia: University of Pennsylvania Press.

Roberts, John M., and Jeffrey C. Hayes. 1987. "Young Adult Male Categorizations of Fifty Arabic Proverbs." *Anthropological Linguistics* 29:1, 35–48.

Rosenberg, Bruce A. 1970. *The Art of the American Folk Preacher.* New York: Oxford University Press.

Roventa-Frumusani, Daniela. 1985. "Le proverbe e(s)t énonciation econcée." *Revue Roumaine de Linguistique* 30:2, 159–167.

Ruef, Hans. 1983. "Understanding Proverbs: Scene Development as a Process of Motivation." *Linguistic Agency University of Trier*, series A, no. 111: 1–14.

Sackheim, Eric, ed. 1969. *The Blues Line.* New York: Schirmer Books.

Sarma, Nabin Ch. 1986. "Study of a Few Assamese Proverbs from the Contextual Point of View." *Folklore* (Calcutta), 27: 4, 71–77.

Schmidt-Radefeldt, Jürgen. 1986. "Structure argumentative, reference et contextualité du proverbe." In *Stylistique, rhétorique et poétique dans les langues romanes*, ed. Jean-Claude Bovier, pp. 87–102. Aix-en-Provence: Université de Provence.

Searle, John R. 1969. *Speech Acts.* Cambridge: Cambridge University Press.

Seitel, Peter. 1969. "Proverbs: A Social Use of Metaphor." *Genre* 2: 143–161. Reprinted in *The Wisdom of Many: Essays on the Proverb*, ed. Wolfgang Mieder and Alan Dundes, pp. 122–139. New York: Garland Publishing Inc., 1981.

———. 1977. "Saying Haya Sayings: Two Categories of Proverb Use." In *The Social Use of Metaphor: Essays in the Anthropology of Rhetoric*, ed. David Sapir and J. Christopher, pp. 75–99. Philadelphia: University of Pennsylvania Press.

Silverman-Weinreich, Beatrice. 1978. "Towards a Structural Analysis of Yiddish Proverbs." *Yivo Annual of Jewish Social Science* 17: 1–20. Reprinted in *The Wisdom of Many: Essays on the Proverb*, ed. Wolfgang Mieder and Alan Dundes, pp. 65–85. New York: Garland Publishing, 1981.

Simpson, John A. [1982] 1992. *The Concise Oxford Dictionary of Proverbs*. Oxford: Oxford University Press.

Smith, Barbara Herrnstein. 1978. *On the Margins of Discourse*. Chicago: University of Chicago Press.

Smitherman, Geneva. [1977] 1986. *Talkin and Testifyin: The Language of Black America*. Boston: Houghton Mifflin. Reprint, Detroit: Wayne State University Press.

Snapp, Emma L. 1933. "Proverbial Lore in Nebraska." Lincoln, Neb.: *University of Nebraska Studies in Language, Literature, and Criticism* 13: 53–112.

Spaulding, Henry D., ed. 1972. *Encyclopedia of Black Folklore and Humor*. New York: Jonathan David Publishers.

Sport, Kathryn and Bert Hitchcock, eds. 1991. *De Remnant Truth: Tales of Jake Mitchell and Robert Wilton Burton*. Tuscaloosa: The University of Alabama Press.

Stafford, A. O. 1916. "The Mind of the African Negro as Reflected in His Proverbs." *Journal of American Folklore* 1: 42–48.

Stedje, Astrid. 1987. "Sprecherstrategien im Spiegel der Phraseologie." In *Beiträge zur allgemeinen und germanistischen Phraseologieforschung*, ed. Jarmo Korhonen, pp. 91–109. Oulu: Oulun Yliopisto.

Stevenson, Burton E. 1965. *The Macmillan Book of Proverbs, Maxims and Familiar Phrases*. New York: Macmillan.

Szwed, John F., and Roger D. Abrahams. 1977. "After the Myth: Studying Afro-American Cultural Patterns in the Plantation Literature." In *African Folklore in the New World*, ed. Daniel J. Crowley, pp. 65–86. Austin: University of Texas Press.

———. 1978. *Afro-American Folk Culture*. Philadelphia: Institute for the Study of Human Issues. (A bibliography.)

Taft, Michael. 1979. "Four Possible Factors in the Formation of Bound Expressions." *Lore and Language* 2: 10–24.

———. 1994. "Proverbs in the Blues: How Freqent Is Frequent?" *Proverbium* 11: 227–258.

Taylor, Archer. 1950a. "Proverb." In *Standard Dictionary of Folklore, Mythology and Legend*, ed. Maria Leach, pp. 902–905. New York: Funk and Wagnalls.

———. 1950b. "Proverbial Phrases." In *Standard Dictionary of Folklore, Mythology and Legend*, ed. Maria Leach, pp. 906. New York: Funk and Wagnalls.

———. 1962. *The Proverb and an Index to the Proverb*. Hatboro, Pa.: Folklore Associates.

———. 1969–1970. " 'To Hoe One's Row' in Africa." *American Notes and Queries* 8: 7–8.

———. 1973. "Small Remarks." *Proverbium* 22: 807.

———. 1975. " 'Neither Fish nor Flesh' and Its Variations." In *Selected Writings on Proverbs by Archer Taylor*, ed. Wolfgang Mieder, pp. 122–128. Helsinki: Suomalainen Tiedaekatemia.

Taylor, Archer, and B. J. Whiting. 1958. *A Dictionary of American Proverbs and Proverbial Phrases, 1820–1880*. Cambridge, Mass.: Belknap Press of Harvard University Press.

Tedlock, Dennis. 1972. "On the Translation of Style of Oral Narrative." In *Toward New Perspectives in Folklore*, ed. Americo Paredes and Richard Bauman, pp. 114–133. Austin: Texas University Press.

———. 1983. *The Spoken Word and the Work of Interpretation*. Philadelphia: University of Pennsylvania Press.

Thomas, Nigel H. 1988. *From Folklore to Fiction: A Study of Folk Heroes and Rituals in the Black American Novel*. New York: Greenwood Press.

Tilley, Morris P. 1950. *A Dictionary of the Proverbs in England in the Sixteenth and Seventeenth Centuries*. Ann Arbor: University of Michigan Press.

Toelken, Barre. 1979. *Dynamics of Folklore*. Boston: Houghton-Mifflin.

Trench, Richard C. 1852. *Lessons in Proverbs*. London: John W. Parker and Son.

Tutuola, Amos. 1953. *The Palm Wine Drinkard*. New York: Grove Press.

Vlach, John Michael. 1991. *By the Work of Their Hands: Studies in Afro-American Folklife*. Ann Arbor: UMI Research Press.

Watson, Llewellyn B. 1991. *Jamaican Sayings: with Notes on Folklore, Aesthetics, and Social Control*. Tallahassee: Florida A & M University Press.

Westermarck, Edward. 1931. *Wit and Wisdom in Morocco*. New York: Horace Liveright.

White, Newman I. 1928. *American Negro Folk-Songs*. Cambridge, Mass.: Harvard University Press.

Whiting, B. J. 1931. "The Origin of the Proverb." *Harvard Studies and Notes in Philology and Literature* 13: 47–80.

———. 1934a. *Chaucer's Use of Proverbs*. Cambridge, Mass.: Harvard University Press.

———. 1934b. "Proverbial Material in the Popular Ballad." *Journal of American Folklore* 47:22–44.

———. 1952a. "Proverbs and Proverbial Sayings." In *The Frank C. Brown Collection of North Carolina Folklore*, vol. 1, ed. Wayland Hand, pp. 329–501. Durham: Duke University Press.

———. 1952b. "William Johnson of Natchez: Free Negro." *Southern Folklore Quarterly* 16: 145–153.

———. 1977. *Early American Proverbs and Proverbial Phrases*. Cambridge, Mass.: Harvard University Press.

———. 1989. *Modern Proverbs and Proverbial Sayings*. Cambridge, Mass.: Harvard University Press.

Whitten, Norman E., and John F. Szwed. 1970. *Afro-American Anthropology: Contemporary Perspectives.* New York: The Free Press.

Wilson, F. P. 1970. *The Oxford Dictionary of English Proverbs.* Oxford: Clarendon Press.

Work, John W. 1940. *American Negro Songs and Spirituals.* New York: Bonanza Books.

Yankah, Kwesi. 1983. "Toward a Performance-Centered Theory of the Proverb." *Critical Arts* 3: 1, 29–43.

———. 1989a. *The Proverb in the Context of Akan Rhetoric: A Theory of Proverb Praxis.* New York: Peter Lang.

———. 1989b. "Proverbs: The Aesthetics of Traditional Communication." *Research in African Literature* 20: 3, 325–346.

———. 1989c. "Proverbs: Problems and Strategies in Field Research." *Proverbium* 6: 165–176.

Yassin, Muhmoud Aziz F. 1988. "Spoken Arabic Proverbs." *Bulletin of the School of Oriental and African Studies-University of London* 51:59–68.

Yates, Irene. 1947. "A Collection of Proverbs and Proverbial Sayings from South Carolina Literature." *Southern Folklore Quarterly* 11: 187–199.

Index

Recent Titles in the Publications of the

American Folklore Society, New Series

Conway, Cecilia. *African Banjo Echoes in Appalachia: A Study of Black Folk Traditions and Influences.* Knoxville: University of Tennessee Press.

Giray, Eren. *Nsiirin! Nsiirin! Jula Folktales from West Africa.* Michigan State University Press.

Gower, Herschel and James Porter. *The Transformative Voice: Life and Songs of Jeannie Robertson.* Knoxville: University of Tennessee Press.

Hufford, Mary, ed. *Conserving Culture: The Emergent Discourse on Heritage.* Urbana: University of Illinois Press.

Jones, Michael Owen. *Putting Folklore to Use: Essays on Applied Folkloristics.* Lexington: University of Kentucky Press.

McCarthy, William B. *Jack in Two Worlds: Contemporary North American Tales and Their Tellers.* Chapel Hill: University of North Carolina Press.

O'Connor, Bonnie. *Healing Traditions: Alternative Medicine and the Health Professions.* Philadelphia: University of Pennsylvania Press.

Toelken, Barre. *Morning Dew and Roses: Nuance, Metaphor, and Meaning in Folksongs.* Urbana: University of Illinois Press.